Man's Best Friend

On the Road Again with

A Selective Guide to Mid-Atlantic State's Bed and Breakfasts, Inns, Hotels, and Resorts that Welcome You and Your Dog

MAN'S BEST FRIEND
ON THE ROAD AGAIN WITH

A Selective Guide to Mid-Atlantic State's Bed and Breakfasts, Inns, Hotels, and Resorts that Welcome You and Your Dog

DAWN AND ROBERT HABGOOD

Macmillan•USA

Illustrations: Glynn Brannan
Cindy Frost

Editor: Barbara Hayes

Macmillan General Reference
A Prentice Hall Macmillan Company
15 Columbus Circle
New York, NY 10023

Howell Book House
MACMILLAN is a registered trademark of Macmillan, Inc.

ISBN 0-87605-706-7

Manufactured in the United States of America

10 9 8 7 6 5 4 3 2 1

TO SAM AND BUCKY
A BOY AND HIS DOG

CONTENTS

THE BEST OF THE REST
Hotels and Motels that Accept Dogs

MAPS

TOLL FREE 800 TELEPHONE NUMBERS

INDEX

INTRODUCTION

Americans have a truly special relationship with their dogs and, more often than not, our dogs become members of the family. Unfortunately, what many are discovering is that when trying to take a vacation with their dogs, problems begin to arise. All of the charming Bed and Breakfasts, inns, hotels, and resorts that have welcomed guests without a dog, often do not welcome them and their canine companion with the same open arms. Thus, planning even a simple trip with a dog has required culling out information from Chambers of Commerce and many general interest guidebooks, all in the hopes of locating accommodations that *might* accept canine cohorts. Some of these materials do offer listings of the motels and motor lodges that welcome pets; however, these are merely generic lists and rarely give armchair travelers any feeling for what they can actually expect to find once they have arrived. Even after combing through all of these resources, many discover that they still have a lot of work ahead. They must make further telephone calls, obtain brochures, decide which establishment is best for them — all this before making a reservation. Sometimes all of this work can result in finding a jewel, but more often than not, even the most diligent travelers are forced to compromise on their ultimate accommodation selections.

As dog lovers ourselves, with two Golden Retrievers, we didn't think travelers should have to spend so much time finding suitable accommodations, nor should anyone end up by compromising on lodgings that simply "make do." Travelers seeking to explore the unique highways and byways of the many regions of the United States should not be forced to leave their canine companions at home when going on a sojourn or compromise on the quality of their accommodations in order to bring "Bowser" along. We knew that there had to be an easier and better way to locate quality accommodations that welcome dogs. Thus, we set out to investigate this problem.

Our solution to this dilemma is a series of travel guides entitled *On The Road Again with Man's Best Friend*. For the last ten years we have written these books, which focus on B&Bs, inns, hotels, and resorts that welcome you and your dog in the Mid-Atlantic states, on the West Coast, and in the New England area. We have looked at thousands of establishments throughout these regions, have **personally visited each of them**, and have then selected the finest and/or most interesting for each of these books. Some are exclusive hotels and resorts, where guests are treated like royalty and the amenities are virtually endless. Others are intimate B&Bs which offer very personalized overnight accommodations. Still others are romantic country inns, often with fireplaces, down comforters, and picturesque views. There are detailed overviews of the accommodations, amenities, and services to be found at each of these establishments. After reading any given selection, readers can more easily make decisions on which place best fits their particular needs. Also included are interesting activities that both humans, and their four-legged counterparts, can enjoy — both on the premises or in the nearby area. Finally, there is a comprehensive appendix that outlines all the motor lodges, motels, and chain hotels that also welcome dogs, as well as a list of all the toll-free 800 telephone numbers.

We have carefully researched and triple-checked the information that appears in these books to ensure that all the information contained herein is up to date, and to ensure that each of the establishments appearing in the *On the Road Again with Man's Best Friend* series of books does welcome dogs. We sent questionnaires to hundreds of accommodations and selected those that truly seemed appropriate for guests traveling with a a canine companion. We then telephoned each of them before making a personal visit to reconfirm that these are establishments that indeed welcome Bowser. As one final check, each of the entries was telephoned shortly before the book went to press to verify all the details, and any policies concerning dogs. Although some establishments will inevitably be forced to change their pet policies, we are confident that travelers can sit back and enjoy planning their itinerary, secure in the knowledge that Bowser will be as happy as they are while exploring the Mid-Atlantic States.

MAKING A RESERVATION

After selecting an accommodation, prospective guests should *always* call ahead to make a reservation. During the conversation with the host or manager it is important to mention that your dog (lovingly referred to herein as, "Bowser") will be coming along. The manager might want to know how big the dog is, is s/he house-trained, a barker, well-mannered, good with other dogs, etc.

We have, over the years, heard numerous stories about dog visits gone awry, forcing innkeepers, hosts, and managers to reconsider their pet policy. We can only stress that it is ultimately up the individual guests to show extra courtesy when bringing their dog. For instance, an animal who constantly barks or is high-strung when at home is not going to be any better when traveling. To expect him or her to behave differently while on vacation would be unfair to everyone involved.

HELPFUL HINTS

PRE-VACATION TIPS

Here is a list of suggestions, some obvious and others not so obvious, of things to take on the trip:

1) A leash and collar with ID tags.
2) A few play toys, chew bones, treats, etc.
3) A container of fresh water.
4) Food and watering bowls.
5) Dog bedding (towel, mat, pillow) or travel crate (kennel).
6) Grooming aids (comb, brush, flea powder, etc.).
7) Prescription medication. If your dog is currently on any medication or is a nervous traveler in the car, you may wish to consult your veterinarian prior to departure.
8) As an added precaution, some may wish to bring their dog's vaccination records in case of emergency.

EN ROUTE

WARNING: Do not leave a dog in the car for a long period of time on hot days. Make sure the car is well ventilated, preferably parked in the shade, and that the dog has plenty of water to drink. An unventilated car acts very much like an oven and can heat up to well over 100 degrees in a very short time causing heat stroke, brain damage, or even death.

VACATION-TIME TIPS

The following is a brief list of general policies and concerns expressed by innkeepers that we wanted to pass along to prospective guests:

1) Guests should keep their dogs leashed while on the grounds.
2) Dogs should not be left alone in the bedroom, even the best behaved dog at home might cause a problem when left for long periods of time.
3) Owners should try to walk their dogs away from the establishment's grounds and clean up after their dog.
4) Most would prefer that owners bring their dog's bedding to keep them comfortable and lessen the chance of damage to the furnishings.

KEY TO ABBREVIATIONS

RATES

Range from the least expensive to the most expensive bedroom and/or suite. Sales tax has not been included in the rate schedules nor mandatory tipping (the tax rates vary from state to state). Every establishment offers either family rates, weekend and weekly packages, or low off-season rates. *When making your reservation, you should always inquire about any special discounts or packages.*

PLANS

1. (B&B): Bed and Breakfast; usually includes a Continental breakfast.
2. (EP): European Plan; does not include any meals.
3. (AP): American Plan; rates are often listed on a per person basis and include all meals
4. (MAP): Modified American Plan: rates are often listed on a per person basis and include both breakfastand dinner.

PAYMENT

AE: American Express; CB: Carte Blanche; DSC: Discover; DC: Diners Club; ENR: En Route; JCB: Japanese Credit Bank; MC: Master Card; VISA: Visa. When no credit cards are accepted, guests may pay their deposit or final bill with personal checks, traveler's checks, or cash.

NEW YORK

MANSION HILL INN

115 Philip Street at Park Avenue
Albany, New York 12202
(518) 465-2038, (518) 434-2334
Innkeepers: Maryellen, Elizabeth, and Steve Stofelano, Jr.
Rooms: 6 doubles, 2 suites
Rates: Doubles $95, Suites $155
Payment: AE, DC, MC, and Visa
Children: Welcome (cribs and babysitters are available)
Dogs: Well-behaved dogs are welcome
Open: All year

During our travels through upstate New York, we kept hearing about this wonderful little inn in Albany, that offered comfortable guest rooms and excellent food. In fact, there are many people who regularly drive down from Saratoga Springs to have dinner or brunch at the inn's intimate restaurant. Now, for anyone who has ever driven through Albany, or spent a night here, they might wonder where this gem has been hiding in a city dominated by motels and low-budget hotels. As it turns out, the Mansion Hill Inn is just around the corner from the State Capitol buildings and within a short walk of the shopping and business districts.

The inn is comprised of four buildings located in an historic, yet transitional, neighborhood. It is obvious that the turn-of-the century clapboard and Victorian row houses have gone through a period of neglect, only to be resurrected in more recent years. Visitors will still find an even mix of the disheveled and the newly renovated. Those who are used to more suburban surroundings, might not be totally comfortable wandering around the neighborhood late at night; however, those with an urban background will find it to be reminiscent of the residential neighborhoods in any big city.

During the day, though, everyone will enjoy walking the streets around the Mansion Hill Inn, as they come alive with activity. The centerpiece for the neighborhood is the inn's restaurant, which attracts as many locals as it does guests of the inn. Historically, this spot has always been a favorite gathering place for the area, as it was formerly the South End's local tavern. Over the years, it has served Albany's extended families, including the most recent owners, the Stofelano family. Steve and Maryellen bought the dilapidated row house in 1984, at the time learning that it was originally built in 1861 for an Albany brush maker named Daniel Brown. They spent the next year or so renovating this structure and ultimately buying three others to create the complex that exists today. A lush courtyard not only ties the buildings together, but also sparkles at night, lit by tiny white lights draped along the tree branches. This is a particularly festive scene for guests to look out on from their rooms.

As one might imagine, there are a variety of doubles and suites available to overnight visitors. Each has been decorated in a slightly different style, some are feminine with floral prints and frilly curtains framing the windows, while others offer a more tailored masculine look. Darkly-stained reproduction English furnishings are set amid comfortable sitting chairs and functional writing desks. In the process of furnishing the rooms, Maryellen did not overlook the personal touches such as bottles of Saratoga Spring water and seasonal fresh flowers. Nooks and crannies, often holding a few collectibles, provide more character in some instances than the decor. Cable televisions, individually controlled heating and cooling systems, and telephones complete the modern amenities. Families might appreciate the adjoining rooms or the huge suites. The latter offers a master bedroom that is complemented by a living room and den along with a well-appointed kitchen. Some of the suites even have balconies or views of the mountains or the Hudson River. Every standard room or suite offers a private bath which, like the rest of the accommodations, is newly refurbished and extremely clean. Constantly adapting, Steve says that one of their most recent projects is trying to cultivate flower gardens on the premises to provide fresh flower arrangements for the guest chambers and restaurant.

Flowers are just one part of the overall light and airy decor guests will find in the restaurant. The ambiance is enhanced even further by a crackling fireplace. Each morning, a full breakfast is served to guests of the inn. However, the favorite choice for many people is the four-star dinner menu. Patrons may wish to select an appetizer such as the coconut shrimp with a raspberry coulis, the homemade sausage of the day, or the marinated artichokes, roasted red peppers, and sun dried tomatoes on mixed greens. The menu often has an extensive array of pasta offerings. Fusili pasta sauteed in a white wine sauce of fresh salmon, tomatoes, artichoke hearts, and capers or the red pepper and basil penne pasta with sauteed spinach and mushrooms in a gorgonzola cream sauce are well worth trying. Other options include the roasted half duck, medallions of veal with sherried tart cherries and scallions, and the chargrilled filet mignon topped with a wild mushroom demiglace. The desserts are always homemade and can be enjoyed with capuccino or espresso.

Bowser will want to explore the local Lincoln Park, or more distant Corning Preserve that runs along the Hudson River. The neighborhood is also conducive to short walks, and a bit further afield visitors can investigate historic sites such as the Governor's, the Ten Broeck, and the Schuyler mansions.

The Stofelanos' pride themselves on service and on the fact that this is a family-run establishment, which enables them to quickly heed special requests and provide helpful suggestions to those who are in need of assistance. The only quirky exception to this is when prospective guests try to telephone the inn. On many occasions, we have had difficulty getting anyone to answer the telephone; we thought they might be busy taking care of their in-house guests. Our advice is be patient and continue trying, because the ultimate experience is well worth any additional effort one might have to make.

MULLIGAN FARM BED & BREAKFAST

5403 Barber Road
Avon, New York 14414
(716) 226-6412, (716) 226-3780
Innkeepers: Lesa Sobolewski and Jeffrey Mulligan
Rooms: 4 doubles
Rates: $55
Payment: Personal checks
Children: Not appropriate for children under the age of four
Dogs: Welcome with advance notice and prior approval
Open: All year

Some find that the perfect antidote to life's day-to-day stresses is to get away from the routine and take a relaxing vacation in the country. For those who want a true sampling of farm life, there is the Mulligan Farm. It is a 1,200 acre expanse of land that Jeff and his wife Lesa run as a working farm, with registered Holsteins and an assortment of sheep, horses, and chickens. The elegant Greek Revival homestead was actually built in the mid-1800s by a wealthy banker as his country home. Jeffrey's grandfather, E.D. Mulligan, bought the farm in 1920 and spent years raising horses and both Guernsey and Angus cattle. His passion was for fox hunting though, and he ultimately became the master of the Geneseo Valley Hunt, the second oldest organized hunt in the United States. In keeping with this sixty year tradition, Lesa and Jeff continue to hold the hunt each year.

Although the hunting tradition is interesting, today's visitors are far more likely to find Lesa and Jeff hard at work tending to their cows, completing various chores, and caring for their guests. While this might seem to be a juggling act for some, it is clear, after meeting Lesa, that she is blessed with a seemingly endless amount of energy. When we arrived, she was busy single-handedly cooking a full farm breakfast for her eight guests. From her huge farmhouse kitchen, she was able to butter the toast, cook the scrambled eggs, start a second pot of her special organic coffee, and sustain a running conversation with us. While her guests were eating, she provided a leisurely grand tour of the farmhouse.

From the exterior, the main house is elegant with its columns, white clapboards, and black shutters. There is little sense that this is actually a country farmhouse. The building, and in fact the entire property, have been listed on the National Register of Historic Places ensuring that it will always maintain its sense of history. Those who are new to the Mulligan Farm, will first come upon a grouping of barns and outbuildings, which are separated from the farmhouse by beautiful perennial, herb, and vegetable gardens, that can be fully appreciated in the height of the summer.

Once inside the house, guests will find the spacious dining and living rooms. The former has a fireplace, which not only adds charm to this chamber, but also provides a good deal of warmth on cool days and nights. A wall of paned windows overlooks the back of the property and the in-ground swimming pool. Just beyond the dining room, through an enormous arch, is the living room. This is another comfortable place with walls of bookshelves that lend an air of formality to the otherwise simply furnished room. A doorway off the living room brings guests to the screened-in porch. Many find this to be one of their favorite gathering spots during the summer months, as it affords them pretty views of the countryside and refreshing breezes. There is even a special hard-bottomed hammock that some guests have been known to sleep on during a hot summer's night.

Upstairs, there are four individually decorated and furnished bedrooms, with many of the pieces coming from Jeff's grandparents' collection. Our favorite room is situated at the top of the stairs. Its four-poster bed has a down comforter on it and the walls are papered in a traditional old-fashioned floral print. Another good-sized room is found at the front of the house and is furnished with twin beds and has the same quaint decor. Families or couples traveling together might choose this room as it adjoins a second bedroom, that is accessed by way of a bathroom and short hallway. The fourth guest room has been more recently refurbished with a contemporary bold navy blue and white patterned wallpaper that replaced the original fading one. This double-bedded chamber also shares a bathroom.

Each morning, guests are invited downstairs for a full country breakfast. This hearty repast varies, although the pancake and egg dishes are always made with eggs gathered from the farm's chickens. These offerings are usually complemented by fresh fruit, bacon, sausage, homemade muffins, and coffee cake. Those who enjoy their coffee will certainly be intrigued with Lesa's organic variety, although she also offers tea for anyone who prefers that.

Most come to the Mulligan Farm to get away from the hustle and bustle of their busy lives. In the summer months, there is a swimming pool that is most refreshing, as well as acres of woods and pastures for meandering through. The farm is located just off a relatively quiet country road that is great for taking walks with Bowser. The region around Avon is primarily farmland which offers a bucolic setting for long walks, bicycle rides, or just exploring by way of car. The B&B is also close to the wineries and the Finger Lakes of upstate New York. In the winter months, when the local life is quiet, guests will spend more time indoors next to a fire or perhaps head out for a little cross-country skiing. Letchworth State Park is close to Mulligan Farm, as are a couple downhill ski areas. Those who want a dose of the city can visit nearby Rochester.

But what many will find the most endearing about Mulligan Farm, are Lesa, Jeff, and their seven-year-old border collie, Callie. Their relaxed manner and lifestyle immediately makes people feel comfortable and quite at home, often causing guests to either extend their stay or re-book for many years to come.

THE SEDGWICK INN

Box 250
Berlin, New York 12022
(518) 658-2334
Innkeeper: Edith Evans
Rooms: 10 doubles, 1 suite
Rates: Doubles $65-85, Suite $100
Payment: AE, CB, DC, MC, and Visa
Children: Welcome in the motel units only
Dogs: Welcome with advance notice in the motel units
Open: All year

The Sedgwick Inn has been in existence since 1791, when it served primarily as a stagecoach stop for travelers. Today, major interstates draw traffic away from this small valley, except during foliage season when the back roads become the preferred choice of travel for the leisurely leaf peepers. When we first came upon the white clapboard and black shuttered Colonial building, we quickly checked our map to see if we were still in New York state because the inn and its surroundings were more reminiscent of a classic New England setting. As we turned into the dirt drive, we could see that behind the inn there were also several outbuildings. We soon learned from Edie that the inn has served many functions and undergone a few additions and transformations since the 1700s. At one time, it was the private summer residence for a New York family and then, because of its proximity to Route 22, it became the ideal location for The Ranch Tavern. Additions to the property over the years included a small, neo-classical building dating back to 1834. This structure is completely lined with tin and in previous incarnations was a Civil War recruiting station, a doctor's office and a feed store. The Carriage House has been converted into a gift and crafts shop. Finally, there is a low lying building that contains the six motel units. These rooms are actually full of character and do accommodate those traveling with a dog.

We don't like to use the word motel because it conjures up images of cookie cutter units and sterile surroundings. This group of Colonial style rooms have lace curtains framing the windows that overlook the attractive grounds and beyond to a small stream. Upon opening the windows, guests will hear the sounds of the buoy chimes as they swing in response to the refreshing breezes. While the rooms are not overly spacious, they do have a certain country charm. The furnishings are primarily Cushman, with old-fashioned maple headboards, along with writing desks and bedside tables. Although the wallpaper is a subdued rust and brown Colonial pattern, it somehow befits the eclectic collection of lamps and paintings. A glass water pitcher is set next to the bed so that guests can help themselves to a drink of water during the night. A clock radio, private telephone, and black and white television are welcome conveniences. The bathrooms are very clean and offer a nice array of Calisto shampoos and soaps.

Obviously, the motel units do not provide the same antique charm found within the main house; however, what guests loose in ambiance they make up for in quietness, as these rooms are set well back from the main road. Those who stay in the motel rooms are invited to take advantage of all of the inn's amenities. This often begins in the morning on the sun porch, when Edie serves a Continental breakfast of juice, freshly brewed coffee, and homemade muffins and rolls. During the quieter times, she will add an egg dish or pancakes to her repertoire, enticing guests to stay a bit longer. Lunch can also be enjoyed, here, with warm Yankee pot roast sandwiches served with a horseradish sauce or smoked-turkey sandwiches with raspberry mayonnaise topping the menu choices. After these hearty repasts, many wander up to the Carriage House to browse through the collectibles.

Guests soon learn that Edie, and her late husband Bob, started the restaurant as a service to their guests but the quality was such that they finally had to open the doors to the public. Today, diners make The Sedgwick Inn's restaurant a part of their itinerary when traveling through this region. Candlelight, low ceilings, and a fresh rose on every table set the tone for the meal to follow. The menu changes regularly, but a sampling might include artichoke bottoms stuffed with lobster, shrimp and bell peppers, smoked seafood medley, or a Shaker pease porridge. We think the entrees are particularly interesting. During our visit, roast game hen with a black currant sauce, grilled swordfish seasoned with sorrel and chive, and the Osso Buco romano with sundried tomatoes were on the menu. The simple Black Angus filet mignon and the carbonnade of beef a la flamande appeal to heartier appetites. The desserts are worth a mention, because the double chocolate raspberry tart, the hazelnut strawberry shortcakes, and the strawberry rhubarb creme brulee are difficult for most to pass up. The wine cellar is excellent, with guests often perusing the bottles and picking one of their favorites themselves. Live music on Friday and Saturday nights cause most to linger far longer than they ever imagined.

After dinner, there are several common rooms that patrons find appealing. One particular favorite is filled with books and comfortable furnishings, along with a selection of games and puzzles. Some guests are so tired they just drift up to their antique furnished bedrooms, located on the second floor. While the motel accommodations are perfectly nice, anyone traveling without Bowser should think about reserving a room in the main inn since these rooms overflow with antique charm. Our favorites were those on the back of the house because they were quiet, although those who want a view of the Berkshires might select a bedroom on the front of the house.

During the day, Bowser will certainly find many ways to stay entertained. The property offers many nooks and crannies to explore. Slightly further afield, there are hikes to be enjoyed throughout the Berkshires. Williamstown is another favorite destination in the summer months because of the tremendous summer theater program. The Williams College campus here is as enjoyable for Bowser to explore as it is for his two-footed friends. In the winter months, visitors come to this area for the picturesque cross-country skiing, the intimate ski resorts, and the scenery that Norman Rockwell made famous.

ONTEORA, THE MOUNTAIN HOUSE

Box 356
Piney Point Road
Boiceville, New York 12412
(914) 657-6233, Fax: (914) 657-6233
Innkeepers: Bob McBroom and Joe Ohe
Rooms: 3 doubles, 1 suite
Rates: Doubles $95, Suite $135 (Weekend and package rates are available)
Payment: Personal checks
Children: Children over 12 years of age are welcome
Dogs: Welcome with prior approval
Open: All year

It is often the simplest concept or the most universal product that makes great fortunes for entrepreneurs. This was certainly the case for Richard Hellmann who was the great mayonnaise mogul. Hellmann took the millions he made from his mayonnaise empire and retreated to the Catskills in the early 1930s. He found a plot of land that placed him high above the undulating valleys and winding rivers, and just south of an ancient Mohawk Indian trail that cut its way through a valley called Onteora or *the land in the sky*. Here, he built a stunning mountain retreat in the style of many of the great Adirondack cottages of the era.

This place is big and it is built to maximize the views that give the retreat its name. The great room with its tall, cathedral ceiling is dominated by a massive fieldstone fireplace. The walls of windows, which include an enormous picture window, seem to bring the breathtaking mountain views right into this space. Just off the great room, Hellmann designed a 40-foot screened-in porch and an expansive deck, both of which offer even more spectacular views of the Esopus Valley. Another observation deck was constructed to fit into the roofline of the main house, allowing for the most panoramic vistas of the Catskill mountains and park. Finally, he had four guest rooms built in the comparatively smaller wings of the house, that are stepped back from the main section.

Bob and Joe found the house and its rundown gardens in 1991, and spent over a year bringing the entire property back to its former elegance. The two-story shingled mountain cottage is now a retreat for those who are in need of complete rest and relaxation. Although the house has antiques (some of them Korean) scattered about it, there is also a rather fresh, contemporary look to the decor and many of the other furnishings. Simple wood furniture is complemented by a collection of Asian pottery and accented by hand wrought iron fixtures, all of which lends an eclectic feeling to the B&B.

Relatively speaking, the guest rooms were designed on a much smaller scale than the common areas at The Mountain House. Fortunately, the cathedral ceilings in each of the chambers create an additional sense of space, and specially selected antiques add to the feeling of authenticity. The suite is the most requested room because it offers the most privacy. The private porch is ideal for enjoying the fresh mountain air, while the gas fireplace creates an ambiance that most people remember long after they leave. Other bedrooms offer fabulous views of the valley, and all enjoy the luxury of down comforters on the queen-size beds. With the exception of the suite, there are no private baths, just the two shared bathrooms and sinks with mirrors in all the bedrooms.

After a good night's sleep, many awaken feeling refreshed and ready for the filling breakfast which is served on the glassed-in porch. This is a leisurely affair, offered between the hours of 8:30 and 10:30 a.m., giving guests the chance to start the day at their own pace. Joe is the chef and offers a meal to rival any fine restaurant. Depending upon the morning, the selections might include Eggs Benedict, served with a special mayonnaise sauce and accompanied by potatoes and baked tomatoes, crepes prepared in a variety of ways, or corn pancakes combined with a red pepper sauce and turkey sausage. Of course, those who are craving plain scrambled eggs (he does throw in herbs from their garden) or simple buttermilk pancakes, can request them as well. All of this is beautifully presented and garnished with fresh fruit. Afterward, guests will find plenty of things to keep them occupied.

If the day is inclement, people can often be found in the library reading or sitting in front of the fire in the common room. The screened-in porch is an equally appealing spot in the summer months. Others might be tempted to head into the billiards room, with its dark wood and heavy Spanish influence, to play a little pool on the vintage table. If the day is warm, the fifty-foot heated swimming pool, complete with a charming twig gazebo, is a very inviting place. Given the opportunity, we are certain Bowser would decline all of this and opt for a walk along the trails that wend through the property. For guests who prefer more strenuous hikes, there is the nearby Catskills Park which is comprised of 1,000 acres of wilderness that has been placed in a preservation trust. Anglers can test their prowess on Esopus Creek, a spot legendary for its trout fishing. Those who want to stay put can always opt for one of the lawn games available at the house.

Finally, for those who want the ultimate in privacy, there will soon be a separate cottage available on the property. Joe is in the process of renovating the building and should have it ready in the next year for people to rent by the week or by the month. This will allow repeat guests, and those who fall in love with the area, to extend their stay and gain a sense of what Mr. Hellmann and others have discovered over the years — that this truly is a unique and spectacular mountain setting.

MAPLE RIDGE INN

Box 372
R.D. 1, Box 391
Cambridge, New York 12816
(518) 677-3674
Host: Ken Riney
Rooms: 10 doubles, 1 suite
Rates: Doubles $175-200, Suite $250
Payment: Personal checks
Children: Welcome provided they are closely supervised. Our personal thoughts are that the inn may be too formal for small children unless they are exceptionally well-behaved.
Dogs: Well-behaved dogs are welcome as long as they are well supervised
Open: All year

Some years ago, Ken Riney took a traditional 32-room Victorian mansion, filled it with exquisite antiques, added a bit of Southern hospitality, and imbued it with New England charm by calling it the Maple Ridge Inn. Since then, he has expanded upon the amenities and the grounds, creating a little piece of paradise in the hills of upstate New York. When we arrived, the staff was preparing the inn for the beginning of the horse racing season in Saratoga Springs. The perennial gardens were in full bloom around the inn, urns and planters were overflowing with geraniums and assorted annuals, the leaves on the huge shade trees had all come in, and the adjacent corn fields were thick with new growth.

We were granted access to the inn through the glassed-in porch, which was also filled with plants. The height of the ceilings, a good 20 feet, provided a feeling for what was to follow. As we entered the foyer our eyes were drawn to the mahogany staircase which gracefully curved toward the upper floors. A breakfast room lay off to one side, and our attention was immediately drawn to the formally set table and large sideboard containing a sterling silver tea service. On the other side of the foyer was the even more ceremonial dining room. The focal points for this room were two huge, glass-topped tables, through which one could see the decorative china bases. The sideboard, flanked by a pair of waist-high blue and white urns, contained bone china edged with gold leaf. Soft light was provided by an enormous brass chandelier, imported from England. The walls were papered in a dark blue paisley print wallpaper which proved to be a terrific backdrop for the original oil paintings and other important pieces of artwork.

Those who have come to the Maple Ridge Inn to totally relax will discover all sorts of places to do so. Some migrate to the cozy sitting room, found just off the dining room. As with the other rooms at the inn, original artwork set amid fabulous antiques set the overall tone; however, here one's eye is drawn to the ornate, multi-tiered silver candelabra. Assorted nooks and crannies contain more collectibles, knickknacks, and antique silver pieces. Just beyond this chamber is the expansive sun porch, which is filled with comfortable rattan sofas and chairs. The ceiling has been draped with colorful fabrics adding a festive tone to the room. The walls of windows overlook the tree-lined pond and undulating fields.

Bedroom options include the four upstairs rooms and the Carriage House rooms. Those looking for a bedroom which is furnished in the same decorative style as the public rooms will probably opt for one in the mansion, as these are furnished with antiques from around the world amid a setting of high ceilings and ornate trim. The most luxurious chamber is the recently renovated Penthouse, which utilizes the entire top floor of the mansion. Those who stay here not only enjoy complete privacy, but also panoramic views of the surrounding countryside. Two queen-size bedrooms have been exquisitely decorated. These are adjoined by a sitting room, complete with a television equipped with a VCR and a coffee bar. Guests who stay here can ask for freshly brewed coffee and/or breakfast to be delivered to the room, complete with a newspaper. Wrapped in soft bathrobes, some enjoy their morning coffee and read the paper while the sun streams in through the stained glass window.

A different set of accommodations can be found in a quaint converted building located to the rear of the property. It is separated from the mansion by a huge barn and carriage house filled with yet more antiques. Here, each of the bed chambers boasts separate outside entrances, making it easy to take Bowser for an impromptu walk. Although the bedrooms lack the same intrinsic details found at the mansion, they are beautifully decorated with a mix of antiques, wicker, and rattan furnishings. Some rooms contain day beds and others double beds with carved wood headboards. The walls have been painted a rich burgundy, with accents provided by brass lamps, framed mirrors, and a scattering of collectibles. The lush carpeting dampens people's footsteps (and Bowser's) and brings an additional sense of coziness to these chambers.

While adventuring with Bowser, guests are treated to the sight of all sorts of domesticated fowl and other wildlife. Rabbits and chickens can be found in a special enclosure, while ducks, geese, and other waterfowl tend to congregate around the pond. The perfect thing to do on a warm summer's afternoon is to either rock to and fro on the wooden swing or recline on the rope hammock.

Guests will find the service at the Maple Ridge Inn to be as exquisite as the decor and furnishings. Breakfast is served buffet style each morning, with homemade muffins and breads, unusual jams, and a special coffee or tea being provided. The staff goes out of their way to fulfill every request. For instance, arrangements can always be made for a limousine to take people antiquing or to a horse race in Saratoga Springs. A traditional high English tea is also available by reservation. Guests are treated to delicate finger sandwiches, pastries, and an assortment of teas and the special house coffee. Those who prefer a less formal repast will always find special desserts, coffee, and tea available in the afternoon. One of the truly special culinary experiences is a multi-course gourmet dinner, which is created by a chef that Ken brings in specifically for the event.

There is plenty for Bowser and his/her human companions to do in the area. The two brooks that run through the property are as scenic as they are cooling to the feet on a hot summer's day. There are also plenty of back roads to explore, or explorations may be limited to the 22-acres of land surrounding the inn. Trout fishing is one of the most popular pastimes on the local Battenkill river. Cambridge is renowned for antiquing, with an entire district that has been named to the National Register of Historic Places. A particularly unusual sight for this rural section of upstate New York are the two wooden gold-domed churches that belong to the local monastery. The inn is also within a few minutes drive of the Vermont border, offering picturesque back country roads to meander along as well as beautiful countryside to marvel at along the way.

THE INN AT THE SHAKER MILL FARM

Route 22
Canaan, New York 12029
(518) 794-9345, Fax: (518) 794-9344
Innkeeper: Ingram Paperny
Rooms: 18 doubles, 2 suites
Rates: $75-100 per person (MAP), B&B rates of $45 are also available
      during the week
Payment: MC and Visa
Children: Welcome
Dogs: Welcome
Open: All year

Over the years, in the process of researching our books, we have run across every type of innkeeper one could imagine and have seen some extremely unusual accommodations. The most original was a kind of communal situation in Northern California, where guests stayed in teepees, Yurts (rounded canvas tents with clear tops), and even an enormous converted wine cask. We have just found the second most unusual place, as much for the informal and fascinating owner as for the simple yet eclectic accommodations.

The inn is actually situated on a lane, right off Route 22, about halfway between Canaan and New Lebanon. In many respects, it has more in common with its Berkshires' neighbors in Lenox and Stockbridge and the nearby Hancock Shaker Village, than with anything surrounding it in New York State. Set on a gently sloping knoll, the rambling homestead seems a natural part of its woodland setting, seemingly melding into the waterfall that drops gently into a stream that flows through the property. Guests from around the world come here to unwind, walk the paths, and meet some of the Americans who have developed a penchant for the simple, rustic experience that Ingram offers his guests. Newcomers will discover that Ingram is a man who moves to his own beat, and guests are welcome to come along for the ride. He knows how to make people feel comfortable, is well-versed on just about any subject, and is a gifted craftsman. His early years were spent with the United Nations; however, for the last quarter century he has been entertaining guests in his rustic retreat.

When making reservations, people are sometimes puzzled by the rate schedule. It is based on single occupancy and has full, modified, and three-day weekend plans, along with the usual one day B&B plan. Breakfast and dinner are usually included, as well. Broken down in simple terms, this means you are getting a good deal, particularly when Ingram throws in a third night of lodging and breakfast for a mere $25. Now, keep in mind, this is an old Shaker mill that Ingram has converted over the years into 20 bedrooms and a few common rooms. Wood beams and stone walls create the desired effect in some bedrooms, while others have smooth plaster walls. Some chambers are quite spacious and ideal for a large family and others are intimate and inviting for just two. They are all clean and comfortable and have private bathrooms. Some offer fireplaces, others kitchenettes, but all are sparsely furnished in the traditional Shaker manner.

There are some who come to the inn to relax and be reclusive, which is fine, although they are inevitably drawn into the convivial atmosphere which seems to permeate the place. Many look forward to the afternoon, when guests tend to congregate in the common room and enjoy conversation along with the cookies and fruit laid alongside the herbal teas and coffee. Those who miss this opportunity to meet some of the other house guests then will certainly get the chance in the evening, when many gather around the circular fireplace in the barrel-ceilinged great room. Dinner is served at different times depending on the night and the schedule of the guests. The menu varies and is dependent on Ingram's culinary mood. His International cuisine is noteworthy and often includes vegetarian specialties.

In the morning, a full breakfast is awaiting guests. Breads, muffins, and bagels are complemented by cream cheese and hard cheeses. Fresh fruits and yogurt appeal to some and assorted egg dishes to others. Juice and a wide variety of herbal and fruit teas, along with coffee are, of course, also available. During the day, many people head to the Hancock Shaker Village to gain a better appreciation for the Shaker culture. Some might also be interested in taking a longer drive up to Williamstown, Massachusetts for summer stock theater, or investigate the quintessential New England towns of Lenox and Stockbridge. Culturally, the area is rich and diverse; however, Bowser might prefer a tour of the local trout stream, a swim in Queechy lake, or hiking in the local Berkshires. In the winter months there are two nice downhill ski resorts at Jiminy Peak and Bosquet, along with nearby Brodie. Cross-country skiing is also easily accessible, with a sauna found back at the inn to rejuvenate tired muscles.

In these hectic and often too serious times in which we all live, it is nice to know there exists a place where the dress is always informal, the food is always unusual, the guest list is always International, and the innkeeper is always unpredictably entertaining. Those who need to know every detail about an inn, down to the color of the sheets, will probably not like it here. Those who can accept the fact that "check-in time is whenever you arrive and checkout time is whenever you leave," will truly have an appreciation for this wonderfully unusual inn and its magnanimous host.

LINCKLAEN HOUSE

79 Albany Street, Box 36
Cazenovia, New York 13035
(315) 655-3461
Manager: Howard M. Kaler
Rooms: 18 doubles, 3 suites
Rates: Doubles $84-99, Suites $115-130
Payment: MC and VISA
Children: Welcome, no charge for children under 12 years of age when they are
           sharing a room with their parents (cribs, cots, babysitters, and
           highchairs are available)
Dogs: Welcome
Open: All year

Travelers have all sorts of reasons for stopping in Cazenovia, whether to visit someone at one of the three nearby colleges, to take a refreshing break from the heat of the city, or to do a bit of antiquing. Historically, Cazenovia has always attracted visitors, hence the reason for building The Lincklaen House in 1836 as a place to house those coming through the area by stagecoach. Today's guests can even find one of the original hitching posts in front of the inn. The three-story Federal style inn is situated on a corner of Cazenovia's main street. Over the years, it has been owned by a variety of people, each adding their own personal touches to the structure. Since 1956, various members of the Tobin family have overseen the operation of the inn, creating a sense of continuity for those staying here over the years.

Either of the two entrances lead guests into an airy lobby, complete with high, coffered ceilings, paneled walls, and elegant Federal style antiques, all of which set the tone for the entire hotel. Guests register at an equally formal, old-fashioned front desk. While waiting to be escorted upstairs, some might want to peek into the East Room, where a crackling fire is usually set in the ornate fireplace. It is here that a Continental breakfast is served each morning and tea in the afternoon.

A long circular staircase leads guests upstairs to the bedrooms, or they may take the elevator. Our favorite rooms were on the front of the building, as they all had high ceilings and were quite sunny. As an aside, the closets in these front rooms are deeper than all the others in the hotel. This is because when the building was originally designed, hoop skirts were fashionable and the women needed a closet with enough space to store them. While these, and many other, historic touches have been maintained, certain features have been expanded upon. Several of the small rooms have been enlarged and all of the bathrooms have been updated with new fixtures and tiling. Also during the Tobins' tenure, Mrs. Tobin created different stencil patterns for each of the bedrooms, giving them crisp and colorful motifs while also maintaining the traditional ambiance of the inn.

Although each bedroom is quite different, guests can expect to find jabots in varying floral patterns at the huge paned windows, white Bates spreads on the beds, and attractive reproduction Queen Anne furnishings. The little extras, such as decorative containers filled with potpourri and Gilchrist and Soames soaps and shampoos are most welcome additions. A telephone, cable television, and air conditioning are modern conveniences not always offered in historic inns, but they are standard amenities at the Lincklaen House. While most of bed chambers are quite spacious, some of the older twin-bedded rooms are rather small. Guests who are looking for the most modern accommodations will find the third floor rooms to their liking. The bathrooms definitely vary in size, so if big bathrooms are an important item then by all means, request a room with one.

Although there are some fine restaurants in Cazenovia, the Lincklaen House has also developed a reputation for serving good food. In the afternoon, the intimate Courtyard is a favorite spot with its flower gardens and huge shade trees. Dinner is always served in the equally cozy main dining room with its high ceilings, supported by large white columns. White clothed tables set with fine china and silverware are surrounded by Windsor-backed chairs. The menu changes seasonally; however, it is difficult to resist starting one's meal with the inn's famous seafood bisque. Aside from choosing an entree from one of the daily specials, guests will be pleased with the more standard offerings such as the medallions of duck, peppercorn lamb, and the Caribbean Cornish game hen. The seafood linguine is also a favorite as it is a combination of shrimp, scallops, and sundried tomatoes in a tomato cream sauce. Delicious popovers accompany every meal.

After a summer dinner it is fun to stroll through town and down to the scenic Cazenovia Lake. A return trip could take visitors along the quiet side streets of this mostly residential community. Depending upon the time of year, guests who choose to wander further afield with Bowser will find hiking, skating, and cross-country skiing available to them. Apple picking and cider making are popular fall events, while spring brings maple sugaring and trout fishing opportunities. After all is said and done though, guests are always happy to return to the warmth and hospitality of the Lincklaen House.

CRABTREE'S KITTLE HOUSE INN

11 Kittle Road
Chappaqua, New York 10514
(914) 666-8044, Fax: (914) 666-2684
Owners: Richard and John Crabtree
Rooms: 11 doubles
Rates: $85
Payment: AE, CB, DC, DSC, ENR, MC, and Visa
Children: Welcome (cribs, cots, and highchairs are available)
Dogs: Welcome with advance notice
Open: All year

Crabtree's Kittle House Inn is most notable for its fine food and wine, which is what initially drew people to this secluded Westchester County inn. It is located in a quiet, residential part of affluent Chappaqua. Built in 1790, the house was originally called the Reisig and Hexamer's Barn on Ivy Hill Farm, which was a 600-acre nursery and fruit farm. Over the centuries, this simple building has been altered many times to meet the needs of its owners. At the turn of the century, a wealthy financier made the most extensive changes, transforming the barn into a 17-room carriage house that was to be a present to his newly married daughter and her husband. She rejected the idea of living in a converted "barn," opting instead for a real house a few miles away. In the late 1920s, the estate was sold and parceled off, leaving the Kittle House as a separate entity that was used as a roadhouse during prohibition. The 1930s ushered in another change for the building as an unsuccessful school for girls. Finally, in 1936, the Lawrence family bought it and transformed it into a restaurant and guest house called the Kittle House and Lawrence Farms Inn, commencing, what has become almost a 60-year tradition of innkeeping.

Although the inn has had several owners over the last half-century, the most current ones being Richard and John Crabtree, it has always managed to attract a distinguished clientele. Some of the more notable guests have included Henry Fonda, Tallulah Bankhead, and Margaret Sullivan, who were then little known actors performing at the adjacent Mt. Kisco Little Theater. Today, the restaurant is renowned for its fabulous wine cellar (over 1,000 vintage wines) and an exceptional and everchanging American Continental cuisine.

Guests approach the entrance to Crabtree's Kittle House Inn through white stone pillars, which lead down a drive to a four-story stucco building with Colonial overtones. Upon entering the inn, it is hard to tell the structure was ever a barn, except for perhaps the rustic, dark woods that are still apparent in the tap room and main dining room. Off to one side, there is a polished oak bar, a subtle reminder of the roadhouse days. Further into the building is a cavernous dining room, which overlooks the back of the property. As guests head downstairs to the greenhouse dining room, they will discover this spacious room exudes an entirely different atmosphere than the upstairs room with its abundant sunlight and more modern trappings.

We could spend pages discussing their extensive lunch and dinner menus, but must be content to offer just a sampling of the dinner entrees guests may expect. A few of the appetizer selections include a roquefort and walnut salad, halibut and salmon gravlax tartare, and penne with Maine sea scallops. A shiitake foie gras oreo on baby spinach, grilled Portobello mushrooms, and the onion soup with Jarlsberg cheese are additional options. Entrees offer many palate pleasing options. Pecan crusted loin of lamb with a Kentucky bourbon sauce, organic free range chicken with a lemon thyme sauce, and the pheasant with couscous and honey thyme sauce are three interesting choices. A sesame-crusted filet of Norwegian salmon with balsamic butter, Connecticut Peking duckling with a black currant sauce, and filet mignon on a kataifi crouton with a Beaujolais wine sauce are additional favorites of many patrons.

After dinner, a steep flight of stairs will bring overnight guests to their simply furnished and decorated rooms. These are rather Spartan, with a decor centered around a Colonial theme. Each is somewhat unique, but all offer standard amenities such as private baths, telephones, and color cable-televisions. We have to stress, there is nothing fancy about the bedrooms; however, they are very clean and comfortable and provide a nice atmosphere for which to get a good night's sleep. In the morning, guests are treated to pretty views of the woods that rest along the perimeter of the sprawling grounds.

After enjoying a substantial Continental breakfast, many are anxious to take Bowser out for a little exercise. There are acres of land to explore, as well as hilly terrain surrounding the inn. The streets in this neighborhood are quiet, making it very conducive for early morning and late evening walks. Many people also choose to explore this lovely community with its rock walls, exquisite homes, and rolling countryside.

ATHENAEUM HOTEL

Box 66, Route 384
Chautauqua, New York 14722
(716) 357-4444
General Manager: Thomas Smith
Rooms: 160 doubles
Rates: Doubles $88-130 per person, double occupancy (AP)
Payment: Personal or travelers checks
Children: Welcome
Dogs: Welcome, provided they follow the rules outlined by the Institute
Open: During the season, late June - August

To be completely honest, we had very little idea what the Chautauqua Institute was all about until we arrived there one hot summer afternoon. We bought our gate pass (obligatory to even be allowed admittance to this gated community) and upon passing by the guards, seemingly entered into a bygone era. Here, on the banks of Lake Chautauqua, lay an old-fashioned Victorian summer community, complete with colorful gingerbread houses, narrow winding streets, grassy covered plazas, and an impressive outdoor amphitheater. People strolled with their children down to the water, rode bicycles, or could be seen relaxing in their rocking chairs on front porches. We felt quite at ease and were eager to learn more about a place that seemingly had such a serendipitous effect upon its residents.

The Chautauqua Institution was founded in 1874, specifically to instruct Sunday school teachers. This Christian foundation is still in evidence today, although it has been expanded to encompass all faiths. Ten or so of the hundreds of cottages are designated as Denominational Houses, where ministers, their families, and the public are welcome to stay for a small fee. It is important to understand that this sleepy year round community of 500 or so expands into the thousands during the busy summer season.

Guests of the Chautauqua Institution may choose to spend their time listening to lectures on arts and the humanities, global ethics and the environment, or on education and the American character. Those who are interested in attending summer school will find Schools of Art, Dance, Music, Theater and Special Studies. Literary enthusiasts may be interested in the Chautauqua Literary and Scientific Circle, the oldest continuous book club in America. Some of their many lecturers over the years have included many Pulitzer-Prize winning authors. Recreation abounds for children of all ages, who can take advantage of the supervised day camp programs. While the arts are an integral part of the Institute, so are the outdoor recreation opportunities. We were beginning to understand why everyone we encountered was so pleasant and relaxed.

While there are a hundred or so accommodations to choose from in Chautauqua, ranging from a single room in a private home to hotels, the crown jewel for the entire community is the very impressive Athenaeum Hotel, which was completely restored in the mid-1980s. The hotel is separated from the lake by huge expanses of lawn. This majestic Victorian hotel, with its Mansard roof and floor-to-ceiling Palladian windows, was built in the style of many of the grand old summer resorts. A pair of stately staircases lead guests up to the sprawling front porch, which extends 50 feet or so to either side of the main entrance. Some guests had already settled into the green wicker rocking chairs when we passed by, basking in the warmth of the summer sun.

As we stepped inside the hotel, the grand scale was no less awesome. The lobby is truly cavernous, with ceilings soaring up 30-feet or more. The good-sized brown wicker chairs are usually occupied by twosomes engaged in conversation. Here, brass Victorian chandeliers with glass sconces cast soft light on the lustrous patina that emanates from the woodworking, wainscoting, and hardwood floors. Just off the lobby is our favorite common room, a long formal parlor, painted a soft yellow hue and lit by three enormous crystal chandeliers. Off-white wicker chairs and sofas, with comfortable cushions, set the scene for this convivial chamber. The room runs half the length of the hotel with floor-to-ceiling glass windows offering expansive views of the lake. The Blue Room, just off the parlor, is much smaller than any of the other public rooms, and is furnished in a more Victorian manner.

Just across from the parlor is the formal dining room. There is a dress code here for dinner, which seems a fitting custom for this particular hotel and its clientele. Luncheon on the day of our visit was a multi-course meal starting with consomme and Count Pitty Pats crab soup. Three of the entree selections included trout, tenderloin of beef, and salmon with arrugula, tomatoes, and capers. A time honored tradition of two desserts was also included — this day the offering was an almond amaretto cheesecake, a raspberry vanilla torte, or the lemon chiffon pie. The rather formal atmosphere was made all the more inviting by the charming old-fashioned floral wallpaper, Queen-Anne style furnishings, and elegant place settings.

The guest rooms can be reached by any number of staircases ascending from the first floor, or by an old-fashioned elevator. Wide, high-ceilinged hallways lead to bedrooms with similar ceiling heights. These have all been decorated with the muted tones of Victorian-era wallpapers. Simple furnishings also are reflective of the era, and include oak beds and bureaus with a scattering of wicker chairs. Bathrooms are all private and quite clean, but don't expect any special frills or amenities. Although neat and tidy, there is a sense of Puritan simplicity about the guest rooms that we found refreshing. The windows are usually the centerpiece for the bedroom, offering lovely views of the garden court or lake front. There are many who end up spending very little time in their chambers, as they are usually quite busy with an art class, lecture, or concert. The botanical setting of the second floor outdoor terrace, is also a draw for many of the guests.

During our visit, there seemed to be an older clientele in residence. Perhaps the formal nature of the restaurant and public areas lends itself to adults without young children; however, this should not dissuade young families or couples of any age from enjoying a truly unique experience. Bowser is certain to feel welcome at the hotel and on the grounds. There were many other dogs in the community during our visit, who all seemed to be having a wonderful time cavorting along paths, swimming (but not from the public beaches), and keeping pace with their human counterparts, who were bicycling. This is also a very safe place for Bowser to vacation as cars are frowned upon and walking is the preferred mode of transportation. The hotel is within an easy stroll of the village center, which offers a variety of shops. Tennis is available on any of the eight Har Tru courts, and a diverse selection of recreational options can be found at the Sports Club. Golf enthusiasts will surely be tempted to test their skill on the 27-hole course located just across from the main gates.

The Chautauqua Institute is truly the perfect spot for those who want a vacation destination that satisfies them mentally and physically. With all of the educational programs offered by the Institute, even rainy days can be quite enlightening and rewarding.

Pet Policy: The owners of cats and dogs need to register them with the Finance Office in the Colonnade Buildings. There is a $1 fee. Dogs must be leashed when on the grounds. Check to see where dogs are and are not permitted.

HUDSON HOUSE

Two Main Street
Cold Spring, New York 10516
(914) 265-9355
Innkeepers: Robert Contiguglia and Kathleen Dennison
Rooms: 11 doubles, 2 suites
Rates: Doubles $80-150, Suites $105-200
Payment: AE, DC, MC, and Visa
Children: Welcome
Dogs: Well-behaved dogs are welcome
Open: All year

Set on one of the most majestic sections of the Hudson River is the Hudson House. Since 1832 it has occupied this scenic location, privy to resplendent views of boats traveling along the river, from the era of Robert Fulton's steamboat to today's modern vessels. The hotel has undergone as many changes over the years as it has names. The original name was the Pacific, eventually changing to the Simonson Hotel, then to the Hudson View Inn, and finally to its present name — Hudson House. Dressed in clapboards, with a cypress foundation and a mansard roof, the hotel still offers one of the most enviable views of the Hudson River and the surrounding mountains from its intimate wraparound porches and original paned windows and doors.

Guests can arrive at the inn by way of boat, train, or more often by car. The train is situated a block or so from the inn, although aside from an occasional whistle, guests remain fairly unaware of its existence. An intimate restaurant and bar occupy most of the Hudson House's first floor. The small dining room is broken up into cozy seating areas. In the summertime, the tables are covered with chintz overlays and small glass vases hold single yellow roses. The menu is quite extensive and good, drawing people from all over the region. Guests may choose from appetizers such as Maryland lobster and crab cakes, grilled marinated shrimp and scallops on lobster coulee, or the lemon and black pepper pasta with artichokes, eggplant, and sun-dried tomatoes. The entree selection is no less varied. Roast Long Island duck served with sour cherries and fresh thyme, tenderloin of pork roasted with oranges and pine nuts, and Colorado Monfort shell steak served with frizzled onions are some good options. After dinner, some people might want to relax before the fire in the cozy living room. There is also a television and VCR, but most are content to just visit with each other or read one of the many periodicals.

Although there may seem to be more of an emphasis on the food here than the bedrooms, overnight guests will be quite pleased with what they discover. Our favorite choices are those located on the river side of the building. These chambers, on the second floor, have French doors leading out to balconies. Each is uniquely decorated with fresh country print wallpapers, some tend to be rather contemporary in flavor and others a bit more old-fashioned. One bedroom might have white wicker with navy blue accents as the predominate theme, while another has a huge painted brass bedstead with a yellow floral comforter. Folded quilts rest at the base of the beds and there is always an assortment of country antiques placed about the chambers. The bedrooms without closets boast of antique pine armoires, which are set amid solid oak antique bureaus and lovely oak bedside tables topped with pottery reading lamps. Tie-back curtains, fashioned from prints which complement the wallpapers, frame the windows. The bathrooms are mostly private, clean, and outfitted with Hudson House soaps and shampoos. Some of the guest rooms are quite small; however, what they lose in size they make up for in height as the ceilings (on both floors) are 15 feet. There are two suites at the inn, one is a queen-bedded chamber that adjoins a guest room with a pair of twin beds by way of a central bathroom. The other suite has a twin-bedded room adjoining a bedroom with both a double bed and a bathroom, all of which have lovely views of the river. During our visit, it was hot and steamy, making the air conditioner and ceiling fan an especially welcome amenity.

For those who are wondering what they might want to do in Cold Springs, there are plenty of options. The town park is just across the way, with a small, red roofed gazebo and grassy lawn leading down to the river's edge. The town has the plans and the funding for a restoration of the area. The result will be a beautiful park, extending down to the Hudson, where there will be a children's playground, more grassy areas, public rest rooms, and antique street lamps, all in a style of the 1800s. Guests may also wish to walk Bowser along the quiet waterfront, or head up the hill for a bit of window shopping at any of the antique stores lining the quaint main street. This is a rather sleepy town, often closing up shops on Monday and Tuesday and then gearing up again on Wednesday for the upcoming weekend. Cold Spring has a little ice cream parlor, a handful of good restaurants, and best of all, a genuine small-town atmosphere. Those who prefer hiking will find a myriad of trails and hills to climb at nearby Bear Mountain, Storm King, and Bull Hill. Local hiking maps are available at the bookstore. Anyone searching for an escape from the city, or who is visiting nearby West Point, should definitely consider stopping in for a night or two at the Hudson House.

DE BRUCE COUNTRY INN
on the Willowemoc

Route 23
R.D. 1, Box 286A
DeBruce, New York 12758
(914) 439-3900
Innkeepers: Ron and Marilyn Lusker
Rooms: 15 doubles
Rates: $140-170 double occupancy (MAP)
Payment: AE, MC, and Visa
Children: Welcome
Dogs: Welcome with advance notice and a $25 deposit
Open: All year, except from December 15 through April 1

As we were driving toward the De Bruce Country Inn along the scenic Willowemoc River, it was easy to see why Marilyn and Ron felt comfortable leaving the confines of New York city for the simpler and more peaceful lifestyle of the Catskills. Here, they felt they could combine both their artistic talents and their experience in restoring old buildings into creating a successful country inn.

The couple had spent well over twenty years visiting the area before finally locating an ideal building which could be transformed into an inn. Originally built by a German family in the early 1900s, today the mustard color De Bruce Country Inn lies hidden from the road by bushes and trees. Its facade is rather unassuming, standing tall and square; however, the extensive interior renovations and artistic flair of the Luskers have dramatically transformed this building into an unusual restaurant and overnight accommodations that is literally filled with unusual pieces of art and handmade crafts.

We entered by way of the dining room, which is a large chamber with a number of windows overlooking the swimming pool and the mountains beyond. Rose colored tablecloths cover the smattering of tables, but what really attracts one's attention are the assorted paintings adorning the walls. This is just one of the many rooms which display artists' works. This rather sprawling gallery is changed twice a month, each time imbuing the inn with new life. Beyond the restaurant is one of our favorite spots, the glassed-in porch, which offers panoramic views of the Catskills. The reflective red tile floors are cool to the touch in the summertime, with the open windows allowing the refreshing breezes to move freely through the house. Guests will discover that breakfast is often served here on summer mornings. While the menu is ever changing, patrons may choose a lighter fare of whole grain cereals, muffins, and fresh fruit or try some of the hot dishes, which could include pancakes, blintzes, omelettes, or French toast.

All but one of the bedrooms are located on the top two floors. The hardwood floors and clean lines of these rooms gave Marilyn and Ron the opportunity to provide special decorative touches. The rather Spartan chambers are furnished with one or two carefully selected country antiques, which are often painted to complement a quilt or original painting, silkscreen, or lithograph. What really intrigued us were the quilts that had come to them by way of Thailand. The sophisticated patterns and beautiful colors (teal green and red, pale pinks and greens, and varying hues of blue) were what drew us to these unique quilts and it wasn't until closer inspection that we noticed the intricate handstitching.

The guest rooms are available in a variety of sizes; however, our favorites were those to the rear of the building with views of the mountains. One pairing of rooms on the second floor turned out to be an ideal suite for families. Another favorite guest chamber was tucked away on the first floor, decorated with lovely country antiques, and open to the warmth of daylong sunlight.

Visitors are certain to be charmed by the same things that drew Marilyn and Ron to the area. Guests need only walk down a path and across a small bridge, before finding themselves on the other side of the renowned Willowemoc trout stream. In addition to assisting anglers in their technique, guides are also available to lead them along the extensive trail systems or to escort them on hunting expeditions.

While the fall brings hunters to the area, it also draws its fair share of leaf peepers and those who prefer to do their "hunting" through the lens of a camera. The winter months attract those with a love for the outdoors who are interested in exploring the seemingly endless trails by way of their cross-country skis. Bowser is certain to enjoy a fair amount of freedom in this wilderness region. After a busy day in the hot sun, many look forward to returning to the inn and relaxing in the gazebo, set idyllically next to the stream. Others prefer a rejuvenating dip in the pool and then a steam in the sauna. A volleyball net is also set up for anyone interested in playing.

One of our favorite spots in the evening is the "Dry Fly" lounge, which is an antique bar located in the basement of the inn. Sipping a hot toddy and putting one's feet up next to the fireplace seems to be the perfect way to end a thoroughly enjoyable day. There is usually a small selection of edible goodies which can often serve as late evening snacks for some of the guests as well. Another corner of the inn offers an old-fashioned parlor which lies just beyond a pair of French doors off the reception area. Here, comfortable couches and chairs are gathered around a wonderful fieldstone fireplace that is usually crackling and popping on cold Catskill nights. Grab a book from the small library and settle back for evening reading.

As we have mentioned, Ron and Marilyn are very creative. Although they enjoy being around people, they are equally content when all is quiet as it allows them to enjoy the beautiful surroundings and indulge in their true passion — art.

OLD DROVERS INN

Old Route 22
Dover Plains, New York 12522
(914) 832-9311
Innkeepers: Alice Pitcher and Kemper Peacock
Rooms: 4 doubles
Rates: $110-170
Payment: DC, MC, and VISA
Children: Very well-behaved children are welcome
Dogs: Welcome if they have been groomed recently, are friendly, and are
      walked off the property ($10 daily fee)
Open: All year except the first two weeks in January

If we had to pick one spot in the southern Berkshires for the perfect romantic getaway it would be the Old Drovers Inn. This historic inn has been taking care of travellers for over 250 years, and as with fine antiques, it literally glows with a unique charm that only time can bestow on fine things.

The inn was built in 1750 and was then known as the Clear Water Tavern. It housed cattle drovers — "a group of professional middlemen who purchased herds of cattle and swine from New England farmers, drove the animals down the post roads to New York city markets, and sold the cattle for as good a price as they could get." Along the way they stopped for food and drink and occasionally to sleep. Today's visitors come seeking the same respite, except instead of being on their way to New York city to sell their wares, they are usually escaping from the pressures of business for the quiet of the country.

Although the inn is conveniently located about a half mile from busy Route 22, guests have a sense of stepping back in time. Huge shade trees overhang the white clapboard inn and 12-acres of grounds. Day lilies, lilacs, and a profusion of other perennials are abundant in this naturalized setting. Small wooden tables and benches are set about the grounds, allowing guests to enjoy a sense of solitude. Those who are patient will see rabbits and other woodland creatures coming out to roam in the early morning and evening hours.

Most overnight guests enter the inn through the charming sitting area. Here, they are enveloped by a sense of history. Truly classic mahogany antiques surround the huge down sofa, which is perfectly positioned to take advantage of the warmth from the fireplace. A narrow, winding staircase leads to the second floor bedrooms and the intimate common areas. Each of the four bed chambers is loaded with antiques and a good deal of charm. The largest and most unusual is the Meeting Room, aptly named for the meetings which were held here until the mid-1800s by the Dover Plains' selectmen. Today, guests will find chintz-covered wing chairs facing the elegant white brick fireplace. Two antique double beds rest under the high barrel-vaulted ceiling. Hues of yellow can be found throughout, from the floral curtains at the windows to the coverlets on the puffy comforters. Our personal favorite is the Sleigh Room, whose focal point is a sleigh bed which faces the fireplace. Others may prefer to relax in one of the two wing chairs set before the fire. The Cherry Room, with its matching cherry-wood beds and abundance of English antiques, is more reminiscent of the English countryside than of New York State, giving guests a further sense of being in another place. The coziest of the four is the Rose Room, which does not offer a fireplace but whose charm more than makes up for this omission. The Colonial paneling (found in two chambers), wide board floors, English chintzes, and lovely antiques make these chambers some of the coziest and most inviting we have ever seen. It is only after guests settle into their rooms that they will begin to notice the especially thoughtful amenities such as small makeup mirrors, special soaps and shampoos in the bathrooms, and evening trays filled with chocolates, fruit, and bottles of water.

While only a select few are able to enjoy the pleasures of staying at the Old Drovers Inn, many more can sample the excellent and innovative cuisine served in the dining room. This is located in what many would think of as the basement of the building, but which is actually the original tap room for the inn. The low-beamed ceilings and original stone walls are illuminated by the flickering candlelight emanating from the hurricane lanterns which dot the linen covered tables. The centerpiece for the dining room is a massive stone fireplace which imparts as much charm as it does warmth. While some might choose to mention the huge drinks that are served in elegant crystal glasses, others prefer to dwell on the seasonally changing menu. Cheddar cheese soup is the inn's specialty and a traditional favorite; however, the house smoked salmon and goat cheese purses covered in a lobster vinaigrette, or the crayfish, artichokes, and lemon aioli are equally appealing. Entree selections are also unusual and extensive with choices such as the Guinea hen-truffle oil and breast of Magret duck covered in a red wine oxtail sauce. A saddle of rabbit au jus or the Black Angus Cowboy steak with tobacco onions and red-eye gravy round out the distinctive menu. Those who have a penchant for peppermint stick ice cream will find the locally made version served at the inn to be unparalleled, although the Key Lime pie and chocolate pecan pate have their fans as well.

In the morning, breakfast is served in the Federal Room, which is usually warmed by a fire. The focal point here is the charming mural painted by Edward Paine in 1941 depicting the inn, West Point, and Hyde Park. The hearty repast to follow may include selections such as Belgian malted waffles, French toast baguette, Shepherd's eggs on hash browns, and delicate, delectable egg dishes.

While the walking is quite peaceful on the grounds and immediately adjacent to the property, there are also plenty of things to do in the vicinity. For those who want to experience wine tasting, there are two vineyards nearby, one in Amenia and the other in Millbrook. Also in Millbrook, visitors will discover the Mary Flagler Cary Arboretum with nature trails and collections of plants. Of course, there are also plenty of backroads to explore and pleasant parks to visit as well. But what draws most people to the Old Drovers Inn is the refined and gracious setting in which they can relax and do nothing at all.

BASSETT HOUSE

P.O. Box 1426
128 Montauk Highway
East Hampton, New York 11937
(516) 324-6127
Owner: Michael Bassett
Rooms: 10 doubles, 2 suites
Rates: Doubles $75-175, Suites $165-175
Payment: AE, MC, and Visa
Children: Well-behaved children are welcome (cribs and cots available)
Dogs: Welcome with advance notice and prior approval and a $15 fee
Open: All year

East Hampton has long been known for its exclusive summer colonies and magnificent oceanfront beaches, seemingly inaccessible to tourists. The town has much to offer in the way of wonderful stores and restaurants, and yes, there are ways to gain access to the beaches. Unfortunately, there are not a lot of places to stay that are reasonably priced and want Bowser as a guest. We ran across one spot that was, relatively speaking, moderately priced, unpretentious, and welcomes guests of the four-legged variety — The Bassett House.

Set back from the very busy Montauk Highway, this B&B is framed by several shade trees and a picket fence. Built in 1830, the original Colonial style house has experienced many additions over the years with the culmination being a much extended version of the original. An old iron basset hound guards the entrance to the inn, providing some insight to the often eclectic, and sometimes amusing, furnishings and decor inside. There is still a feeling of antiquity throughout the first floor, with moldings and hardwood floors; however, the original small rooms are no longer in evidence. Existing doorways have either been enlarged or have disappeared altogether to be replaced by an arch, causing the three rooms to flow together. The first sitting area offers a comfortable couch and chairs, circa 1950s, along with a not so state-of-the-art television. Down a step is the large living room, whose centerpieces during our visit were a turn-of-the-century cookstove and an old fashioned dentist's chair festooned with balloons. Collectibles of all periods abound with a variety of art deco clocks, signs, and glassware displayed throughout. The French doors off the living room lead into a long dining room, whose back wall of windows overlook the lawn and gardens. This is a favorite spot for guests, who sit at the immense table each morning and visit, while Michael whips up a full breakfast for them. He has a way of making people feel so comfortable that the mood around the breakfast table is always most convivial. For those who enjoy catching a few extra winks, don't despair, breakfast hour stretches to 11:00 a.m.

After a very hearty meal, guests usually feel the need to get out and stretch their legs. Surprisingly, there is quite a bit of land attached to the inn, providing more than enough space for throwing a ball for Bowser. There are also chairs set on the patio for those who would rather sit and read the Sunday paper while "you know who" basks in the sun. Taking the Sunday paper back to be read in bed is also a popular option.

The second floor bedrooms are located off a long, narrow hallway scattered with rose patterned area rugs. Many of these chambers are painted in old fashioned colors, such as pale greens and roses. Some bedrooms might have a Victorian motif with carved wooden or spindle headboards and matching bureaus. Towels are draped over old-fashioned wooden towel racks and often there is some sort of sitting chair set next to a window. Our favorite rooms were those on the back of the house, as they were furthest from the street noise. We were particularly fond of the third floor attic rooms resting comfortably among the eaves, with windows overlooking the backyard. A cozy private sitting area can also be found up here, with bulging bookshelves and comfortable places to read. One of our favorite rooms lay at the end of the house, offering the most privacy and an immense amount of sun streaming in through the windows. Some of the bathrooms are shared and others private, but all are extremely clean.

B&Bs offer different things for different people. Some guests go to soak up the ambiance and be surrounded by antiques, others just want to get away and completely unwind in a private setting, and still others look for a place where they can meet new people, share stimulating conversations, and savor a slice of life they don't often experience. The Bassett House offers the latter experience, with Michael being the catalyst for everyone's good time.

Those who are looking for a few unusual excursions during their stay in East Hampton might want to try the East Hampton Nature Trail. They can also head over to the Animal Rescue Fund Adoption Center in East Hampton, borrow a friend for Bowser, and follow one of their trails through the woods. Cedar Point Park in East Hampton is another favorite spot for walks. At the end of the day, it is nice to know that a wonderful, comforting, and casual evening is awaiting guests of the Bassett House.

THE PINK HOUSE

26 James Lane
East Hampton, New York 11937
(516) 324-3400
Managers: Sue Calden and Ron Steinhilber
Rooms: 4 doubles, 1 suite
Rates: Doubles $185-235, Suite $260-420
Payment: Personal checks
Children: Not appropriate for small children
Dogs: Very nice, relaxed dogs are welcome. Must get along with Cody who
     is their friendly yellow lab/retriever
Open: All year

The Pink House is truly a special find, as much for the B&B as for Sue and Ron, the two people who run it. Hidden behind a huge privet hedge, it is easy to mistake this coral pink 1850s Colonial for a private residence. Tinkling bronze Salari bells welcome guests to the front porch, with its comfortable wicker chairs. After stepping through the main entrance and into the foyer, we knew we had stumbled upon a treasure, one that had been refurbished with a fine eye toward detail. We soon discovered that Sue and Ron have advertising and architectural backgrounds, with Ron providing the conceptual and woodworking skills. Nothing about the inn is overdone, yet it maintains a sense of sophistication. The clean simple lines of the house have not been obscured by excess clutter, thereby allowing such features as the original built-in cabinets and detailed moldings to stand out.

One of the more memorable aspects of The Pink House are the fresh flowers displayed in every room and alcove, along with the watercolors that adorn the walls. The living room is one of our favorite common areas. When we arrived, there was melodious background music playing softly for guests, who had settled into the two sofas flanking the fireplace. A profusion of flowers on the coffee table is the centerpiece of color for this room, while a collection of decoys, resting on a long table against the wall, provide an interesting accent. Just beyond the living room is the intimate dining room, which in addition to some charming antique collectibles also features a good sized model of a boat. Breakfast is served here each morning, a multi-course affair that begins with homemade granola, yogurt, and an assortment of freshly baked breads and muffins. Of course, fresh fruit, juice, and strong European coffee are also integral parts of this meal. Those with even the healthiest dose of willpower will find it difficult to resist the banana walnut pancakes, Belgian waffles, and sourdough French toast that are usually offered as well. On cool mornings, a fire warms the entire room, enticing most to linger well after the meal is concluded. On warm mornings, this hearty repast is served on a large table on the back porch that overlooks the gardens and swimming pool.

The gardens surrounding the inn are reminiscent of the English countryside. An enormous, mature privet hedge surrounds the property, affording all the more privacy for the inn's guests. A croquet course is separated from the swimming pool by a cutting garden, resplendent in vibrant colors. The pool is the perfect size for swimming laps, or for just taking a refreshing dip on a hot summer day. Chaise lounges are set about the perimeter of the pool, making for an ideal spot for sunning or reading the morning paper.

Set off to the side of the cutting garden is one of our favorite chambers, The Garden Room. This suite has a private outside entrance (ideal for Bowser) that opens onto a small patio surrounded by flowers. It is decorated in a sophisticated style that is similar to the B&B's other bedrooms, although as we later discovered, each chamber does have a distinct personality. The Blue Room is brightest, with an inviting oak pencil post bed resting on polished oak floors. The afternoon sun streaming into this chamber beckons most to rest awhile on the cushioned window seat. The Twin Room offers twin beds (which can be pushed together to make a king) and an even more elegant ambiance, with pink and green fabrics setting the tone. The huge secretary set off to the side is the focal point for the room, as is a wall of collectibles. One of the smallest guest chambers is decorated in blue and yellow Pierre Deux fabrics. This bedroom, with its nooks and crannies, small window seat, and out-of-the-way location, feels like a secret hideaway for many of the guests. The Green Room is located on the end of the house, is furnished with wicker and also offers some of the best views of the gardens. All of the bathrooms have been redone with the same luxurious touch, that includes marble accents and antique mirrors. Added to this are a deluxe selection of toiletries, as well as thick cotton bathrobes to lounge in after a bath or shower.

Although we didn't have a chance to visit with Sue, Ron was a most gracious host who was extremely friendly and willing to accommodate any special requests. His dog Cody, a very friendly yellow lab/retriever, has been known on occasion to jump up into a willing guest's lap for a rub behind the ears. When it comes time to explore the surrounding area, guests may head off in just about any direction and find something to entertain them. The inn is only a short distance from town, allowing for terrific window shopping opportunities. A turn in another direction brings visitors into one of East Hampton's most beautiful and exclusive residential sections and beyond to the beach. There are also numerous town parks to explore and Hook Pond, which is a leisurely stroll from the inn. A trip in the car will lead to some of the extensive trail systems in the area, including the Northwest Woods, Indian Field, and Hither Hills and Woods (a map is available in the town clerk's office). Upon returning to The Pink House, guests will discover tempting homemade breads and a variety of refreshments have been thoughtfully laid out for afternoon tea.

In a short time, Ron and Sue have proven successful in providing just the right combination of ingredients for their guests. The charming accommodations, their proximity to the village of East Hampton, and the low-key, unpretentious atmosphere allows people to truly unwind.

RIVER RUN

Box D-4
Main Street
Fleischmanns, New York 12430
(914) 254-4884
Hosts: Larry Miller and Jeanne Palmer
Rooms: 8 doubles, 2 apartments
Rates: Doubles $40-90, Apartments $50
Payment: MC and Visa
Children: Welcome
Dogs: Welcome and are considered to be "special guests". If left alone, crates
    can be provided for them. A $5 nightly fee is requested.
Open: All year

In all our years of researching inns, we have yet to come across a place that actually encourages guests to travel with their canine companions. Obviously, there are plenty of inns and hotels which welcome and accept this arrangement, but very few have hosts who actually go so far as to make the dogs almost as comfortable as their human counterparts. River Run is the first, and as far as we know, the only establishment to truly want guests to bring their four-legged friends.

For those who might worry that this is merely a glorified doggie hotel, rest assured it is far from it. This is a charming 20-room B&B, located in Fleischmanns village. Those arriving at night will be entranced by the white lights draped along the branches of the spruce trees that mark the entrance to River Run. When we arrived, Larry's sweet cocker spaniel, Ruffian, was waiting patiently on the front porch for Larry to return. Shortly thereafter, Larry came strolling up the front walk (he wasn't expecting us), and the two of them led us inside.

We soon learned that Larry and Jeanne purchased the inn in 1992 from another couple who needed a break from the innkeeping business. It was an ideal situation for Larry who was also in need of a change, but his was from the pressures of the New York advertising world. Larry teamed up with Jeanne, and together they bought this 1887 Victorian B&B. Larry and Ruffian moved to Fleischmanns permanently, while Jeanne has kept her job at a large publishing house in the city and commutes up on weekends. What makes River Run work is that Larry and Jeanne each bring something different to the B&B, whether it be an eye for details, culinary expertise, or their easy rapport with the guests.

Physically, River Run retains many of its original Victorian features. Stained glass windows can be found in many of the bedrooms and are the highlight of the dining room, where they light up the room with color each morning. The parlor is equally inviting, with its wall of built-in shelves that are literally packed with books that we suspect are a sampling of those produced at Jeanne's publishing house. Music is usually playing in the background, and a fire blazing in the fireplace, when guests return from their daytime excursions. In the winter months, cookies and hot drinks are laid out here, while in the summer time, the front porch is the preferred gathering spot for iced tea and lemonade. Guests have also been known to take their repast down to the private riverside garden, where they may recline in the comfortable lawn chairs or in the most inviting hammock.

If the weather is not conducive to being outside, guests can always follow the handcarved bannister that curves gracefully up to the third floor. On the top floor, aside from some guest rooms, there is a parlor created specifically with Bowser in mind. For various reasons it is not practical to let Bowser roam around the first-floor parlor, therefore, this equally comfortable space was created. Here, guests will be just as happy relaxing on the sofa or soft side chairs, while their four-legged friend sleeps at their feet or visits with some of the other canine residents.

The eight guest rooms in the main house are easy to find, as each has been given a name based on a river in the region. Just as each river has its own unique characteristics, so do the bedrooms. Whether in the Delaware, Esopus, or Beaverkill, guests are certain to find early American antiques predominating. Brass or oak headboards can be found on most of the beds, with furnishings consisting of mirrored oak bureaus set alongside rocking chairs or armchairs. Lace curtains serve to define the stained glass windows, which provide a profusion of color across the hardwood floors. As with everything else at the inn, the private and shared bathrooms are spotless and offer lightly scented glycerine soaps. Those who relish their sense of space, will want to stay in the second floor rooms as their ceilings are high and the bedrooms quite spacious. The Delaware is one of our favorite chambers with its king-size brass bed and pink floral wallpaper. Third floor chambers are set into the eaves, offering much in the way of charm. Cable television is also available in some of the bedrooms, a nicety for those who don't want to completely lose touch with the real world.

Downstairs, in a separate part of the B&B, there is the retro-wing with two 1950s' apartments. While they do not have the same antique ambiance as the rooms in the upper levels of the main house, they do give guests a little more independence. A kitchen is available for meal preparation and separate outside entrances makes it easy to take Bowser for leisurely walks. Finally, most families will also find these particular accommodations ideally meet their needs.

On the weekends, Jeanne organizes breakfast, which she has perfectly planned down to the last raspberry. Our menu was handwritten, providing us with a glimpse of what was to come. This hearty affair began with granola, cantaloupe, juice, and strawberry bread. While this would satisfy most Continental breakfast goers, there was more to follow. Resisting both the black raspberry whole wheat pancakes and the apricot plum torte was an impossibility, so we vowed to skip lunch and enjoyed every bite of this delicious meal. Another of the B&B's morning specialities is a traditional English breakfast, consisting of scones, grilled tomatoes, an egg dish, and bacon.

Although River Run has been operational for only two years, a lot of thought has obviously gone into creating an environment truly conducive to meeting the needs of the guests who choose to bring a dog. There is no sense of having to keep Bowser in hiding, in fact Ruffian enjoys meeting her overnight visitors. Those who want to go out for dinner can make Bowser comfortable in one of the kennels made available by the inn. Larry and Jeanne have even gone so far as to create a lengthy *pet philosophy* so that everyone knows, in advance, what to expect. This goes so far as to tell them about towels, which are available at the front door, for drying off Bowser should he get wet during his walk. All of this planning allows for a truly comfortable and relaxed stay for all.

Larry and Jeanne have also put together an extensive list of things to do while in the area. For instance in Arkville, there is the Delaware and Ulster Rail Ride which allows dogs. Devil's Tombstone is a rock formation resembling a large tombstone, a natural wonder that many find intriguing. The Ashokan Reservoir provides fishing and picnicking opportunities. The Pakatakan Hiking Trail in Margaretville is another good prospect on a warm summer's day, as are any of the other hiking trails in the Catskill Forest Preserve. We found this part of the Catskills to be surprisingly scenic and peaceful and River Run to be one of the best finds for dog lovers.

GARDEN CITY HOTEL

45 Seventh Street
Garden City, New York 11530
(800) 547-0400, (516) 747-3000, Fax: (516) 747-1414
General Manager: Catherine Nalkin
Rooms: 264 doubles, 16 suites
Rates: Doubles $175-340, Suites $400-850
Payment: AE, CB, DC, JCB, MC, and Visa
Children: Welcome (cribs and cots are available)
Dogs: Small dogs are welcome with advance notice
Open: All year

Those with any historical knowledge of Long Island will certainly remember the luxurious and elegant Garden City Hotel, which occupied this same site for over 100 years and played host to an array of millionaires, business moguls, and society's most elite. The hotel was recreated in the early 1980s, and reopened in 1983. What exists here today is, in many respects, a rebirth of the original Georgian building with a contemporary twist. Two long nine-story brick wings are joined in the middle by a massive clock tower. A white cupola, encircled by Palladian windows and topped by a spire adds further architectural interest to the exterior of the building.

This same sense of refinement is evident from the moment guests step through the revolving door and into the lobby, which is awash in pale pink imported marble. The foyer is perhaps the most striking part of the public areas because of its centerpiece, a French, Louis XIII bombe front chest. An ornately carved gilded mirror hangs behind the chest, which is backed by richly polished mahogany walls. The collection of French antiques and reproductions is made all the more striking by the massive flower arrangements that fill the hand-painted porcelain bowls. In rebuilding the hotel, there was an emphasis on the details, whether this involved crafting the ornate pillars that mark the entrance to a ballroom or finding just the right 19th-century sconce or chandelier to hang in a restaurant. The hotel is not completely steeped in the old traditions though, as there exists a fair amount of brass, glass, and sharp angles that contrast with the softer and more elegant lines of the French furnishings.

The bedrooms maintain many of the same themes and attention to detail found in the public areas of the hotel. Pale peach and green Clarence House or Schumacher floral fabrics set the primary color schemes in the bedrooms. These coordinated fabrics are utilized on the beds and at the windows, presenting a very tailored backdrop to the equally traditional Drexel furnishings. Brass reading lamps, some original works of art, and an occasional antique piece give each bedroom additional character. King-bedded rooms offer separate sitting areas with sofas and graceful armchairs. The marble bathrooms are well stocked with plush cotton towels, blow dryers, and a selection of fine toiletries. The amenities are just what most would expect from a hotel of this nature with multiple telephones, cable televisions, and wet bars in some of the suites. Mints are placed upon the pillows after the nightly turndown service.

As with any full-service hotel, there is a restaurant and a variety of small shops on the premises. The Polo Grill offers contemporary American cuisine, but with some intriguing twists. The appetizer selection includes the Creole Louisiana shrimp with a melange of greens, pepper and corncake, and a jalapeno remoulade; the pan-seared quail salad with a wild mushroom polenta, ragout of beans, and crispy dumplings; or the organic field greens and fresh herbs with assisi nuts, pralines, and sundried blueberries. Some patrons could easily make a substantial meal out of the appetizers; however, it is well worth investigating the entree selections as well. The free range veal is served with saffron glazed fennel and a medley of baby vegetables with a saffron sauce; the rack of lamb is accompanied by a gateau of braised onion, herbed spatzle, and an Armagnac thyme pan jus; and the pan seared swordfish has a honey and mint carrot cake and pineapple salsa on the side. After dinner, some enjoy working off their indulgences at G's, the dance club in the hotel. The GC Spa is also a popular destination within the building, providing workout equipment and free weights, along with an indoor pool, whirlpool, Jacuzzi, and sauna. Guests can even request the service of a personal trainer to guide them through their regime. The juice bar supplies refreshing drinks at the end of a workout.

Some might ask why the Garden City Hotel still maintains its popularity. One of the reasons is its central location, just 20 minutes from La Guardia and JFK and a mere 40 minutes by train into Manhattan. The railroad station is located just across the street from the hotel. The Nassau Coliseum, Westbury Music Fair, and the Jones Beach Theater are also within a short driving distance of the hotel. Even though the hotel is centrally located to these destinations and to an assortment of shopping options nearby, Bowser might be more thrilled with walks on the property, heading north or south to one of Long Island's beaches, or investigating one of the local parks. Guests have many reasons for coming to stay at the Garden City Hotel, but what surprises just about everyone is the level of luxury and service they encounter.

BENN CONGER INN

206 West Cortland Street
Groton, New York 13073
(607) 898-5817
Innkeepers: Peter and Alison van der Meulen
Rooms: 2 doubles, 3 suites
Rates: Doubles $90-120, Suites $110-220
Payment: AE, DSC, MC, and Visa
Children: Small children are not appropriate
Dogs: Extremely well-behaved dogs are welcome, females are preferred as
    they have a three-year old male Akita, Bushi.
Open: All year

The Finger Lakes region distinguishes itself from other parts of New York for many reasons. Thousands of years ago, glaciers cut deep, narrow swaths in the landscape and created natural gullies that today form the 11 Finger Lakes. Although most of the lakes are separated from one another by high ridges, virtually void of forestation, this is where the similarities end. The towns surrounding the lakes have developed their own distinct personalities over the years. Some areas are known for their wineries and agriculture, while others are primarily artists' colonies. The region has also been home to a number of well-to-do industrialists over the years, one of whom was responsible for building what is now the Benn Conger Inn.

In 1921, Benn Conger, a New York State senator and entrepreneur, built a Greek Revival mansion in the heart of the Finger Lakes region. With white clapboards, green shutters, and two-story columns supporting an enormous portico, its style seemed more befitting a Southern plantation. He chose the charming hamlet of Groton and founded his company, the Corona Corporation which later became known as Smith-Corona. Conger did not lead a quiet rural life though, as he was known to have been good friends with the famous bootlegger and numbers' racketeer, Dutch Schultz.

Many years later, the house was bought by a couple who transformed it into an inn. Peter and Alison are relatively new arrivals to the area and the business. Four years ago, they left their high pressure careers in New York City for the more pastoral setting of upstate New York. This does not mean for a moment that their lives are less hectic, as they have funnelled their energies into running a first-class inn and restaurant. Although the guest rooms are sensational, it is the restaurant that has won most of the accolades. The dining rooms reflect a French-country motif, combined with the bright colors of English chintz. Of the four dining rooms, our favorite is the Conservatory. Here, green tiles and trim coupled with three walls of floor-to-ceiling Palladian windows and doors make this chamber very light and airy. The main dining room is also inviting, with its intimate groupings of tables and crackling fire filling the marble fireplace. Aside from winning awards from *Wine Spectator* for their phenomenal wine cellar, Peter has also turned his skills as a chef toward developing the Mediterranean-style cuisine.

The seasonally changing menu offers such appetizers as polenta served with shiitaki and crimini mushrooms in an herb butter sauce, Coquilles St. Jacques, or shrimp sauteed in a white wine and garlic sauce. Entree choices could include the shrimp, scallops, and mussels with tomatoes, shallots, and basil in a cognac cream and served over a black lobster-filled ravioli. The roasted rack of lamb encrusted with fresh herbs and served with a raspberry-mint sauce or the roasted pork tenderloin with an apples and port demiglace are equally enticing. After dinner, many like to retire to the cozy library, where there is a wonderful dark hardwood bar and fireplace that are particularly conducive to intimate conversation over a favorite nightcap.

Of course, those fortunate few who have also reserved a room at the inn, need do nothing more than head upstairs to the second floor and their elegant accommodations. Keep in mind, this was built as a private mansion with enormous, uniquely configured rooms that were meant to house the icons of industry and politics. The period details were therefore in evidence and ready for Alison's creative touch. In keeping with the mood of the house, Alison looked to Elsie de Wolfe, a famous decorator in the 1920s who reputedly brought decorating out of the dark, heavy, ponderous Victorian age into a lighter and more cheerful Edwardian period. As a result, the bedrooms feature delicate tie-back curtains rather than heavy draperies, bright floral fabrics versus heavy damask, and fine furnishings. Period antiques are highlighted by brass or sleigh beds, pine chests, bureaus, and delicate armchairs. The three double bedrooms and suites share a private common area that is a delightful place for reading or visiting with the other guests. The amenities are many, but one of the nicest was the silky soft 350 thread-count cotton imported linens on the beds.

Each morning, a full, gourmet breakfast is served in the Morning Room. This is a lavish affair, often extending to four or five courses and leaving most guests feeling sated for much of the day (that is until afternoon teatime). After breakfast, many people choose to explore the 18 acres surrounding the inn. The property is a combination of deep green lawns, flowering gardens, and a beech tree grove. Toward one end of the grounds there is a creek and beaver pond that many guests, and Bowser, find rather fascinating. Further afield there is Cayuga Lake, which becomes warm enough in the late summer for swimming and boating. There are also five state parks within 20 miles of the inn. Some of these have huge natural gorges and others hiking and picnicking opportunities. Peter and Alison have an Akita, Bushi, who might have discovered some additional spots of interest. Finally, Alison told us that she would prefer very well-behaved female dogs, as Bushi is a male and would probably find females less confrontational. If, for some reason, the pairing does not work, there is a wonderful kennel just across the road, where Bowser would be very comfortable during the evening hours.

SANDY CREEK MANOR HOUSE

1960 Redman Road
Hamlin, New York 14464-9635
(716) 964-7528
Innkeepers: Shirley Hollink and James Krempasky
Rooms: 3 doubles
Rates: $45-65
Payment: DSC, MC, and Visa
Children: Not appropriate for children under the age of 12
Dogs: Welcome with prior approval
Open: All year

Those who have occasion to be in the far upper reaches of New York state, virtually on the banks of Lake Ontario, should look into a Bed and Breakfast called the Sandy Creek Manor House. This turn-of-the-century English Tudor-style home lies on six-acres of woodlands and gardens and even has a picturesque creek running through the property. It is apparent, from the moment guests drive onto the property, that Shirley has a penchant for gardening as a profusion of bulbs, flowering plants, and perennials create a palette of color throughout the grounds. Azaleas, lilacs, and an array of spring bulbs supply the early season color, which is later picked up by the irises, day lilies, and mums that predominate the four new perennial beds found in the clearing by the creek. According to their most recent newsletter, James has also been improving their "Paradise Path" by thinning out many of the trees that seemed to be encroaching upon this favorite walk. As guests and Bowser explore their new surroundings, they may run across one of the four resident cats who, Shirley assures us, always maintain a very safe distance from any visiting dogs.

On a cool day, it is always nice to meander into the living room and warm oneself by the fireplace. Here, as in the rest of the house, a few antiques complement the comfortable furnishings. One of the standouts is the antique player piano, which has over 1,000 rolls of music that guests are welcome to play. In the afternoon, tea and baked goodies are served here, which is a natural time for guests to gather and get acquainted.

The three bedrooms are all named. Guests can choose from the Rope Room, which is dominated by a black lacquered and gold stenciled antique rope bedroom set. The cozy 3/4 size bed is covered with an Amish quilt and is often ideal for those romantic getaways. For those who think it might be too small, we recommend the Sunrise Room. Here, feather pillows rest against the brass bedstead and a decorative quilt complements the room's color scheme. Finally, there is the Parlor which is furnished with both a double and a single pineapple bed, making it ideal for a small family. All of the bedrooms have air conditioning, and two offer the added convenience of television. Shirley and James also recently added a third bathroom so that all of their guests can have private baths.

Although the bedrooms are inviting, it is the breakfasts that guests seem to remember the most about their stay. Shirley is usually up early every morning preparing a hearty feast that leaves everyone sated. She told us that although she has an extensive repertoire, she needs to continually add to it because of her repeat business. A sampling of some items include a puffed apple pancake, a plantation pancake (actually a lightly sweetened souffle), Italian eggs served with freshly baked muffins and breads, an amaretto flavored eggnog French toast, and the egg strata. Fresh coffee, juices, and fruit accompany each meal. Afterwards, many are tempted to lounge on the front porch; however, it is not long before Bowser decides it is time to explore.

Lake Ontario is a five-minute drive from Sandy Creek. Here, anglers will discover salmon fishing to be quite popular, although they can also stay right on the property to catch this popular fish along with steelhead, trout, and bass. Those who want to venture out on Lake Ontario should be able to take advantage of the special packages Shirley has arranged with the local sport fisheries groups. The historic Erie Canal and the Seaway Trail are also situated within close proximity to the B&B. Antique stores are plentiful in this area, just ask Shirley where to go. During the winter months, many guests opt to take an old fashioned sleigh ride that is drawn by some magnificent Clydesdales. Finally, if the day is inclement, guests can often convince Shirley to give them an impromptu craft lesson, teaching them how to weave a split reed seat for benches or chairs.

A visit to the Sandy Creek Manor House is truly a memorable experience, as much for the fine food and gardens as for the warm and relaxed demeanor of the hosts, Shirley and Jim. It is little wonder that so many of their guests come back to visit every year.

SWISS HUTTE

Route 23
Hillsdale, New York 12529
(518) 325-3333
Owners: Gert and Cindy Alper
Rooms: 15 doubles, 1 suite
Rates: $140-160 double occupancy (MAP)
Payment: MC and Visa
Children: Welcome
Dogs: Welcome with a $10 fee
Open: All year except from mid-March to mid-April

We were drawn to the Swiss Hutte with the knowledge that the accommodations were modeled more after a motel than an inn; but we had also heard the restaurant was what many guests remembered long after their stay. We visited the inn during the summertime, when the tiny ski resort of Catamount Mountain was closed for the season. The patrons at the Swiss Hutte did not seem to mind though as they had come to sample the restaurant fare and enjoy the pretty views of the mountain and the picturesque pond, through plate glass windows. What looked most inviting that day was the gazebo and the comfortable chairs it contained.

The motel rooms are located next to the restaurant in a two-story building that resembles a Swiss chalet. Each bedroom has a separate outside entrance and a small terrace or balcony whose railings are festooned with window boxes overflowing with summer flowers. These units have been recently refurbished and are quite attractive. The furnishings are made from a lightly stained pickled pine, creating a rather sophisticated Scandinavian motif. Many of the pairs of queen-size beds in each room are backed by wooden headboards detailed with dental moldings. A table and chairs are set before the plate glass windows, offering perhaps some of the nicest views of Catamount. The bathrooms are good sized and have separate areas for showers. Standard amenities such as cable television, air conditioning, and a telephone are found in each room. There is a sense of intimacy that has been created at the Swiss Hutte, which almost makes one forget that these are technically motel rooms.

A small resort atmosphere is what set the Swiss Hutte apart from other accommodations of this type. Obviously, in the wintertime the primary focus is skiing. The great thing about the Swiss Hutte is that downhill skiing is within walking distance of the inn. During the summer months there are even a wider array of diversions from which to choose. The swimming pool, set off to the side of the restaurant, is just as appealing as either of the two spring-fed ponds with sandy beaches. Those who prefer tennis will find two courts awaiting them. Even golfers should be pleased with the local selection of courses, with four facilities situated closeby and a putting green available on site. Those who are more interested in exploring the grounds with Bowser will find the perennial gardens are in full bloom most of the summer with over 150 varieties of plantings. Of course, Bowser might enjoy a little more rigorous exercise and choose one of the local hiking trails or venture up Catamount for some scenic vistas. Most of the diversions should help guests work up a healthy appetite for any of the inn's meals.

The ambiance of the restaurant is almost as enticing as the entrees. Guests walk into an intimate bar area with a fireplace and a smattering of tables. Just beyond this space is a light and airy room that is spacious and offers the best views of the mountains through plate glass windows. The tables are set with linen, crystal and china. It is difficult to summarize the menu as it is ever-changing, with selections appearing daily on a chalkboard. On any given day, patrons might dine on smoked salmon on a bed of baby greens and avocadoes or curried shrimp and scallops as appetizers. Entrees might include grilled salmon with sun dried tomatoes and basil butter, liver terrine armagnac and truffles, wild mushroom ragout in a puff pastry, and roast duck a l'orange. Desserts also vary depending upon the day; however, many rave about the raspberry cream pie.

Those contemplating a stay at the Swiss Hutte should expect very pleasant accommodations, excellent food, and beautiful surroundings; however, they should also bear in mind that this is not a classic inn but rather an unpretentious establishment which everyone, including Bowser, can enjoy.

LA TOURELLE

1150 Danby Road, Route 96B
Ithaca, New York 14850
(607) 273-2734
Manager: Leslie Leonard
Rooms: 35 doubles
Rates: $75-125
Payment: AE, MC, and Visa
Children: Welcome
Dogs: Welcome
Open: All year

The name La Tourelle certainly conjures up images of the French countryside; however, most will be surprised to learn that this inn and its award winning restaurant lie in the heart of New York State. Occupying a scenic hilltop setting, and within walking distance of Ithaca College, the inn is difficult to miss. The exterior style is definitely reminiscent of the chateaus of France with its white stucco walls, while the airy interior has a rather modern twist. The two-story lobby is comprised of French doors, burnt red tile floors, pale pink walls, and pickled wood furnishings. Live plants, vases overflowing with flowers, and primitive sculptures and artwork create an interesting blend of periods and styles. In the summertime this is a cool and inviting space and during the cooler months, the floor-to-ceiling rock fireplace makes the reception area all the more inviting.

The bedrooms can be found off any of the long hallways leading from the reception area. Those who are tired of matchbox sized hotel rooms will be pleased with the accommodations at La Tourelle. Each bedroom, from the luxurious fireplace suite to the queen- and king-size guest rooms, is spacious. The floor-to-ceiling windows (quite remarkable since the ceilings are twenty feet high or vaulted) further increase the sense of openness. Our favorite bedrooms overlook the back of the property and the distant rolling hills that surround Ithaca. The soft pinks found in the lobby are carried through into most of the guest chambers. Sparsely furnished, given the size of these spaces, the chairs, tables, and bureaus have been authentically recreated in a formal French style. Bathrooms are nicely appointed and have the usual complement of soaps and shampoos. In the French tradition, a bottle of wine is set out in a cooler along with two glasses. In the morning, a Continental breakfast is awaiting and can be enjoyed at a small table in front of the windows.

Those who come in search of athletic diversions, will find a covered tennis court located to the rear of the property. A pond lies off to the side, hidden inconspicuously behind some trees. When we visited, someone was attempting a bit of fishing. On the 70 acres surrounding the inn, there are ample grassy areas to exercise Bowser. Many guests enjoy venturing off the property for their recreational pursuits. One option is Stuart Park, which is located on Cayuga Lake. While there is a carousel and rose gardens here, Bowser would be more apt to find the Fuertes Wild Fowl Preserve to be more interesting. Another suggestion is a trip to the Taughannock Falls State Park. The waterfalls are over 200 feet high and are flanked by an even deeper gorge. Visitors can either hike along the trails at the edge of the gorge or swim in the waters below. Other gorges worth visiting are bisected by the Cascadilla and Six Mile creeks.

After a busy day, guests look forward to their return as an excuse to relax at the white, wrought iron tables set on a small courtyard. Here, they can sample the wide array of appetizers and perhaps enjoy something to drink. Most of the guests at La Tourelle make reservations at the award winning restaurant, L' Auberge. Housed in a one-story antique cottage on La Tourelle's grounds, patrons will be tempted by the diverse fare offered. Although the menu is frequently changing, a sampling might include the chilled honeydew and raspberry soup, a wild mushroom fettucine, or the juniper crusted gravlax. Entree selections range from a tender filet mignon or a New York strip steak smothered with shallots and mushrooms to capellini with chicken, asparagus, and sun-dried tomatoes or the salmon saffron. At the end of an evening, the short walk back to La Tourelle is just what most guests need before settling into a long night of sleep.

STAGECOACH INN

370 Old Military Rd.
Lake Placid, New York 12946
(518) 523-9474
Host: Peter Moreau
Rooms: 9 doubles
Rates: $65-85
Payment: Visa
Children: Welcome
Dogs: Welcome in two guest rooms
Open: All year

Often, when people think of Lake Placid they associate it with the 1980 Winter Olympics. When visiting the town, one is certainly struck by all of the physical reminders of this historic event. For instance, it would be difficult to miss the enormous, man-made ski jumps that mark the entrance to town (when coming from the east), or the sport's complex, shops, and hotels that line the lake. For those who opt to be in the center of activity, there are a number of diverse accommodations to choose from; however, we preferred a little place that is just slightly off the beaten track and which offers a great deal of charm and personality — the Stagecoach Inn.

Since 1833, the inn has been opening its doors to guests. Time and the 20th-century has changed much of the Adirondacks, but it has done little to alter the inn. As guests walk along the covered porch running the length of the inn, they can imagine the echoing sounds of boots worn by weary travelers who must have made the stagecoach trek nearly 200 years ago. One enters the inn by way of a dutch door, which leads into an intimate, wood-paneled reception area. One's eye is drawn to a backlit, stained glass window of a stagecoach and horses that serves as the focal point for the room. While returning guests may expect to see Lynn, and her English sheepdog the Bearoness Theodora, they have moved on and now the inn is being run by its owner of the last 20 years, Peter Moreau, and his Australian Shepherd.

Although the innkeepers have changed, the ambiance has not. All of the bedrooms are simply, yet classically decorated, in a style synonymous with the Adirondacks. Brass and white iron bedsteads, antique pine bureaus with beveled mirrors, and an occasional delicately carved chair or two fill the cozy rooms. Tie-back curtains made from fresh calico fabrics, frame the paned windows. Each bedroom has a unique character. For instance, the two upstairs chambers, which each share a bathroom (complete with copper claw-footed bathtubs), are quite intimate. Alcoves built into the eaves might contain pottery or artwork or teddy bears, while baskets of peppermints and bottles of potpourri rest on the dressers.

Two of our favorite guest rooms are located on the first floor of the building and have private entrances, which are perfect for those traveling with Bowser. Both of these rooms offer windows on all sides, and are positioned at each end of the long porch. They are simply, but attractively decorated with country antiques and offer brick fireplaces. The bathrooms are private, giving guests the feeling they are occupying a private suite. In fact, many of the rooms are accessed by different sets of stairs and doors, further increasing the overall sense of privacy people have when staying here.

In the evening, guests will often return to find a fire blazing in the living room fireplace. This chamber is truly reminiscent of an Adirondack hunting lodge, with its vertical board walls, a deer head mounted above the fireplace, and its comfortable chairs and sofas. While most of the rooms at the inn have fairly low ceilings, the living room is open to the second floor, providing an increased sense of spaciousness. Here, guests can usually be found relaxing in front of the television, reading a good book, or just putting their feet up and doing nothing at all.

Peter, while competent in many areas, does not claim to be a chef. A friend of his, who is actually a trained chef, handles breakfast duty. Each day the meal varies, but guests can usually expect some sort of egg dish, French toast, homemade breads, juice, and great coffee. Afterwards, it is time to head off for some skiing, or for those who are visiting in the summertime, a trip to one of the many lakes dotting the region. The lakes offer a myriad of boating, swimming, windsurfing, and sailing opportunities. Day hikes can easily be planned, with no two days being alike as there are 2.3 million acres of wilderness in the Adirondacks.

The Stagecoach Inn occupies merely a small piece of this vast space, with the stands of trees and grassland immediately surrounding the inn serving as a microcosm for that which lies beyond it. It provides guests with a quiet spot for enjoying the seasons, while the inn recreates a bit of history they are not likely to experience again anytime soon.

THE HORNED DORSET INN

Route 8
Leonardsville, New York 13364
(315) 855-7898
Owners: Harold Davies, Kingsley and Bruce Wratten, and Donald Lentz
Rooms: 2 doubles, 2 suites
Rates: Doubles $75, Suites $95
Payment: MC and Visa
Children: Appropriate for children over the age of 12
Dogs: Welcome
Open: All year, closed on Monday

We must admit that when we read about the excellent cuisine and unusual accommodations at The Horned Dorset Inn, we were very intrigued. As we drove along the rural country roads leading to Leonardsville, we began to sense that people came to the inn and restaurant seeking a total escape from the city. The Horned Dorset Inn is located on the main street of this quiet farm community. The building housing the restaurant is completely void of ornamentation, in the style of a Quaker meeting house. Step into the courtyard though and visitors will soon gain an appreciation for the inn's intrinsic charms. On one side of the courtyard, there are the huge Palladian windows of the restaurant, while on the other is the ornate 1875 Italianate home with its wide porches, cornices, and pillars.

The inn and restaurant are owned by four people, two ex-professors and two ex-teachers. The home originally belonged to the grandmother of one of the owners; however, it has long since been renovated and converted into guest rooms and the other building into a gourmet restaurant. The latter features exquisite multi-course meals that often last for several hours.

French doors lead into the foyer of the architecturally exquisite Italianate home, where guests will see a small table with a telephone and guest book. The sitting room, found just off the foyer, is the focal point for the house. A piano awaits those who might want to tickle the ivories, while a library of books is housed behind glass cabinet doors. Comfortable couches are just right for relaxing, usually after a very filling meal at the restaurant. The intricate moldings and antiques lend an air of formality to the house; however, guests will definitely find that an unpretentious atmosphere pervades.

Two of the bedrooms are located on the first floor. Both are adorned with furnishings that are in keeping with the character and scale of the house. The huge pieces are almost dwarfed by the high ceilings and spacious rooms. One of the bedrooms offers a queen-size bed and large bathroom. Another bedroom has twin beds and a similar assortment of antiques. Those who desire a bit more space, or who are traveling with either another couple or children, will appreciate the pair of upstairs suites. These are accessed by following the gentle curves of an elegant cherry staircase from the foyer to the second level. Each suite offers a sitting room with a pullout couch bed, a private bathroom the size of most normal bedrooms, and a spacious king-bedded chamber. A small table, set in an alcove, is just the spot for enjoying the morning's Continental breakfast. This is a simple affair of croissants, freshly squeezed juice, and coffee or tea. Downstairs, there is also a full kitchen that guests are invited to use for storing snacks or creating lunch. As self-sufficient as this might make one feel, most people often opt to dine at the restaurant each evening.

As we mentioned before, from the exterior the dining room appears to be huge and rather stark; however, once inside, patrons will see a pair of cozy dining rooms. Each of these chambers is equally sophisticated; however, the one with the rock fireplace and Palladian windows is our favorite. The other has the ambiance of a formal library, as the seating is on two levels, separated by an open railing. Tables are set with white linen, crystal, and silver flatware.

Silver-plated wine decanters keep the wine and champagne at just the right temperature (they have an extensive wine cellar). The French inspired menu is presented verbally, and changes daily. But if the sampling of the fare during our visit is any indication, even those who consider themselves to be culinary sophisticates will be most pleased. Escargot served in a puff pastry with sauteed frog's legs and a garlic cream sauce may not be for everyone, but it is one of the more unusual appetizer selections. The rabbit pate, or shrimp and scallop crepe served with a lobster sauce are more mainstream offerings. Entrees could include rack of lamb with ginger and raisins, poussin rolled with an artichoke and pimento puree and drizzled with a Calvados cream sauce, and a breast of duckling with a cassis or fig sauce. One truly decadent creation, which may be a cholesterol watchers demise, are the medallions of veal garnished with a mushroom mousse, slices of avocado, bleu cheese, and a Hollandaise cream sauce. After a rich meal, the sorbets are always a good choice for dessert, but those who are craving a little more indulgent sweet will want to contemplate the bombe au chocolat, blueberry and strawberry pastry, or the chilled Grand Marnier souffle.

There are plenty of reasons to visit this area, whether it be to see a student at nearby Colgate or Hamilton colleges, to explore this diverse agricultural region, or to investigate some of the antique stores in the area. Bowser is certain to feel quite comfortable in this rather lavish setting, and guests should feel comfortable knowing that the yard around the inn is fenced. Just outside the gates, there are plenty of country lanes to investigate as well.

THE BOXTREE HOTEL

250 East 49th Street
New York, New York 10017
(212) 758-8320
Manager: Nina Fuenmayor
Rooms: 11 junior suites, 1 penthouse
Rates: Junior suites $290, Penthouse $320, Rates include Continental breakfast
    and a $100 dining credit
Payment: AE
Children: Not appropriate for children under 10 years of age
Dogs: Welcome
Open: All year

Much has been written about The Boxtree Hotel, an eclectic spot where museum quality furnishings abound amid unusual pieces of art, some of which have become a permanent part of the building's architecture. A bit of history is needed to fully appreciate The Boxtree Hotel, which is located in the heart of the historic enclave of Turtle Bay. A good deal of the hotel's appeal and success is due exclusively to the hotel's flamboyant owner, Augustin Paege.

Mr. Paege, a native of Bulgaria, moved to the United States after having lived in Paris for a number of years. In the early 1980s, he opened his now-famous Boxtree Restaurant. What took place, from that moment forward, could only be called a metamorphosis.

Today, guests will literally find a catacomb of rooms in the two brownstones. The first and second floors house a series of exquisite and unusual private dining rooms, while the uppermost floors contain the suites. To gain access to the hotel, one must look carefully for the copper and wrought iron canopy overhanging the door. Once inside, the cool brick floors and deep green walls envelope guests. Antique treasures literally spill from every corner, although the standouts are the 17th-century vargueno (a Spanish campaign chest with individual drawers that hold notes for guests) and the Louis XIII sedan-style chair. The chair is a brown leather domed piece, which provides a private nook for guests to read. The fireplace has an ornately carved mantelpiece with two, 18th-century porcelain figures flanking it.

Although most could while away their time in the foyer, there are more treasures to be discovered on the upper floors. Narrow, winding stairs lead to the bedrooms. The doors marking these private dominions have delicate flowers painted on them with unique furnishings and objects d'art awaiting on the other side. For instance, The Contessa's Room is more than just reminiscent of a Parisian flat - it is one. In addition to its French antiques, all of the mouldings and paneling were taken from a flat in Paris and brought to the United States to be installed in The Boxtree. The same applies for the antique bed, which like all the other beds in the hotel, is set into a separate alcove. The Japanese Room, on the other hand, has a more minimalist decor with its black lacquered furniture, clean lines, and elegant black velvet draperies trimmed in red. The Chinese Suite offers more in the way of colors, with salmon and grey walls complementing the chintz fabric, Chinese porcelains, and 19th-century Chinese tables and chairs. But the highlight for most has to be the King Boris Suite, which has actually been inhabited by the ex-king of Bulgaria. Here, the deep royal blue walls are accented by gold leaf paneling and intricately carved crown moldings. Light emanates from a gold chandelier and crystal and gold wall sconces. Focal points are the floral marquetry screen and the gold and sterling cabinet.

As unique and unusual as each room is, there are certain constants. The ends of the beds are always draped with soft animal furs and overstuffed couches rest in front of the working fireplaces. The bathrooms, although small, are also works of art with marble tiles, lots of glass, European shower heads and fixtures, and both terry cloth robes and an assortment of fine toiletries. But many guests find they are most impressed with the simple details, such as the silver Tiffany pens, the cuff links for men, and the Irish linens and oversized bath sheets, all of which truly reflect Augustus Paege's penchant for perfection.

This penchant extends, of course, to the food. While breakfast is a culinary treat, it is the dinner menu which continues to inspire restaurant reviewers. There are a few private dining rooms, such as the Music Room, with its huge fireplace flanked by ornate columns inset with colored glass. The turn of the century stained-glass window at the far end of the room is another visual standout, as is the Jacobean oak table. Other dining rooms are set on different levels and are linked by a truly grand and equally unusual staircase. It was carved on-site by David Mills (who, incidentally, is responsible for all the other ornately carved architectural delights in the hotel) and then covered in plaster. The whole masterpiece just flows from one level to the next. Once diners have taken in their wonderful surroundings, they can then focus on the food.

The menu is constantly changing. Appetizer samplings include such delicacies as a wild boar proscuitto with figs, a terrine of duck livers foie gras, or the lobster bisque. The mallard duck with a cassis sauce, lobster mornay, or roast pheasant with a juniper berry sauce were just a few of the many entrees available during our visit. For dessert, a terrine of chestnuts and chocolate, medjool dates steeped in port and raspberries, or a pear poached in burgundy were some of the choices. As a final note, guests should understand that their room price includes breakfast and a $100 credit they may use toward dinner or lunch at the hotel.

Finally, we must admit that it is difficult to give potential guests a complete overview of The Boxtree Hotel, purely because a stay here is so visual and the attention so personal. It can be said though, that the unique accommodations at The Boxtree Hotel far surpass anything the New York boutique hotels can offer.

THE CARLYLE

Madison Avenue at 76th Street
New York, New York 10021
(800) 227-5737, (212) 744-1600
General Manager: Dan Camp
Rooms: 135 doubles, 55 suites
Rates: Doubles $275-375, Suites $500-1,250
Payment: AE, CB, DC, MC, and Visa
Children: Welcome
Dogs: Welcome
Open: All year

Surprisingly, New York City has no shortage of hotels which welcome guests traveling with a dog, although it is the first-class hotels that seem particularly fond of those who choose to bring Bowser along. On the more intimate side of luxury, there are a few standouts, and one that immediately comes to mind is The Carlyle.

Situated in the heart of the Upper East Side, just steps from Central Park and the boutiques and fine restaurants on Madison Avenue, is The Carlyle. Housed in one of the city's pre-war buildings, the hotel makes the most of its assets. Highlights include the intricate hand-worked moldings and cornices, vaulted ceilings, expansive marble floors in the public areas, and original parquet floors in the guest rooms. Exquisitely decorated, each public and private room in the hotel holds some treasure, whether in the form of an antique, rare or original work of art, or exquisite Oriental rug. With the exception of the high ceilings and some enormous flower arrangements artfully arranged in Oriental vases of equal proportion, the lobby, restaurant, and cafe remain intimate. Bemelmans Bar is a favorite hangout for guests of The Carlyle and resident New Yorkers. The curved walls surrounding the bar's patrons hold whimsical murals painted in 1947 by artist Ludwig Bemelman (the author/illustrator of the children's book series, *Madeline*).

While the public is of course welcome in the restaurants and bar at The Carlyle, the rest of the hotel is the exclusive domain of its guests and those who own private co-operatives in the building. Each room or suite has a distinct personality, and to ensure that things remain just so, five or six rooms are taken out of commission every two months for a total renovation. While one bedroom might feature English chintzes covering fine antique reproductions, traditional botanical prints, and Oriental rugs covering the hardwood floors, another will be decorated in an equally sophisticated French style. Colors can be as bold as deep reds and forest greens or as subtle as pale yellows and pinks.

Along with the elegant rooms and suites, what guests will find, without exception, are first class amenities. Living rooms and bedrooms feature huge, state-of-the art televisions, equipped with VCRs and elaborate stereo/CD systems. While honor bars are fairly standard in most of the better hotels, The Carlyle goes beyond that and creates a small pantry, which contains a fully stocked wet bar. The refrigerator has a full complement of fine liquors and liqueurs, along with imported chocolates and French butter cookies. The bathrooms are equally well-appointed. The usual assortment of luxurious soaps, shampoos, and bath salts are perfect for leisurely bathing, although the extra thick terry cloth robes make the after-bath experience just as appealing. The liberal use of glass gives the illusion that these good-sized bathrooms are almost cavernous. The European bidet is a welcome addition for many.

For those who want to work off the excesses of their indulgences (perhaps a butter cookie or two), there is a newly completed state of the art private fitness center on the premises. This is the private domain of the guests and is fully equipped with workout equipment, massage rooms, and a sauna.

As exquisite as The Carlyle is, Bowser is certain to prefer his/her walks along Park and Madison avenues or around Central Park. There is almost always a dog walker contingency which gathers in the mornings and evenings in the Park. One of the wonderful attributes about staying at The Carlyle, is that after a day of exploring, shopping, and sight-seeing one has the distinct feeling of coming home again —just one of the many qualities that sets The Carlyle apart from most of New York's more impersonal grand hotels.

FOUR SEASONS HOTEL

57 East 57th Street
New York, New York 10022
(800) 332-3442, (212) 758-5700, Fax: (212) 758-5711
General Manager: Thomas Gurtner
Rooms: 309 doubles, 58 one- and two-bedroom suites
Rates: Doubles $325-445, Suites $555-3,030
Payment: AE, CB, DC, DSC, MC, and Visa
Children: Welcome (cribs, cots, babysitters, and special children's amenities
        are available)
Dogs: Welcome
Open: All year

Leave it to the Four Seasons to continue to create benchmark hotels, with one of their newest offerings situated in the heart of mid-town Manhattan. Opening in the summer of 1993, the facade for this rather imposing building "reflects the style of architect I.M. Pei." Those who are unfamiliar with Pei should note the clean lines and the overall lack of ornamentation. Definition in the building is created by grouping blocks of floors together thereby creating independent sections of rooms. These are seemingly put together, almost as one would build a Lego building, with a wide base that finally narrows to one tall group of floors at the uppermost level. This unusual structure allows for a variety of private terraces off some of the guest rooms. French limestone, used on both interior and exterior surfaces, produces a smooth finish and increases the overall sense of openness. Inside the hotel, 60-foot ceilings create enormous areas which are somewhat broken up by different levels in the lobby lounge. While many of the hotels in New York have fabulous flower arrangements, those at the Four Seasons are some of the most impressive we have seen. During our visit, exquisite displays of pink and purple flowers rose 15 feet from the massive pewter pots that held them. These arrangements were placed in such a way to further create a sense of intimacy in a common area that offered little other ornamentation.

At first glance, the bedrooms appear to be just as understated, although after further examination we were certain this was not the case. Guests enter their bed chambers by walking down a short hallway, accented by an alove with a marble topped mini-bar. Passing by the bathroom, it is clear that there was no shortage of marble when it came to designing this spacious room. Everything, from the floors to the vanities, is covered in a rich reddish-brown marble or with expanses of mirrors, the latter adding dimension to the room. The oversized bathtubs are also state-of-the-art, filling in less than 60-seconds. Slippers and terry cloth robes are easily accessible for a little after-bath lounging. Hair-dryers, makeup mirrors, a small television, and full array of toiletries complete the bathing amenities.

The bedroom, however, is no less noteworthy. Draperies open electronically, which allows the sun to further accentuate the room's already warm, sandy tones. The furnishings are contemporary and very attractive, with brass and glass coffee tables, brass lamps, and sleek sofas and armchairs. Telephones can be found next to the bed, on the desk, and in the bathroom. An armoire conceals the television and radio, making the room that much more uncluttered and comfortable. All of the guest chambers are big, very big in fact, averaging 600 square feet. This emphasis on ample dimensions extends to the dressing area's wall of built-in closets and drawers. Twenty-three bedrooms and suites have the added luxury of exterior terraces that offer commanding views of the city. Bowser will easily feel at home, as will those human friends who accompany him.

The Four Seasons Hotel is also long on service amenities, including the standard 24-hour concierge and room services. Their Fitness Center, while not immense, does provide all of the state-of-the-art equipment anyone might need for a complete workout. There is also a full service spa for those who would like a massage. Those garments which need pressing will be taken care of in an hour, and scuffed shoes shined free of charge. A full complement of newspapers are available through the front desk and can be delivered to guest rooms each morning. The staff is well-equipped to provide many other special services people might need during their stay.

While the hotel is within easy walking distance of any number of restaurants, there is also an excellent alternative within the building. The 5757 Restaurant is reminiscent of the 1920s Art Deco period. As guests ascend the wide, open staircase to the eatery, they will be drawn to the huge round window of frosted glass that dominates the back wall of the room. Dramatically set under this is a Bosendorfer grand piano, which is often in use during the late afternoon and evening. One side of this space contains the restaurant and the other a wonderful bar. The latter offers, among other drinks, seven different types of martinis. The wall behind the bar has an original painting of a carousel by Kimon Nicolaides, with the framed studies for the final picture lining the other walls. There is also a huge glass etching of the painting adorning another wall. The restaurant serves a Continental fare with menu items ranging from smoked salmon with artichokes, carpaccio of salmon, and soft shell crab with mustard greens to an Atlantic seafood stew, grilled lamb chops, and mushroom and spinach raviolis covered with a tomato tarragon broth.

After dinner, a walk along Madison Avenue or Park Avenue is always appealing. The former for its window shopping and the latter for its green areas. Central Park is also an easy stroll from the hotel. New York City has countless diversions, sights, and attractions, including the old favorites, the Statue of Liberty and Ellis Island.

HOTEL PLAZA ATHENEE

37 East 64th Street
New York, New York 10021
(800) 225-5843, (212) 734-9100, Fax: (212) 772-0958
General Manager: Bernard Lackner
Rooms: 130 doubles, 30 suites
Rates: Doubles $320-400, Suites $590-895
Payment: AE, CB, DC, MC, and Visa
Children: Welcome (cribs, cots, and babysitters are available)
Dogs: Small to medium-size dogs are welcome
Open: All year

From the beginning, there have been high expectations for the Hotel Plaza Athenee in New York City. Its sister hotel in Paris has been a bastion of elegance and sophistication since the 1800s, and has had such an impact on Europeans that those who travel to the United States often seek out this smaller version of the original. Located on 64th Street, between Madison and Park Avenues, one might miss this rather unobtrusive building except for the crimson red awnings on the first floor windows and the portico, which is accented with the national flags for France and the United States.

Glass doors rimmed in brass open into a truly intimate reception area. Pale, polished Italian marble floors are inlaid with black marble tile, that complement the detail found in the coffered ceilings. Classic French armchairs are upholstered in black leather and the round tables in a black veneer, all of which have gold leaf accents. Ornate brass sconces and chandeliers enhance the already lovely decor. But what attracts the most attention are the hand-painted murals that frame the elevators. Woodland scenes in muted colors stand out against a pale blue backdrop of sky. Huge vases of fresh flowers merely add to the serenity of this seemingly pastoral setting. The intricately woven carpets soften guests' footsteps as they enter the piano lounge, where subdued deep green and brown color schemes virtually transport them into the forests of the mural.

The bed rooms are located on the upper 17 floors. The staff prides itself on protecting their guests' privacy, and people will discover they are catered to in a most discreet and formal manner. There is a continued sense of reserve, both from the staff and in the ambiance, as one walks along densely carpeted halls to the chambers. The sense of formality is strong, without the florals and bright colors of the French countryside. Instead there is a very classic approach to the decor, with sage green and taupe having been chosen as a color scheme for some of the accommodations and deep rust tones and ecru for others. Artwork is kept to the minimum, with a few important pieces gracing each room. Draped tables are topped by Oriental vase lamps and armoires conceal the televisions. Irish Navian carpets on the floors and richly textured draperies at the windows tie each bedroom together. As with other luxury hotels in New York, the bathrooms are bathed in marble, Aurora Rose Portuguese marble to be precise. Plush towels and French terry cloth robes are wonderful for wrapping up in after a hot bath with the luxurious Lanvin toiletries. It is clear that only the very finest will do at the Hotel Plaza Athenee.

The Hotel Plaza Athenee has a high staff to guest ratio, allowing them to provide a level of service well beyond an ordinary luxury hotel. Just about anything, from a multi-course, gourmet midnight feast to a forgotten toiletry, can be arranged. For a truly unforgettable experience though, if only for the opulence of the surroundings, guests should plan to spend an evening in the hotel's premiere restaurant, Le Regence. Amid crystal, gold leaf, green marblized paneled walls, and murals, guests dine on exceptional Continental cuisine. A sampling of items for a particular Thanksgiving meal included a duck liver terrine with a salad of apple and a pumpkin ravioli with truffles. Medallions of veal with wild mushrooms or lobster in a sauterne wine sauce were just two of the entrees. The dessert cart is always decadent with tortes of fresh fruit and rich chocolate or petit fours perfectly accenting the delicious, French coffees.

While a walk through Central Park might appeal to Bowser, many guests are more intrigued with the window shopping along Madison and Fifth Avenues. From a dog's standpoint, the hotel may pale in comparison to a romp in the Park, just as from his/her owner's perspective, the Hotel Plaza Athenee rises above the rest of the Upper East Side boutique hotels in upholding a French tradition.

INCENTRA VILLAGE HOUSE

32 Eighth Avenue
New York, New York 10014
(212) 206-0007
Manager: John O'Connors
Rooms: 12 doubles and suites
Rates: Doubles $99, Suites $120-140
Payment: AE, MC, and Visa
Children: Welcome
Dogs: Well-behaved dogs are welcome
Open: All year

The Incentra Village House is inextricably tied to Greenwich Village, and is, in many ways, merely a reflection of the world outside its doors. That is, if you can find the main doors. There are no signs to guide travelers to the Incentra Village House, merely the understated number 32 marking the entrance to the two red brick buildings which house the guest rooms. Ring the bell and someone will appear to help with luggage and check-in.

A small sitting room, furnished with a baby grand piano, comfortable sofas and chairs, and decorated with original works of modern art, provides the only communal space in the house. Other than that, the bedrooms and suites exist on a multitude of levels. This is probably due to the fact that the 1840s townhouses have undergone extensive renovations over the years and were, at one point, even converted into apartments. Although, their purpose is slightly different today, most of the kitchenettes remain intact, allowing guests to cook and create their own meals should they be so inclined. While the staff at the inn is very helpful and keeps everything exceptionally clean, amenities like room service, a concierge, nightly bed turn down, and bedside mints are absent here. Instead, guests are allowed to be self-sufficient.

Of the twelve available accommodations, ten offer fireplaces and most are furnished with double beds. Each chamber has been named after a place in the world visited by the owner. The India Room is a good example of the simplest guest room at the Incentra Village House. Guests will find a double mattress resting on an intricate iron bedstead which has been placed to take advantage of the warmth from the fireplace and the assortment of trinkets from India displayed about the room. A stuffed elephant rests in one corner and a mirror framed in carved wood adorns a wall. The Dakota Room has a similar atmosphere, but with a Native American Indian motif. The Maine Room has the traditional pencil post bed covered in a striped coverlet and is surrounded by charming country antiques. One of our favorite rooms is a one-bedroom suite overlooking a quiet courtyard. The living room is quite comfortable with a sofa and side chairs placed around the fireplace. Walk down a few steps into a well equipped kitchenette and then up a few more steps into the sleeping loft area. One constant throughout the Incentra Village House is the preponderance of interesting modern art that can be found displayed both in the hallways and in the bedrooms.

For those who are not familiar with Greenwich Village, there is a fascinating world outside the doors of the Incentra Village House. Bowser will enjoy the many green areas around the inn such as Abdingdon Square and a bit further afield, the Washington Square Park. The streets in parts of the Village are narrow and tree-lined with gracious early nineteenth century townhouses that, for the most part, have been well preserved. Other parts are more commercial with tiny restaurants, art and antique stores, bookstores, and off-Broadway theaters. There is a tremendous amount of diversity among the residents of the area, with an incredible ethnic, social, and professional mix of people. This creates a rich and vibrant environment into which visitors can easily assimilate.

As a final note, the Incentra Village House is one of the more reasonably priced and popular overnight spots in Greenwich Village, as a result they are often booked well in advance. It would be best, if planning to stay here, to call and make reservations as soon as your dates are confirmed.

THE LOWELL NEW YORK

28 East 63rd Street
New York, New York 10021-8088
(800) 221-4444, (212) 838-1400, Fax: (212) 319-4230
General Manager: Martin Hale
Rooms: 4 singles, 9 doubles, 48 suites
Rates: Singles $260, Doubles $320, Suites $420-1,500
Payment: AE, CB, DC, ENR, MC, and Visa
Children: Welcome
Dogs: Welcome with advance notice and prior approval
Open: All year

There are New York's five-star hotels and there are boutique hotels, and then there is The Lowell. Ideal for anyone with particularly discriminating tastes, The Lowell offers the ultimate in privacy and personal attention. Built in 1926, just before the great Depression, the hotel was originally designed as a seventeen-story apartment hotel. Over the years it has housed notable figures such as F. Scott and Zelda Fitzgerald, Eugene O'Neill, Noel Coward, and Dorothy Parker. More recently the owners infused $25 million dollars into an extensive renovation hoping to bring it back to its former standards. Today, its Art Deco/Moderne facade integrates surprisingly well with the late nineteenth and twentieth century buildings in this quiet Upper East Side enclave.

Although the lobby is tiny, the images it contains are powerful. Marble floors merely set the scene for the French Empire-style furniture and chiaroscuro walls, all of which reflect a strong Art Deco theme. Perhaps the most inspiring piece is the front desk with its richly polished woods, cubby holes housing guests' messages, and neatly arranged books, making it appear more like a library than a reception area. The cumbersome task of check-in is virtually ignored, as guests are quickly whisked to their rooms by an always attentive and discreet staff member.

On each floor, elevators open to narrow, winding hallways which are broken up occasionally by doorways. Open any one of these bedroom doors and a jewel box of images meets the eye. Each suite has its own personality, where French, English, and Art Deco motifs somehow mix with a smattering of Oriental pieces to create a stunning effect. Pale yellows and blues might combine with English chintzes and striped satins on bed coverlets and antique chairs. Fluffy down comforters and mountains of pillows turn each bed into its own inviting retreat. Gilded mirrors are interspersed with black lacquered pieces, Art Deco lamps, and an assortment of hunt and botanical prints. Most of the chambers are quite bright, due to the sunlight pouring in from all the windows. Some of the suites even contain private, tiled terraces, which are bedecked with flowers in full bloom during the warmer months. When the weather turns cold, there are woodburning fireplaces, framed in marble or delicately carved woods, to warm chilly toes.

The many modern conveniences are usually discretely tucked out of sight. Cable televisions, VCRs, clock radios, and PC or fax ports are easily accessible but unobtrusive. Bathrooms are mostly marble with brass fixtures. Thick robes, hairdryers, and make-up mirrors are a few of the standard accoutrements, as are the Crabtree and Evelyn soaps and shampoos, along with assorted amenities from Saks Fifth Avenue. For those who are seeking the ultimate in fitness and comfort, there is the Gym Suite. This unique king-bedded chamber not only has magnificent views of Manhattan but also offers his and her bathrooms and a separate workout room, equipped with a treadmill, Stairmaster, bicycle, Nautilus system, and free weights (word has it that Madonna convinced them to add this luxurious chamber). Finally, all of the suites offer kitchens which are completely stocked, with gourmet foods, along with fine china and crystal. This makes it easy for guests to create elaborate snacks or complete meals with ease. However, most choose to dine in The Lowell's very private Pembroke Room, located on the second floor of the hotel.

This room is truly reminiscent of an English tearoom with chintz fabrics and gleaming mahogany furnishings set on thick carpets. Lovely flower arrangements merely add to the elegant effect. Full breakfasts, high tea, and cocktails are not to be missed. Although the room closes for dinner, The Post House next door (accessible through a small door in the lobby), is just the right choice for those who don't want to stray too far from home for an excellent meal. Their wine selection is incredible, with some of the cellar displayed in temperature regulated cases that line the hall on the way in. There is a feeling of dining in an old-fashioned men's club, with the menu reflecting a long list of Post House classics that include filet mignon, filet au poivre, prime rib, triple lamb chops and lobster. Those who prefer a lighter menu, may choose from an array of items which include coconut shrimp with a curry and tomato basil chutney, soft shell crabs, or a chicken breast with pecan corncakes and chili sauce. Those wanting to skip dessert will likely have a tough time passing up the wonderful homemade cookies and bars overflowing from a basket by the door.

While it is easy to talk about the amenities, exquisite antiques, and fine food at The Lowell, what makes this hotel stand out from so many others is the excellent service. The staff is literally willing to honor any and all requests made by their guests. Many of the famous (and not so famous) depend on the staff to respect their privacy, which they do without exception. Housekeeping also does an excellent job, with their twice daily service and triple checking the guests rooms and public areas to ensure they are kept immaculate. With all of this responsibility, it would seem that guests might sense an "attitude" among the staff. Speaking from experience, and as people who are neither rich nor famous, they couldn't have been friendlier.

Bowser will also be well taken care of at The Lowell. Because the hotel is so small, it is easy to get outside for morning and evening walks. Its location is ideal for walks in the Park, along Park Avenue, and even for a bit of window shopping on Madison Avenue.

THE MARK

Madison Avenue at 77th Street
New York, New York 10021
(800) THE-MARK, (212) 744-4300, Fax: (212) 744-2749
General Manager: Raymond N. Bickson
Rooms: 120 doubles, 60 suites
Rates: Doubles $275-325, Suites $525-2,200
Payment: AE, CB, DC, DSC, MC, and Visa
Children: Welcome (cribs, cots, and babysitters are available)
Dogs: Small dogs are welcome with a few stipulations. The Executive
      Offices should be contacted, the dog can weigh no more than 20
      pounds, and should be carried or leashed in the hotel's public areas.
Open: All year

While there are a few size requirements to meet before Bowser is allowed access to The Mark, those dogs who pass inspection are in for a real treat, along with their human counterparts. The edifice housing The Mark has quite a history, having been built in the mid-1920s, it has been used both as private residences and as a hotel over the years. But it was not until the Rafael Group took over the reins, toward the end of the 1980s, and poured tens of millions into refurbishing the property, that it truly began to flourish.

The most distinguishing characteristic to The Mark's Art Deco facade, other than the Palladian windows framed by decorative rosettes and other ornamental plaster work, is the copper tower which caps it. Once inside, the full neo-classic design becomes evident. The reception area is awash with lustrous pale marble floors inset with black marble tiles. Soft wool, Gundolt carpets rest under the Biedermeier furniture (a style of furniture culled from the French Empire period and German painted peasant work, whose adaptable and quaint style lends itself to many contemporary decors). Coffered ceilings are illuminated by sleek light fixtures. Adjacent to the lobby is The Mark's Bar, offering an even more comfortable and clubby atmosphere. Deep green walls are broken up by the richness of mahogany pilasters. The Beidermeier influence is at work here too, although it is interspersed with more classic chintz-covered armchairs. In the bar, there are museum quality, 18th-century Piranesi prints of Roman monuments, vases, candelabra, and bas-reliefs. Guests will also find these drawings in most of the public areas and in all the guest rooms.

Upstairs, just as much care and planning has gone into the decorating and appointing of the bedrooms. Muted green, yellow, and rose tones have been chosen as the predominant color schemes, with soft lighting emanating from overhead fixtures as well as from lamps fashioned from Oriental vases. Beds are covered in sophisticated floral tapestry fabrics; however, guests will undoubtedly be more interested in what lies under the fine tailored bedspreads. The sheets are made of the finest cotton, and come from one of the most exclusive European manufacturers, Frette. Down pillows merely add to an already luxurious experience. The mini-bars are black, high-tech affairs, whose refrigerators are fully stocked with all the chocolates, cookies, caviars, and wines and liqueurs one could imagine. As one would expect, the carefully concealed cable television has its own VCR. The modern amenities and rather contemporary decor are tempered only slightly by the coffered ceilings and detailed moldings inherent in the building.

The bathrooms, on the other hand, are completely state-of-the-art. In some, Italian marble surrounds bathtubs and showers, lines the walls, and forms the vanities. Other bathrooms utilize imported black and white tiles, to create an equally appealing backdrop. A most luxurious array of toiletries are available, including Crabtree and Evelyn soaps, powders, and bath salts, as well as Neutrogena shampoos and boxes of bath oil beads. Those who choose to stay in one of the suites, will appreciate the heated towel racks and additional amenities that include soaking tubs, marble baths, and bidets.

The hotel is located in an ideal section of the Upper East Side, close to Central Park and to countless shopping opportunities, as well as many of the museums in the area. The Metropolitan, The Guggenheim, and The Whitney are all within walking distance. The shops of Madison and Fifth Avenues also merit browsing, and are quite used to welcoming the canine companions who accompany many of their clientele.

MAYFAIR HOTEL BAGLIONI

Park Avenue at 65th Street
New York, New York 10021
(800) 223-0542, (212) 288-0800,
General Manager: Dario Mariotti
Rooms: 96 doubles, 105 suites
Rates: Doubles $295-410, Suites $440-1,170
Payment: AE, CB, DC, MC, and Visa
Children: Welcome
Dogs: Small dogs are welcome with prior approval
Open: All year

Although the Mayfair Hotel has operated under different managements over the years, it has maintained its overall feeling of intimacy and the staff a sense of family. The newest owner is the Cogeta PalaceHotel group. While the building maintains much of its old world charm, the details have all been subtly restored and updated. Old, drafty windows have been replaced with sealed ones, central air conditioning cools the rooms in the summer months, and state of the art telephone equipment keeps travelers in touch with home or office when it is necessary. The modern fitness center makes it easy for guests to continue with their usual workout routine.

Those who have frequented the hotel over the years will be pleased to see that the ornately carved and painted coffered wood ceilings have not been altered, and that the delicately detailed arches, pillars, and Palladian windows still frame the elegant sunken lounge. During our visit, enormous fresh flower arrangements of red lilies and day lilies spilling out of the Oriental vases, formed subtle partitions in the already intimate lobby. This arrangement afforded guests an even more inviting atmosphere to relax and converse.

When newcomers are ready to be escorted to their rooms, the exquisitely carved mahogany elevators and their staff, stand ready to quickly transport guests to the upper floors. Soft carpeting dampens the sounds of footsteps on each floor, with only a doorbell marking the entrance to each bedroom or suite. Return guests are certain to be greeted by fresh flower arrangements or baskets of fruit as they enter the room. It is difficult to describe the average accommodation, other than that they are quite spacious and each has a slightly different shape and ambiance.

There is a distinctly European flavor to the hotel, which is displayed in a variety of ways. Pale blue and peach color tones have been chosen as the primary color schemes in many of the rooms, with detailed ceiling and floor moldings painted in ecru. Some accommodations are decorated with traditional English chintzes, Queen Anne-style furnishings, and an assortment of botanical, nautical, and hunt prints. Other suites favor modern geometric fabrics that have been combined with contemporary furnishings to create quite the opposite, but no less appealing, effect. Marble bathrooms are the standard, and are equipped with a full complement of toiletries and amenities, along with telephones, hair dryers, scales, and bathrobes. The suites, along with many of the bedrooms, have well-stocked butler's pantries, making it easy to entertain in a personal style.

The staff at the Mayfair Hotel is always available to meet any special requests, although most will discover that their needs have already been anticipated. For instance, oversized umbrellas can be found in the closets for the city's inclement days. A choice of International and local newspapers are delivered to the room each morning, along with freshly shined shoes for those who left theirs out the night before. As one would expect, room service is available around the clock; however, it is just as easy to wander downstairs and dine at one of the finest French restaurants in the city, Le Cirque.

One of the many endearing traits about the Mayfair Hotel is its central location. Set between Park and Madison Avenues, guests can easily walk to shopping, restaurants, and to Central Park. There is a purely residential quality to the area that is certain to make people feel as though they have the best of all worlds, the sophistication of New York combined with the charm found in some of the older Upper East Side neighborhoods. Once inside the hotel, a cloak of privacy and seclusion descends on the guest, that many find particularly appealing.

And by the way, Bowser is certainly not the most unusual guest hosted by the hotel. Recently, an animal trainer making an appearance on Good Morning America, stayed here with an exotic menagerie of beasts ranging from a boa constrictor and turtle to some undomesticated African relatives of the cat family. This trainer has also been known to travel with a camel and a one-ton bull — not in the hotel, we trust!! After hosting this group and providing them with the usual high level of service, there is little doubt that the Mayfair Hotel staff will find Bowser to be one of their more mild-mannered guests.

LE PARKER MERIDIEN

118 West 57th Street
New York, New York 10019
(800) 543-4300, (212) 245-5000, Fax: (212) 307-1776
General Manager: Stephen Pipes
Rooms: 494 doubles, 206 suites
Rates: Doubles $245-290, Suites $300-1,500
Payment: AE, CB, DC, DSC, MC, and Visa
Children: Welcome
Dogs: Welcome, but must be placed in a dog crate when left unattended
Open: All year

The Meridien Hotels throughout the world are known for their sophisticated charm, exquisite food, and European style of service. Their hotel in New York City is no exception, although the rather sterile facade may mislead most who pass by the building. This initial impression immediately changes when guests step through the doors into the reception area. The heart of this unusual building soars six floors up to an open-air atrium. Here, sunlight streams in and nurtures the numerous potted plants and trees, as well as the enormous flower arrangements displayed in large Oriental vases. The perimeter of the atrium is comprised of a series of columns, interspersed with enormous arches, balconies, paneled walls, and moldings. Salmon is the predominant color, contrasted against an off-white background. The entire effect is reminiscent of the Roman revival style.

The Meridien has been in the process of updating their hotel, floor by floor, over the last several years. Guest rooms have always been architecturally interesting with bedrooms and small sitting areas separated by walls of built-in cabinets outfitted with paneled doors. Oatmeal and black are the dominant colors, producing a very sophisticated and striking effect. A Biedermeier influence is clearly apparent when looking at the rather masculine furnishings. The bedsteads are covered in tailored, quilted European shams. Woods for the writing desks, chairs, and armoires are polished to a fine luster. Bathrooms, while not enormous, are very well appointed with marble sinks and accents. The usual accoutrements include hair dryers, fine toiletries from Hermes, and terry cloth robes. The newly refurbished rooms were extremely quiet, seemingly impervious to internal and external noise. Our favorite chambers offered spectacular views of the Park, and it would be worthwhile to request one when making a reservation.

Those who do not necessarily want a room with a view, will be equally well served with a visit to the roof deck. Here, guests can lie in the sun, swim in the large indoor swimming pool, or admire the wonderful views of the Park and surrounding skyline while jogging on the outdoor track. Downstairs, there is a literal labyrinth of workout areas for those who want to further tone their bodies. Squash, racquetball, Lifecycles, treadmills, and Nautilus, are just a few of the assorted workout regimes available. The club is well-staffed for those who need assistance with any of these activities, as well as providing instructors for both racquetball and squash along with masseuses who can soothe any tired muscles. Some may prefer to take a rejuvenating sauna or whirlpool, as well.

Bowser will enjoy the leisurely walk from the hotel to Central Park. At this end of the Park there are lakes to explore, rocky knolls to climb over, and an assortment of other dog walkers to visit with. There are many diversions and ways to be entertained in New York City; Le Parker Meridien's mid-town location, exquisite ambiance, and first class accommodations and service should provide a wonderful spot from which to enjoy it all.

THE MICHELANGELO

152 West 51st Street
New York, New York 10019
(800) 237-0990, (212) 765-1900, Fax: (212) 541-6604
General Manager: Laurence Jeffery
Rooms: 126 doubles, 52 suites
Rates: Doubles $240-325, Suites $375-915
Payment: AE, CB, DC, MC, and Visa
Children: Welcome
Dogs: Small, well-behaved dogs are welcome but guests must sign a damage
　　　waiver
Open: All year

As we entered the lobby of The Michelangelo, the rush of wind that accompanied us caused the crystals in the enormous chandelier overhead to chime. The lovely reception area was comprised of marble floors covered with Oriental carpets, intimate seating arrangements, and understated flower arrangements. Here, amid the hustle and bustle of New York's theater district, lies a very peaceful and most inviting enclave. A small bar is discreetly tucked off to the side of the lobby, serving a few patrons. Others could be found conversing in one of the intimate seating arrangements, while the faint ticking from a long case antique clock could be heard in the background. Although the hotel was full the day we arrived, there was little sense of it in the public areas as guests were either in their rooms or out enjoying the myriad of sights and attractions.

Upstairs, floral patterned carpets lead down the long, wide hallways to the newly refurbished bedrooms and suites. Along the way, guests pass lovely sideboards and tables adorned with striking dried flower arrangements and fragrant potpourri placed in Oriental bowls. Doorways open into marble tile entry ways, where new arrivals will discover side tables are set with trays of glasses and Italian sparkling waters. The decorative theme in each bedroom varies from a French Country atmosphere to Art Deco motif, although all have a strong European flavor. The predominate color scheme utilizes peach and pale green color tones. Surprisingly, there are also a number of architectural accents as well, with most of the rooms boasting coffered ceilings, built-in cabinets, and thick crown mouldings. The guest chambers are also quite large, averaging 475 square feet. Televisions are often housed in walnut armoires, while Queen Anne style writing desks are well-stocked with writing paraphernalia. Neutral tone sofas and side chairs are accented with thick throw pillows.

A great deal of attention has also gone into remodeling all of the bathrooms. Once again, Italian marble seems to be the theme with white marble floors and rich green marble counter tops. A toilet and bidet lie side by side, although the focal point for most guests is the oversized bathtub. Extra thick terry cloth robes are just right for wrapping up in afterwards. A full array of toiletries are available, as expected, although the small television was an added treat. Those who choose to watch television from their room can also request a VCR and select videos from the hotel's video library. The services at The Michelangelo are just what one would expect from a first class hotel. A few thoughtful extras include complimentary white gloves for reading the Sunday newspaper, an extensive health club facility, and the complimentary Buon Di Italian Breakfast, consisting of an assortment of delicious Italian pastries and cappuccino or espresso. Lunch and dinner can be found at Bellini by Cipriani, a famous and outstanding, upscale Italian restaurant which attracts an interesting clientele. If nothing else, stop by on a Sunday for brunch and sip a famous Bellini cocktail while watching the world pass by the plate glass windows.

The Michelangelo is a terrific choice for anyone who wants to be within walking distance of the theater district and mid-town Manhattan. Of course, Bowser might be more appreciative of the fact that Central Park is within walking distance of the hotel, although not quite as convenient as some of the other hotels located on the Upper East Side. He might also want to pay a visit to Rockefeller Center and watch the ice skaters twirl and jump.

MORGANS

237 Madison Avenue
New York, New York 10016
(800) 334-3408, (212) 686-0300, Fax: (212) 779-8352
General Manager: Douglas Jacobson
Rooms: 84 doubles, 29 suites
Rates: Doubles $205-235, Suites $275-400
Payment: AE, DC, MC, and Visa
Children: Welcome
Dogs: Small, well-behaved dogs are welcome with advance notice
Open: All year

"Minimalist" is the first word that comes to mind when thinking about Morgans and "inviting" is the second. But first, guests must find the hotel and they must do so by a process of deduction. There are no signs to indicate Morgans even exists, not even a building number that can be seen with the naked eye. We made an educated guess, that a stone columned brick building with double glass doors was the spot, and were warmly greeted by the cordial staff, impeccably dressed in double breasted black suits. While we were waiting to be escorted upstairs, we began to gain some insight as to what Morgans was really all about.

The lobby is an Art Deco experience, decorated in black and shades of gray. The checkerboard patterned floor is perhaps the most intricate part of this room as the only other items in it are some two-story glass and bronze wall treatments amid black leather and chrome chairs. The folks who created Morgans, who, by the way, are also responsible for Studio 54, certainly had a clear vision for the hotel, both in terms of theme and privacy. Elevators whisk guests to the upper levels, leaving anyone in the lobby to merely wonder about what lies in the chambers beyond. Guests emerge onto floors with subdued lighting, dark grey walls, and little else. With under a dozen rooms per floor, the overall effect is very tranquil and oozes exclusivity.

As the doors open into each bedroom, the same Spartan atmosphere prevails, but a stronger sense of sophistication also emerges. The lines are clean, the fabrics neutral, and the furniture handcrafted. The accents are black or white with many shades of gray in between. Some rooms have a window seat, softened with pillows, whose backdrops are the huge domed windows with wooden Venetian blinds. In the winter months, down comforters lie fluffed at the end of the low profile beds, and in the summer there are fuzzy wool checkerboard blankets resting atop Oxford cloth covers. The stereo is playing softly and grey carpeting dampens any sound of footsteps. After the confusion and color of the city, this room is a rather peaceful refuge. The bathrooms consist of black and white imported Japanese tiles, which create a checkerboard effect on the walls and around the tubs. The showers are enclosed with floor-to-ceiling glass. Stainless steel surgical sinks with European fixtures extend from the walls with simple glass shelves housing the custom made toiletries and neatly rolled washcloths. A single flower in a bud vase provides the only spot of color in these rooms. The overall effect is dramatic.

Visually, Morgans has broken with conventional hotel wisdom in so many ways that one might assume it has also done so with the amenities it provides — not so. Color cable television and VCRs (with a library of over 200 films) allow for interesting viewing options; two telephones are placed in each chamber; and a refrigerator holds all the drinks or snacks guests might want. In the evening, beds are turned down and in the morning the *New York Times* is waiting at the door. Guests will also find a state-of-the-art fitness area in the building.

A complimentary breakfast can be delivered to the room each morning or enjoyed in the sunny breakfast room. Those who want to order from a full menu could select items such as Eggs Benedict, Morgans' waffles or griddle cakes, or herbed omelettes. In the evening, many order off the room service menu, making a meal from the interesting array of appetizers. Spicy peanut barbecued shrimp, Maryland crab cakes with a mustard dressing, and the smoked salmon with caviar, sour cream, and red onion are all very tempting. Whether guests need room service or the services of the concierge, both are available 24-hours a day. Morgans truly breaks with standard hotel tradition, but in a carefully crafted way that maintains all of the elements guests depend on — an attentive staff, flexibility to meet guests' needs, and attention to details.

When it comes time to walking Bowser, there are some quiet side streets off Madison Avenue that are just right. Unfortunately, the Park is a rather long walk from here and so dogs staying at Morgans should be comfortable in a city environment.

THE PIERRE

5th Avenue at 61st Street
New York, New York 10021
(800) 743-7734, (212) 940-8101, Fax: (212) 826-0319
General Manager: Herbert Pliessnig
Rooms: 159 doubles, 46 suites
Rates: Doubles $310-440, Suites $600-950
Payment: AE, CB, DC, MC, and Visa
Children: Welcome
Dogs: Small dogs are welcome
Open: All year

While the eighties will always be considered a boom time for the country, and particularly New York City, all the activity did take its toll on the world-renowned Pierre. As the decade came to a close, this matriarch of fine hotels was in need of a major renovation and over the course of two years was painstakingly brought back to its former self.

Although a grand hotel in many ways, The Pierre still manages to hold on to its sense of intimacy. The multi-tiered lobby is immense and dominated by gilded moldings, huge brass chandeliers, Edwardian antiques, and enormous Oriental rugs. Oversized chairs and soft brocade sofas are grouped in intimate seating arrangements. Potted palms frame archways while the sitting areas are broken up by enormous flower arrangements overflowing from Oriental vases. Subdued lighting complements the soft color schemes.

The Rotunda is perhaps the most inspired public area in the building. Murals, reminiscent of Italy, adorn the rounded walls, the two wings of an open staircase, and the ceiling. Painted in the 1930s, these murals are awash in pastels, creating just the right environment for those wishing to enjoy a light lunch, high tea, or cocktails. Just beyond The Rotunda lies the Cafe Pierre whose Art Deco style is also reflected in the contemporary menu. The piano bar is a favorite gathering place well into the late evening hours.

The guest rooms have also received their fair share of attention in the past few years. Staffed elevators bring guests to the upper floors, where there are a mix of bedrooms, suites, and private cooperatives, the latter merely adding to the hotel's residential feeling. One of the many endearing features about The Pierre is the attention to detail that went into building it in the late 1920s. Intricate cornice moldings, paneled walls, and chair rails are painted to bring out their details. Some rooms have rounded walls and all have high ceilings. There is an innate sense of Old World-style about the hotel that would be very difficult to replicate today. This has been accented by the decor and furnishings, which vary dramatically depending upon the room.

Chippendale or Queen Anne-style furnishings dominate most of the bedrooms, taking the form of wing chairs, writing desks, and armoires whose doors are inlaid with beveled glass. Televisions and VCRs are either housed in the armoires or placed in a discrete corner of the room so as not to detract from its character. Subtle color schemes have often been chosen for the wall treatments, probably so they won't compete with the bold chintz fabrics. Some of the bedrooms have been decorated in pale blue and yellow English chintz, while others combine the chintz on a bed coverlet with coordinated plaids on both the overstuffed chairs and the draperies at the windows. One of our favorite suites has views of the courtyard through oversized windows. A richly hued chintz sofa dominates this particular sitting room, reflected in a wall of mirrors that surround a fireplace. The armchairs are covered in leather and ottomans are well placed to rest one's feet. Adjacent to the sitting room is a good-sized bedroom decorated with French Provincial fabrics and a delicately embroidered white coverlet on the bed. Guests are certain to notice the fresh roses which add color and a much appreciated fragrance to the rooms. Bathrooms have been updated as well, with black and white marble tile, expanses of mirrors, and tiny alcoves which hold a vast array of toiletries. Hairdryers and telephones are standard as well. Terry cloth robes await those who look forward to relaxing after bathing.

The hotel's staff to guest ratio is three-to-one, allowing for twice daily maid service, same day valet and laundry service, complimentary shoeshine, secretarial services, and even an unpacking service. The concierge will arrange everything from horseback riding in Central Park to theater tickets, on short notice. Bowser might not appreciate all of the extras that go into making The Pierre a five-star hotel; however, he should relish in the convenience of walking out the front door and across the street to Central Park. Here, he can frolic in the grass, explore one of the many ponds, or fraternize with the other resident dogs. All in all, The Pierre, its staff, and its central location provide guests with everything they might need for a stay on the Upper East Side of New York City.

THE REGENCY HOTEL

540 Park Avenue
New York, New York 10021-7385
(800) 233-2356, (212) 759-4100, Fax: (212) 825-5674
General Manager: Sherry Laveroni
Rooms: 300 doubles, 74 suites
Rates: Doubles $250-375, Suites $550-900
Payment: AE, CB, DC, DSC, ENR, MC, and Visa
Children: Welcome (cribs, cots, and babysitters are available)
Dogs: Welcome provided the guests sign a waiver
Open: All year

What many visitors to New York City often find curious are the large number of dog walkers that can be found on the Upper East Side of Manhattan, anywhere from Central Park to Park Avenue. Mid-morning and early evening, professional dog walkers can often be seen escorting packs of dogs through these wealthy neighborhoods. These are not miniature poodles, but good-sized dogs. For instance, on the day of our visit to The Regency Hotel, four golden retrievers could be seen parading by its main entrance. Situated on the corner of Park Avenue and 61st Street, the Regency Hotel is not one of the trendy boutique hotels, but it certainly does its best to capture the intimate feeling of one. The lobby is the most austere portion of the building, although the austerity is somewhat tempered by the travertine marble floors overlaid with Oriental carpets, French tapestries hanging from some of the walls, and the smattering of French antiques placed throughout. During our visit, the lobby was buzzing with activity; however, once guests are transported to the upper floors they begin to gain a sense of this hotel's appeal.

Having recently undergone a two year and 17 million dollar renovation, the guest rooms now have an elegant residential quality to them with cornices and moldings that are reminiscent of the pre-war buildings lining Park Avenue. Hallways leading to these chambers are lit by crystal chandeliers and walls are defined by a grey damask and coral pink color scheme. The bedrooms, on the other hand, are decorated with warm earth tones which provide a neutral backdrop for the 18th-century reproduction furnishings. Chippendale and Sheraton style reproductions are upholstered with silk and damask fabrics coordinated with the draperies and tailored bedspreads. Two- and four-poster finial beds are flanked by small tables with reading lamps. Classic antique prints provide interesting wall decoration. As one would expect, televisions are concealed in armoires along with refrigerators; an oversized desk provides business travelers with enough space to work; and personal safes are accessible for those wishing to stow their valuables. The ample bathrooms are lined with rose marble and are outfitted with a second telephone, bathrobes, and a host of luxurious toiletries.

While the city offers a myriad of dining options to match any hour of the day, 540 Park is renowned as the place for the power breakfast. Here, amid paneled walls and coffered ceilings illuminated by chandeliers, some of the great business deals of this century have been crafted. Linen covered tables are set with fine china, silver, and crystal. Lovely fresh cut flower arrangements are reflected in the ornate mirrors which decorate the room. Even the Hollywood set finds its way here with such frequency, that the restaurant and hotel have been dubbed Hollywood East. While the breakfast menu is good, and the people watching interesting, it is the elegant dinner menu that truly entices. Appetizer selections include a lobster salad with warm potatoes, wild mushroom ravioli with a wild mushroom gratin, or the seafood risotto. Sauteed venison chops with butternut squash, spinach and fresh cranberries, sauteed lobster and shrimp in a banana curry sauce served with basmati rice and pappadam bread, or the broiled breast of duck with scallion and corn risotto are some of the varied entree selections.

Afterwards, some choose the intimate piano bar setting at the Regency Lounge for an after-dinner drink. Others, who prefer a late dinner or the theater, might want to workout in the hotel's well-equipped fitness center. Here, everything from the Versa Climber "mountaineering machine" to a multi-purpose weight training apparatus is available, along with a whirlpool, sauna, and masseuses for after-workout relaxation. The hotel is located in a rather safe area of the Upper East Side, ideal for evening walks with Bowser and leisurely excursions in Central Park during the daylight hours.

WESTBURY HOTEL

Madison Avenue at 69th Street
New York, New York 10021
(800) 321-1569, (212) 535-2000, Fax: (212) 535-5058
General Manager: Phillipe Leboeuf
Rooms: 179 doubles, 52 suites
Rates: Doubles $275-305, Suites $400-500
Payment: AE, CB, DC, MC, and Visa
Children: Welcome
Dogs: Welcome
Open: All year

The Westbury Hotel is a part of the Forte family of hotels, well located on the corner of 69th Street and Madison Avenue. Those who are familiar with the Forte hotel group know that they have a knack for doing things just right. Forte operates some of the most exclusive hotels around the world, including the two renowned Hotel Plaza Athenees located in Paris and New York. The Westbury, bedecked with bright red awnings, occupies a coveted corner of the Upper East

Side. It is situated in an exclusive residential neighborhood and close to Central Park, Madison Avenue shopping, and a handful of wonderful museums and art galleries. Originally built in the 1920s, the hotel is the epitome of old world elegance. The intimate lobby is steeped in traditional details; its light marble floors contrast beautifully with dark mahogany antiques and the wood paneling in the reception area. Striped silk fabrics cover the sofas set on exquisite Oriental rugs. Potted palms rest in huge porcelain pots and fresh flowers are artfully arranged in glass vases set on pedestals and end tables. Antique tapestries hang on some walls and oil paintings grace others.

This same sense of old-world style permeates the upstairs chambers as well. Here, the detailed moldings and deep set windows provide the basis for the traditional English look that is pervasive. There are 50 different decorating themes found throughout the guest rooms, with one constant, the yards of coordinated fabrics that fill each of these spaces. Striped and chintz designer fabrics predominate, and are usually complemented by dotted Swiss and tapestry-like fabrics. The effect is a true melange of color that is very appealing. Chippendale benches rest at the end of some beds, and a pair of fringe skirted club chairs might be placed off to the side in another. Full-length chintz draperies are coordinated with bed fabrics, or in the case of the suites, with the traditional sofas. Throw pillows are found throughout, whether on the beds or decorating the chairs. A subtle Chinese influence is also present, with Porcelain lamps and bowls placed artfully about the chambers. The wall treatments vary from subtle stripes to those painted in pastel colors. Impressive paintings, prints, and architectural drawings fill many of the walls, and floor-to-ceiling bookshelves occupy others. The overall effect is most impressive, and one that we found quite appealing. The bathrooms in the larger suites are spacious, while those in smaller chambers are often tucked into an appropriate alcove. Each is bathed in marble and stocked with an array of English soaps, shampoos, and bath salts.

The hotel also has a relatively new fitness center. An assortment of state-of-the-art equipment that includes Lifecycles, stair climbers, treadmills, and both free and stationary weights, is a nice precursor to the sauna and steam rooms. Those who prefer a more leisurely pace will enjoy taking Bowser for a walk along Park or Madison Avenues, as well as in Central Park.

Of course, there is no shortage of good restaurants in New York; however, the Westbury also happens to offer a noteworthy menu. The Polo Restaurant is located on the ground floor of the hotel, with its plate glass windows providing good views of the passing street scene. This is decorated in true Polo style, with rust and chocolate brown paisley fabrics covering the booths. The mahogany colored chairs have a rich cordovan leather covering them, and the walls are paneled in dark woods as well. Brass sconces are highlighted by recessed lighting, further enhancing the clubby ambiance. The menu, while not extensive, offers appetizers such as oysters with champagne mignonette and organic rye bread, smoked salmon with Yukon Gold potato salad, mustard and chives, or a lobster cocktail with grilled leeks and parsley sauce. Entrees include such selections as seared spice crusted tuna with Swiss chard and haricots verts in a lemon coulis, the lobster in a minestrone of spring vegetables, or the grilled double lamb chops.

We found The Westbury Hotel to be a wonderful mix between the ultra-luxurious super hotels in mid-town Manhattan and the more intimate boutique hotels found off of Madison Avenue. It is both very elegant and decidedly comfortable, and has a particularly gracious staff who are attentive and, at the same time, very unobtrusive.

CRISLIPS BED AND BREAKFAST

RD 1, Box 57
Ridge Road
Queensbury, New York 12804
(518) 793-6869
Hosts: Ned and Joyce Crislip
Rooms: 3 doubles
Rates: $55-75
Payment: AE, MC, and Visa
Children: Welcome in one guest room
Dogs: Welcome in the first floor bedroom
Open: All year

Built in 1805, this Federal style home is a gracious reminder of the past. We visited in the summertime, when perennial beds around the house were in full bloom and the large shade trees were showing off their dense green foliage. The lawns and gardens were surrounded by rock walls, capping off this picturesque setting. One of the most striking things about this traditional white clapboard house with green shutters is the long, elegant porch with its white rocking chairs and planters of geraniums placed upon the railings. It is difficult looking at the house today, to imagine that it once served as a training ground for young interns by the first doctor of Queensbury.

Although the B&B is situated in a rural part of New York State, it is set next to a fairly busy country road. However, once guests enter the foyer their eyes are drawn instead to the formal English antiques. These have been artfully interspersed with lovely reproductions to create a refined, yet comfortable setting. The living room's old-fashioned floral wallpaper nicely complements the area rugs covering the darkly stained hardwood floors. Our attention was particularly drawn to two special items in here, the grand piano and the Queen-Anne highboy. Just beyond this chamber is the original keeping room, constructed of stone, which has a large cooking fireplace and overlooks the backyard. This adjoins the formal dining room, which is also privy to pretty views of the property through another set of windows. Each morning, guests are served a full breakfast. One day the meal might consist of scrambled eggs, sausage, and English muffins, and on another, buttermilk pancakes topped with fresh blueberries. Juice and coffee or tea always complements the meal.

Those traveling with Bowser are invited to stay in the first floor suite. The canopied bed provides the centerpiece for this chamber, accented by mahogany antiques. Soft carpeting and tied-back draperies give this otherwise spacious room a rather homey feeling. A shelf is well-stocked with a wide variety of books that guests often enjoy reading in the comfortable armchairs. Aside from its ease of access to the outdoors, this room is also ideal for those traveling with a dog as it has a complete kitchenette. This not only facilitates the preparation of a favorite hors d'oeuvre, but it also is a convenient place to prepare meals for Bowser. There are two additional rooms upstairs for those without a dog in tow. The Green and Blue Rooms offer the same mix of mahogany antiques along with king size and canopied beds.

Ned and Joyce prove to be ideal hosts — they are very friendly and as willing to give tours of their house as they are to provide excellent suggestions for things to do in the surrounding area. Both have backgrounds in music, and might be coerced into playing the piano one evening. Lake George is located close to Crislips, offering plenty of aquatic diversions for guests and their canine companion. There is also hiking available in any of the nearby state parks. In the wintertime, Gore and West Mountains open up for skiing, and they also make for interesting hikes in the summer months. At the end of a busy summer's day, a great outdoor place to relax is the secluded brick patio tucked into the side of the inn overlooking the lush perennial gardens. Bowser, might enjoy resting here as well, in anticipation of another busy day exploring the region.

THE INN AT QUOGUE

47 Quogue Street
Quogue, New York 11959
(800) 628-6166, (516) 653-6560, Fax: (516) 653-5313
Manager: Stephanie Winters
Rooms: 70 doubles, suites, and cottages
Rates: $185-275
Payment: AE
Children: Welcome
Dogs: Welcome in the East Building and the Cottages
Open: All year

When thinking of Long Island, visions of the famous Gold Coast, the exclusive Hamptons, or the rather eclectic Fire Island usually come to mind.

The tiny village of Quogue rarely enters the picture because it is primarily a quiet, residential community, without the trendy boutiques and restaurants that usually draw visitors. Here, grand cedar-shake shingled summer houses and smaller clapboard cottages line the lanes that wend through the village. This is not the Hamptons, where mansions lie behind enormous manicured privets. This is, instead, a charming community that is reminiscent of a New England coastal village where white picket fences covered with roses surround picturesque, weathered-shingle summer houses. In the midst of this setting lies The Inn at Quogue, offering exceptional dining and accommodations for the few who know about it. Visitors approach the white clapboard inn, dating back 210 years, along a gravel drive that circles up to the front entrance. Beautifully manicured English perennial gardens can be found throughout the property along with low privets and mature shade trees. The main house holds the inn's three-star restaurant (recently awarded by the *New York Times*) and guest rooms. Because of its antique qualities and the restaurant at the main house, the innkeeper asks that those traveling with a dog stay in one of their two other fine accommodations on the property.

Five years ago, the inn acquired another historical house that lies just across from the main inn. It is 175 years old although it has the freshness of a summer house, albeit a sophisticated one. In stark contrast to the rustic ambiance of a Maine summer "cottage", the light walls in the nine bedrooms are offset by formal English chintzes. The tailored bedskirts and spreads are coordinated with the valances and draperies which frame the paned windows. Without exception, the lines are clean and the furnishings exude a simple elegance. The Shaker bedside tables might be offset by a slightly more formal butler's tray table resting on an area rug woven in pastel colors. Pickled or white wicker furniture can also be found in some chambers, adding to the light and simple formality of the bedrooms. A welcome personal touch are the live plants and fresh flowers that grace most of the bedrooms.

Those searching for a bit more space should consider the cottages. These lack some of the character found in the bedrooms of the East Building and Main Inn; however, they do provide substantially more space and a few additional amenities. Located around the Inn's swimming pool, most of the cottages have been recently redecorated with white wicker furniture. Although kitchenettes are found in some of the cottages, all guests are encouraged to take advantage of the complimentary Continental breakfast served in the restaurant each morning. This lighter version of the morning meal has been added in response to the many requests for a healthier breakfast menu.

Keeping this in mind, the inn also offers a number of activities that will appeal to fitness minded individuals. The solar heated pool is long enough for swimming laps or guests can borrow a bicycle and ride it to Quogue's private beach (the inn supplies the beach passes). Those who are feeling even more industrious, can ride the three miles to the Hampton Athletic Club, present their room key, pay a small fee, and enjoy full use of the spa and workout facilities, along with the tennis courts. Those who arrive by train or private plane and want transportation to some of the boutiques and restaurants in the nearby Hamptons, may also utilize the hotel's limousine service.

At the end of a busy day, most guests choose to have dinner at the inn. As we mentioned previously, the restaurant has been well received and is known for its fine cuisine. A new chef has just come on board as of this writing, and we are certain the quality will continue. A recent Mother's Day menu offered such appetizers as Long Island little necks on the half shell, Maryland crab cakes in a roasted pepper and corn sauce, and a terrine of grilled vegetables with warm goat cheese, basil, and a black olive vinaigrette. Entrees included a roast pork loin accented with mission figs, lemon thyme, and apple fritters accompanied by a wild mushroom ravioli and a spicy tomato coulis with wilted spinach. The loin of lamb had a white peppercorn and port wine sauce and was served with minted white beans, while the pan roasted red snapper was served with a medley of spring vegetables in a saffron garlic broth. For dessert, there were the usual light fruit tarts and sorbets, along with the more decadent triple chocolate mousse cake and warm apple charlotte with apple puree and creme anglaise. Afterward, a walk along the grounds or out to the beach is a delightful way to end the day.

BEEKMAN ARMS

Route 9
Rhinebeck, New York 12572
(914) 876-7077
Manager: Eve Diaz
Rooms: 56 doubles
Rates: $60-95
Payment: AE, DC, MC, and Visa
Children: Welcome in most rooms at the inn (cribs and babysitters are
        available)
Dogs: Welcome in the four motel units
Open: All year

During Colonial times, inns were often situated on important crossroads or along riverbanks. They offered simple food and drink, as well as a place to rest while people awaited the next stagecoach or riverboat. They also frequently served as more than overnight way stations; they were sometimes used to protect travelers during their journey or local residents during military skirmishes. Beekman Arms has served both these purposes during its long and varied history — built in 1766 of thick stone and enormous oak beams, it had humble, wayside beginnings. But it served as a place of refuge during times of war, as well as during times of peace. George Washington, William Jennings

Bryan, and Franklin Delano Roosevelt all have a place in history secured within these walls. Notable events and people aside, the Beekman Arms has spent the bulk of its life serving the public, whether in the cozy tavern or in the guest rooms.

Today, Beekman Arms lies at the busy crossroads of Rhinebeck, a picturesque and sophisticated community set along the Hudson River. The original stone inn, whose walls are three-feet thick, still maintains its intimate feeling after more than 225 years of service. Guests walk on creaky wide pine floors, while overhead dark beamed ceilings provide additional historic authenticity. The inn is filled with a collection of early American antiques, reproductions, and memorabilia. Wooden ladder back chairs and upholstered armchairs are gathered around most of the inn's many fireplaces, creating inviting sitting areas. Those who meander further into the building will discover the Tavern, a place filled with weapons and collectibles from Colonial times. Pistols, sabres, and muskets are interspersed with maps and historic pictures. Here, many are tempted to have a drink in front of a roaring fire and reflect on the lives of people who lived two-centuries ago. Just beyond this chamber is the Greenhouse Restaurant, recently under the direction of a new chef. The former meat and potatoes menu is long gone, and in its place there is a more inspired Continental cuisine.

The appetizers are hearty enough to be considered a meal, with offerings such as the charred carpaccio of beef tenderloin with grilled forest mushrooms, fresh Maine crab cakes with field greens, and homemade mozzarella with crostini of black olive, dried tomato, and a black walnut sage pesto. Although meat dishes are still on the menu, they are much lighter versions than the old style, with selections that include a charred filet of beef with woodsy whipped potatoes and the Adirondack duck served with charred oranges, duck jus, and a gingered sweet potato puree. There is also a good selection of seafood, ranging from the sea scallops with a tropical salsa to the yellowfin tuna crusted with black sesame seeds and served with a julienne of local vegetables. While dinner patrons will not get a full sense of The Greenhouse's ambiance, the luncheon crowd will truly enjoy basking in the warmth of the sun that streams in through the walls of windows.

Beekman Arms has also updated the lodgings as well, creating a variety of bedrooms that are meant to accommodate most types of guests. For instance, chambers in the main building reflect the antique qualities of the inn, featuring antique furnishings and authentic colors. Over the years, the owner has acquired and renovated neighboring properties to create additional guest rooms in the Delamater House and Courtyard, and in the attached Carriage House. These are set well back from the busy road and offer the quietest and most sophisticated guest rooms. All have been decorated with traditional Shaker furnishings and light and airy colors, along with a host of modern amenities.

However, those who want to bring Bowser must stay in one of the four motel units. While these do not reflect the same antique character of the inn, they are also clearly not run-of-the-mill motel rooms. These are located a block from the inn and are also set back from the road. Situated behind an attractive fence topped with latticework, every unit has an outside entrance and a small ivy covered garden planted with shrubs. Each room is slightly different. Some of the walls have been lightened by stain, while others have had their natural vertical board walls "pickled" or brushed with a light, translucent stain. The beds are either covered with hunter green chintz spreads or simple chenille bedspreads. Whether furnishings are made of natural pine or more formal, mahogany toned English reproductions, all of the bedrooms offer Queen-Anne style writing desks and armoires which hide a television. One bed has a lovely Chippendale style bench placed at the end of it. Tie-back draperies in rich fabrics are as attractive as they are functional. The bathrooms are all modern and offer a full array of toiletries.

These rooms are easily accessible to the outside. Bowser will enjoy stretching his/her legs while you check out the boutiques and old-fashioned small town shops that mingle comfortably together. Within two blocks of the inn, there is a quiet residential section which is perfect for early morning and evening walks. Those who want to explore the New England hills to the east and the Catskill Mountains to the west, will find this inn to be the perfect base. There are also the World War I Airdome, the F.D.R. House and Library in Hyde Park, and the Mills and Vanderbilt Mansions to investigate, as well.

Those who are searching for a full antique inn experience with Bowser at their side, will probably not want to consider the Beekman Arms for an overnight stay. However, those who want the flavor of an historic setting in a sophisticated and quaint village, will find such a spot here, in the heart of the Hudson River Valley.

WHISTLEWOOD FARM

11 Pells Road
Rhinebeck, New York 12572
(914) 876-6838
Host: Maggie Myer
Rooms: 2 doubles, 2 suites
Rates: $75-145
Payment: AE accepted but she prefers checks or cash
Children: Welcome with adult supervision and a $10 extra charge (cots are
　　　　available)
Dogs: Welcome with advance notice and prior approval ($10 nightly fee)
Open: All year

Rhinebeck is a sophisticated hamlet; its quaint streets are lined with stores carrying everything from gourmet condiments and preserves to fine antiques and gold baubles. There are excellent restaurants, including one unusual find in a converted church. Although there are seemingly endless ways to spend time and money, there is one good choice for those seeking out-of-the-way accommodations amid pastoral surroundings — the Whistlewood Farm.

The farm offers a sense of isolation when in reality it is only five minutes from Rhinebeck. A long drive wends alongside fenced-in pastures, a barn, stables, and outbuildings, ultimately arriving at Maggie's ranch-style home. From the outside, the gray-stained house is rather unassuming, but step into the tiled sun room and discover an eclectic treasure trove of Western memorabilia, farm tools, and country antiques. Maggie has spent years developing her collection, with notable items that include an extensive number of blue tin bowls, an old wash basin hanging from the wall, a wagon wheel, Victorian chests, and a wonderful dinner bell. A table and chairs placed in the corner of this room is positioned perfectly to take advantage of the expansive views of the distant valley.

The sunken living room is a great place for gathering in the evenings or on cold, overcast days. The grey, cast-iron stove warms the air with an even heat. Antique quilts are one of the many forms of decoration here, hanging on the walls and draped over the backs of the sofas. The Western theme is also pervasive in this room, with saddles draped over the bannister that separates the living room from the rest of the house. This is a great place to converse with other guests, play a few board games after dinner, or just relax with a good book.

One of the things that makes this B&B most conducive to guests are the separate wings of rooms, which give each visitor a sense of privacy. One wing offers three bedrooms, including our favorite, the Sweet Violets room. This ample chamber is furnished with a huge, four poster Sheraton-style bed, covered with a lilac pattern spread, that dwarfs everything around it. This is a very sunny chamber due to the combination of windows and light color scheme. The Juniper Room, while not as bright and cheery, is equally desirable for a different reason — the private patio found just outside the sliding glass doors. This bedroom and the Tumbleweed Room each offer queen-size pencil post beds, with the former providing an extra single bed for those who bring along a friend or child. All the bedrooms also have sturdy antique pine chests of drawers and other attractive furnishings and collectibles. The most requested accommodation is found in another wing. The Wyoming Room is dominated by a pine, four poster pencil post bed whose canopy is fashioned from a blue and white handmade quilt. A sleigh bed rests in the corner with a few chairs set around a side table. A wall of windows offer views of the pastures along with letting in additional light. French doors lead to the bathroom, whose centerpiece is a Jacuzzi bathtub.

Surprisingly, for a rather small house, there are many areas for guests to congregate. As with most houses though, much of the activity centers around the kitchen with its soft, yellow chintz sofas and pine armoire. The kitchen is also home to a player piano, which has a wonderful selection of classic tunes, and an old iron cook stove. In the morning, the smell of fresh coffee and goodies either baking or being warmed in the oven, is enough to raise even the sleepiest of travelers. This aroma is soon followed by a full breakfast of fresh fruit, incredible baked goodies, cereal, and a hot egg dish or waffles and berry-filled pancakes. Late in the day, guests return to find coffee and tea (iced-tea in the summer months) set out on a table that is loaded with more baked treats. During our visit Maggie had obviously already been hard at work creating a savory apple pie, muffins, and a dense chocolate cake.

While Bowser may not be able to sample the baked goodies, s/he definitely will feel at home with all the other creatures who live on the farm. Some of the animals in residence are a black Labrador Retriever called Cherokee and a Doberman, Missy. There are stables complete with heated stalls and enclosed paddocks. Although Maggie is not breeding horses this year, she does board horses and expects to have a few breeding mares again next year. Maggie loves animals and has a knack for making everyone, including her human guests, feel right at home. There are plenty of quiet country roads for walking along and 13 1/2 acres of grounds for guests to meander through. Although Maggie doesn't offer riding at the farm, she can recommend some stables for those guests who want to spend some time on the miles of beautifully maintained horse trails in the area. Nearby Lake Taconic and Wilcox Park are also good options for those who want to swim, fish, or go boating.

RADISSON HOTEL AT ROCHESTER PLAZA

70 State Street
Rochester, New York 14614
(800) 333-3333, (716) 546-3450
General Manager: John Greenwood
Rooms: 348 doubles, 16 suites
Rates: Doubles $89-163, Suites $350
Payment: AE, CB, DC, DSC, JCB, MC, and Visa
Children: Welcome (cribs, cots, and babysitting referral services are available)
Dogs: Small dogs welcome
Open: All year

If business or pleasure ever brings visitors to the Rochester area, or if they are en-route through upstate New York, then a stay at the Rochester Plaza Hotel is certain to be a refreshing change of pace. Located conveniently in the downtown area, the modern, mirrored-windowed building is attractively landscaped with a large patch of grass and flowers in the front and a small elevated park directly behind the hotel, making it easy to walk Bowser any time of day.

Guest rooms are typical of what one might expect at a high-end hotel. The modern decor is streamlined with muted tones of maroon, green, and beige. Oak has been chosen for the armoires, tables, and framed mirrors. But it is not the decor that sets the hotel apart from others, it is the service and amenities. Guests can expect color cable television with a full complement of special channels, thick towels and an array of toiletries in the tiled bathrooms, and complimentary coffee and a newspaper left at the door in the morning.

For those in search of a higher level of service there is the Club Floor. On this floor the amenities have been upgraded. For instance, turndown service is automatic, a complimentary breakfast is served each morning and hors d'oeuvres and beverages at night. Those who develop a late-evening sweet tooth will find desserts waiting in the lounge between 9 and 10 p.m., or they can dip into their personal candy dish in the room. The rooms are also upgraded, with remote controlled televisions and bathrooms fully equipped with scales, makeup mirrors, and bathrobes.

Additional amenities available to all guests of the hotel include a full service health spa, complete with state of the art exercise equipment and an outdoor swimming pool. Those who want a little extra sport, can walk over to the surprisingly well-equipped YMCA. Here guests can take advantage of the indoor track, Nautilus equipment, pool, basketball, and racquetball.

Finally, for those in search of food, there are two informal restaurants within the hotel. The Riverview Cafe offers fare as simple as bacon and cheddar cheese hamburgers, cobb salad, and Caesar salad, along with more elaborate choices that include seared breast of duck, filet mignon, New York strip steak with cabernet butter, and lamb chops. Those who prefer room service, will find it to be expedient and with an emphasis on service.

There is plenty to do in the Rochester area. Inside activities could include a visit to the Strasenburgh Planetarium or any of the nearby museums. These sites and shopping are all within easy walking distance of the hotel. Rochester is also the home of Eastman Kodak, and making a trip to their International Museum of Photography is a must. A bit further afield is the Genesee Country Museum, which offers buildings from the 1800s moved from various sites in New York State to create a village from the past century.

HUFF HOUSE

Route 2
Roscoe, New York 12776
(914) 482-4579, (607) 498-9953, Fax: (607) 498-4200
Owners: Joanne and Joseph Huff Forness
Rooms: 6 singles, 40 doubles, 1 suite
Rates: Doubles $90-125 (weekly rates and AP plans are available)
Payment: AE, MC, and Visa
Children: Welcome (cribs, cots, and babysitters are available)
Dogs: Welcome in specific rooms provided guests observe restrictions
       outlined by hosts
Open: May through October

It is always a treat to discover a place that the clientele have managed to keep secret for generations, as is the case with the Huff House. The small resort has been in the same family for forty years, with Joanne and her husband Joe taking over the reigns in 1982. She explains that most of the return guests have been coming here for years with their families; however, as they get older and can no longer visit, it is time to let a new generation know about the place. Joanne and Joe have also changed gears a bit, and while still attracting the regulars, there are an increasing number who come to enjoy the Huff House fly-fishing, golf, and tennis opportunities.

Reaching the Huff House involves a five-mile trip up a winding mountain road. At the top, guests drive through the informal gates and head down the narrow drive where panoramic views of the Catskills unfold. The resort is rather compact, with three clusters of two story buildings, a few small cottages, and the main farmhouse. A golf course wends through all of this, with mature trees, rock walled flower gardens, and a pond providing scenic accents. New arrivals will park their cars toward the rear of the property and use golf carts to get around or if they prefer, they may walk.

Even newcomers will immediately be struck by the warm family-atmosphere they feel upon arrival. Joanne, Joe, and their 9-year-old female Akita are usually on hand to help guests settle into their rooms. These are rather simple accommodations, uncluttered by knickknacks but favored by most guests as they offer a good deal of privacy, have combinations of bedrooms that are suitable for different size families, and offer separate outside entrances that are very appropriate for Bowser. Our favorites are located in the two smallest cottages with covered porches. These are actually just right for small families as they are composed of two rooms with an adjoining bathroom. As most guests stay for anywhere from a few days to a week, they end up making these chambers feel very much like their home away from home. For the active person, the rooms are almost incidental as there are numerous activities to take advantage of on the premises.

Some like to get up early and play a round of golf and there is certainly never a wait for a tee time. The Huffs have brought in the Roland Stafford Golf School to be a part of the resort, and one can always see people clustered in groups giving each other pointers or asking the pro for some suggestions. However, those who want to do something other than play golf will find two hard courts for tennis, a nice swimming pool, a volleyball court, and bocce. The Huff House is also located close to the world famous Beaverkill and Willowemoc Rivers, regarded by many as the birthplace of fly fishing. Many come to either learn the art of fly fishing or hone their already existing skills. There are also 188 acres to explore, some are wooded while others are wide open and great fun to romp along with your canine cohort. On the rainy days, it is easy to move inside and play backgammon, billiards, cards, or Ping-Pong.

The hub of activity at mealtimes is in the traditional white clapboard and black shuttered Victorian style farmhouse, complete with a front porch filled with rocking chairs. The large common room is quite cozy with chintz covered sofas and chairs artfully arranged to create a few small seating areas around the large fieldstone fireplace. There is an abundance of books to read about golf or fly fishing, while many take a little time before meals to get to know some of the other patrons. For those who are interested, there is a small, social cocktail hour before dinner, as well. The resort is so intimate that guests inevitably develop fast friendships.

Guests are formally seated for meals in the dining room, each family or group of friends enjoying their own table for the duration of their stay. The food is quite good. Along with a set menu, there are also daily specials. The dinner choices during our visit were leg of lamb, roast duck, and trout. The wine cellar is surprisingly well stocked. For dessert there are often fresh berry or pecan pies, brownie sundaes, or ice cream with homemade cookies. In the morning, *The New York Times* is delivered to the table. Breakfast is also a multi-course affair with fresh fruit, excellent homemade granola, and bagels to start one off. What follows is a choice of pancakes, French toast, eggs, and sausage, ham, or bacon. Afterwards, it is time to go out and play, explore the grounds, or just relax in this peaceful pastoral setting.

The Huffs are the perfect hosts. Always accessible and willing to go out of their way to assist their guests. They exude a warmth and genuine friendliness that makes everyone feel most at home and more often than not, very interested in making a return trip in the near future. With all this going for it, it is certain that the Huff House will not remain a well-kept family secret for long.

THE POINT

Star Route, Box 65
Saranac Lake, New York 12983
(800) 255-3530, (518) 891-5674, Fax: (518) 891-1152
Owners: David and Christie Garrett
Rooms: 11 doubles
Rates: $625-775 (AP)
Payment: AE
Children: Not appropriate for children under 18 years of age
Dogs: Welcome
Open: All year except April

As with the mansions of Newport, there continues to exist a certain fascination for the great camps of the Adirondacks. They are associated with an era of opulence when industrialists accumulated vast fortunes and created exclusive retreats for themselves and their families. The Adirondack mountain wilderness appealed to many of these icons of industry who built compounds that subtly conformed to their natural surroundings. Massive lodges and boat houses fashioned from rough hewn logs, natural stone, and slate, were simple, yet imbued with a subtle sense of rustic style and grace.

One of these Great Camps was built in 1933 for William Avery Rockefeller, the reclusive nephew of John D. Rockefeller. Set on a 10-acre peninsula, jutting out into the blue waters of Upper Saranac Lake, this compound consisted of a main lodge, a traditional boat house, and a variety of outbuildings. For many years it remained within the Rockefellers' domain and was known as Camp Wonundra. However, when the Olympics came to Lake Placid in 1980, the buildings were opened to paying guests. Ted Carter, subsequently orchestrated the metamorphosis of this private enclave into an exclusive retreat, which he simply called The Point. Although the years under Carter established The Point's fine reputation, it wasn't until 1986 when David and Christie Garrett bought it, that it really began to flourish.

The clientele who choose to vacation at The Point do so for a variety of reasons, but more often than not it is to escape the pressures of high profile, high pressure lives. To facilitate this "escape," payment is always made in advance and the location of The Point is carefully guarded until final confirmation of a guest's reservation. Therefore, new arrivals are apt to feel as though they are spending their vacation in a fully-staffed private home, where their needs are quietly and efficiently met. Hosts Bill and Claudia McNamee attend to the behind the scenes details, often choosing to stay discreetly in the background (as does most of the unobtrusive staff).

The guest rooms have also been carefully appointed to create just the right mix of casual elegance coupled with wilderness luxury. Large log cabins with slate roofs are outfitted with everything from birch bark furnishings and exquisite fabrics to original artwork on the walls and Oriental rugs and animal skins covering the pine floors. The eleven bedrooms are scattered among four buildings on the property, the most exclusive and private of these being the Boathouse. While the lower level of this building houses the resort's fleet of boats, the upper level has been converted into luxurious accommodations. Richly glowing, inlaid floors outline the room's centerpiece, an enormous canopied bed draped in sheer white fabric. Signal flags line the beamed ceilings, and private sitting areas and alcoves offer either panoramic views of the lake or face inward toward the massive fieldstone fireplace. Those who prefer breakfast in their room, will be delighted with yet another alcove that holds a table and chairs.

Although the Boathouse is certainly a preferred accommodation for many, The Point offers several other standouts as well. Mohawk is one such place, originally designed as the master bedroom for the Rockefellers. The king-size bed faces the massive fieldstone fireplace, while high overhead are intricate beamed ceilings. The decor, as with all of the rooms, is a lovely combination of themes and styles. Some of the beds and rockers are fashioned from bent birchwood, while others have more formal upholstered headboards and intricately woven fabrics covering the sofas and armchairs. Algonquin was originally the library of the lodge, and today the walls of shelves are still heavy with the classics. The rich wood interiors glow in the flickering light from the fireplace, inviting guests to nestle into a deep armchair, rest their feet on the ottoman, and enjoy a good book. The bathroom is equally intriguing, boasting a shower that gives bathers the sensation of standing under a waterfall.

Another of our favorite rooms is Weatherwatch. This is actually one of the largest accommodations, although its alcoves give it a sense of coziness. The king-size bed, draped in richly toned blue and burgundy fabrics, almost seems recessed into one corner of the room. The elegantly subdued effect is enhanced by the natural wood walls and cathedral ceilings. A large picture window provides the panorama to the outside wilderness, while an immense walk-in stone fireplace warms the room and those curled up in the nearby armchairs.

While the decor and the ambiance created in the rooms is beyond reproach, it is the other amenities that truly set The Point apart. The Garretts have made a concerted effort, during their tenure, to concentrate on the cuisine. A three-star chef from Paris, Albert Roux, is the consultant to the kitchen. Bill McNamee, who trained under Roux, is the executive chef and has brought from France other young chefs to work with him. Breakfast is the most casual meal of the day and is often taken in the individual's guest room. However, lunch and dinner are quite formal and are served in the Great Hall, an enormous chamber with a pair of massive fieldstone fireplaces, unblemished Canadian spruce walls and vaulted ceilings, and hand-pegged hardwood floors. Stags' heads are mounted on the walls and zebra skins adorn the floors, creating a rustic and somewhat elegant camp atmosphere.

There is the feeling here that one has stepped back into time, into an era of the formal house party, where people who were previously unknown to one another were chosen by their hosts for a weekend of conversation and diversion. Guests assemble around the meticulously appointed tables for multi-course extravaganzas. It is difficult to describe a typical menu, as there is nothing typical about anything presented here. Let it simply be said that the food is always exquisitely prepared, artfully presented, and fashioned with only the freshest of ingredients flown in from around the world. Guests are invited to let the chef know what they like, and dislike, and he will adapt the menu to meet their needs. Dinner attire is dressy, and two days a week, black tie for the men and gowns for the women are suggested. The wines have been carefully selected and are presented with each of the four courses. After a delicious repast, some choose to relax with cognac in the Great Hall or visit the Pub for billiards or backgammon. As with any good house party, it is often the combination of personalities that creates the mood for the weekend. Even reticent guests often find themselves attracted to the interesting assortment of people who are drawn to The Point.

While some might be content to treat their vacation at The Point as a purely social event interspersed with some private time, others are more inclined to take advantage of the activities and diversions offered to them. There is an entire fleet of boats available for exploring the lake, ranging from a 1950's mahogany Cris-Craft to the more contemporary sailboard. A canoe is the perfect way to quietly investigate the nooks and crannies of Upper Saranac Lake. Many people like to take a box lunch, loaded with gourmet delicacies and fine wine, for their picnic on a private island. Along with all the usual water sports, there is tennis on the premises, golf nearby, and plenty of hiking and riding trails in the area. Bowser can partake in just about all of these adventures away from The Point and also find plenty of acreage to explore right on the property. In the wintertime, guests will be able to outfit themselves with cross-country skis, ice skates and hockey sticks, and even snow shoes for treks through the wilderness. A small ice fishing lodge is also made available to guests.

The Point is truly one of the more unusual and private retreats available to travelers today. While the price might preclude many would be guests from enjoying this spot, one should keep in mind that it does include everything - meals, liquor, activities, gratuities, and tax. More importantly though, anyone who visits will come away feeling completely rejuvenated and carrying with them a glimpse into another era.

UNION GABLES BED & BREAKFAST

55 Union Avenue
Saratoga Springs, New York 12866
(800) 398-1558, (518) 584-1558
Innkeepers: Jody and Tom Roohan
Rooms: 8 doubles, 2 suites
Rates: Doubles $80-100, Suites $90-200
Payment: AE, MC, and Visa
Children: Welcome (cribs and baby-sitters are available)
Dogs: Welcome with advance notice
Open: All year

Saratoga is a virtual hotbed of activity for horse aficionados during the racing season in August and during harness racing season, which runs from April until mid-November. Even non-racing visitors can, and do, get caught up in the frenetic summer social season. However, there is far more to do in Saratoga Springs than just watch horses and attend parties. It is also a beautiful community blessed with numerous cultural attractions, therapeutic mineral springs, and grand turn-of-the-century Victorian homes. The houses were built over the last century by the wealthy families and individuals who came for the summer season. Housed in one of these gabled treasure boxes is the Union Gables Bed and Breakfast, which Jody and Tom not only purchased but also completely renovated just over a year ago.

We have decided that this is a rather unique couple, because aside from undertaking the monumental task of restoring the 1901 Queen Anne Victorian in a short period of time, they also had four young children to care for and Tom a full-time real estate career to maintain. We should also add that this was a true metamorphose for the building which had served many functions since its creation. At one time it was a home to college students and later to disabled adults. As one might imagine, it was somewhat rundown and truly in need of some attention.

Jody and Tom, with the assistance of a group of decorators, have turned the old Victorian into a true showplace, but one where guests also feel completely comfortable. Starting from the ground up, they replaced the disheveled trellises, cleaned the rock foundation that held up the dual pillars supporting the massive wraparound porch, and highlighted the intricate shingled patterns on the turret, eaves, and gables by painting them various shades of slate blue, rust, and cream. Arched and rounded windows also became more pronounced once they were painted in contrasting colors. Overgrown gardens and lawns were tended to, creating a pleasant visual backdrop for the house. An authentic looking gas lamp was even installed, lighting the pathway to the front door.

Inside, tongue and groove fir floors needed to be restored, and in some places replaced, before they could be refinished to their lustrous reddish hues. All the plumbing and heating systems were overhauled and air-conditioning installed. But amid all the updating, the couple felt it was of the utmost importance to preserve the overall Victorian feeling, so authentic reproduction furnishings and wallpapers were selected to reflect the era. And in the end, after a flurry of activity, the home was once again a tribute to its listing on the National Register of Historic Places.

Although Union Gables has only been in operation for a short while, word is already spreading about the charming B&B. The guest rooms are individually decorated making it difficult to describe an average chamber. The multiple eaves and gables create unique guest room configurations, occupying different corners of the B&B or filling the rounded walls of the turret. The suite is an ideal set up for families, with one queen-size bed and two double beds occupying the expansive space. One double bedroom has been decorated in deep green plaids which are nicely accented by several Shaker tables and benches that have been painted in a coordinating hunter green. Red accents in the colorful area rug and on the bed pillows add definition to this crisply decorated chamber, along with dried wreaths and potted ferns. Another bedroom utilizes the traditionally subdued rusts, greens and ecrus from the Victorian era with lovely floral papers and small framed period prints decorating the walls. Those who shy away from subdued colors might want to choose the blue and white bedroom with its chintzes and stripes or perhaps the red and white Adirondack bedroom with its bent willow chairs and white painted vertical board walls. Additional standard amenities include a television, telephone, and even a small refrigerator for storing snacks and drinks. The bathrooms were not overlooked in the renovation; each is modern and offers a bath or shower, and sometimes both, along with an ample supply of soft bath sheets.

In the afternoon, Jody thoughtfully provides baked goodies and coffee, tea, or juice to her guests. They may enjoy their tea on the front porch, surrounded by wicker and hanging plants, or in the fireplaced dining room with its bow window. The living room offers a piano and comfortable Victorian furnishings. In the morning, a Continental breakfast of locally made croissants and muffins, fresh fruit, juices, and coffee or tea is presented. Afterwards, guests enjoy roaming through this lovely residential neighborhood. During the season, the neighboring horse track is always a draw; however, Bowser might be more interested in a trip to the Saratoga National Historical Park, which encompasses over 2,800 acres of forest along the Hudson River. Here, there are trails to explore, picnicking spots to enjoy, and even a scenic driving tour with multiple stopping points that your canine cohort might like to investigate. If Bowser feels like napping for a bit, pay a visit to the National Museum of Dance and the National Museum of Racing and Hall of Fame. The Saratoga Spa State Park is also the host to the New York City Ballet in July and the Philadelphia Orchestra in August. The bathhouses and mineral springs will undoubtedly intrigue human visitors and when Bowser wakes up s/he might want to follow the paths that wind through the property.

THE WIDOW KENDALL HOUSE

10 North Ferry Street
Schenectady, New York 12305
(800) 244-0925, (518) 370-5511, Fax: (518) 382-2640
Hosts: Richard Brown and Matthew Moross
Rooms: 2 doubles, 1 garden suite
Rates: Doubles $95, Suite (to be determined)
Payment: Personal checks
Children: Welcome
Dogs: Welcome
Open: All year

The name Schenectady does not necessarily conjure up images of intimate B&Bs or historic Williamsburg homes. We were rather surprised to learn that the city is undergoing quite a renaissance, where historic buildings are being restored and the urban center is being revitalized. In the midst of all this lies the famous Stockade District, which includes approximately 60 homes that were built between 1700 and 1850 by Dutch settlers. Within the labyrinth of streets and houses, visitors will discover a small yellow tavern that was built in the early 1790s. Here, the Widow Annie Kendall "served cakes and ale" to her visiting patrons. It was not until the early 1980s that Richard started to restore this delightful antique home. Time had taken its toll on the building and it took ten years of hard work to finish the painstaking renovations. What emerged though was so intimate and charming that the idea of keeping it a secret seemed inappropriate, and so in the same tradition as the Widow Kendall, Richard opened his doors to the public.

Those who have stayed at the Widow Kendall House are impressed with many aspects of this charming B&B. If it isn't the gourmet breakfasts, then it certainly is the exquisite gardens. The brick-front Colonial, like many historic homes in the district, lies right next to the street with just enough space for a shade tree and a few decorative plantings. Step through the slightly askew front door, and the history of the house truly begins to unfold. The original wide-plank floors lead guests through the antique filled living room, dining room, and beyond to the gourmet kitchen and breakfast room. From here, new arrivals catch their first glimpse of the perennial gardens which are, in themselves, worth the price of admission. Just beyond the garden gate is the Garden Suite (which is currently being renovated and is expected to be completed in August of 1994) which will certainly be the most private and luxurious of the B&B's accommodations. Unfortunately, it was not completely finished as of this writing, but we are certain it will be at least as lovely as the two other bedrooms.

Upstairs in the main house, guests have the choice of two bedrooms that have been furnished with attractive period antiques Richard has collected over the years. The queen-bedded room might hold the largest bed in the house, but it is the double-bedded room that many guests find provides the most ambiance because it also contains a fireplace. Fresh flowers, cut from the summer garden, are placed in the bedrooms and throughout the house. Air conditioning and televisions are just two of the modern amenities that add to the enjoyable stay. Although the bathroom is shared, it also proves to be a luxurious experience. If we could design an ideal bathroom for this room configuration, this would be it; it is spacious and contains a Jacuzzi and separate shower.

It is easy to feel pampered at the Widow Kendall House, particularly in the morning when a multi-course gourmet meal arrives at the table. The aroma of freshly ground coffee usually alerts deep-sleepers that breakfast will soon be ready. Guests will discover that Richard brings a good deal of artistry to the preparation and presentation of the meal. The fresh fruit cup is almost exotic, and so pretty that guests often study it before sampling it. Those who are watching their diet, might consider cereal, yogurt, and cottage cheese along with the fruit. Others choose to indulge in some of the more hearty offerings. Omelettes can be stuffed with herbed cheeses, mushrooms, onions, or any number of other ingredients. This dish is often accompanied by lightly browned crispy potatoes, turkey bacon, and an assortment of delicate, freshly baked muffins and breads.

Walking through the Stockade District is one good way to start the morning. Afterwards, some may be interested in a trip to Union College. Built in 1795, this attractive campus was the first to be chartered by the New York State board of regents. Bowser may be more interested in exploring the grounds and stretching his legs. During the horse racing season, the B&B provides the perfect base for expeditions to Saratoga. When guests return they will be pleased to find tea and baked confections awaiting them, and if the weather is cool, a fire in the hearth.

VILLAGE LATCH INN

P.O. Box 3000
101 Hill Street
Southampton, New York 11968
(800) 54-LATCH, (516) 283-7048 or 283-2160
Owners: Marta and Martin White
Rooms: 55 doubles, 9 suites, 3 cottages
Rates: Doubles $89-225, Suites $160-350, Cottages $350
Payment: AE, DC, DSC, MC, and Visa
Children: Welcome (cribs and babysitting services are available)
Dogs: Welcome in certain rooms with a one-time fee of $20
Open: All year

For years the Irving Hotel, set on eastern Long Island, was a favorite destination for an exclusive clientele. Although the hotel has long since been demolished, its annex, situated across the street, is now home to the Village Latch Inn. Set back from the road behind a privet hedge and grassy lawn, the inn rests on an estate setting with mature trees, flowers, and shrubs. The inn's overall aura is, as Marta describes it, very "Great Gatsby ... coupled with an eclectic, sophisticated, and international atmosphere." The five-acre property is dominated by the original annex, a white clapboard and black shuttered Colonial style building, which has been enlarged with various wings. A flower covered trellis marks the main door, which oddly enough, is situated to the rear of the building. A long hallway, lined with Marta and Martin's collectibles from around the world, brings guests to the first floor sitting rooms.

Immediately upon entering the building, guests sense this is not an ordinary place whose furnishings set a specific decorative tone. True, there are some English antiques scattered here and there, along with traditional chintz fabrics; however, there are also unusual collectibles, sculptures, and exotic dolls, as well as tables and chairs from South America, and various gourds and bowls from Mexico. Wicker and informal antique furnishings complete the scene, although the latter are not from a noteworthy period. The colors chosen for the backdrop to these pieces are bold, more reflective of the vibrant hues from the Amazon rain forest than the aristocratic traditions of Southampton. Strangely enough, this eclectic and rather zany array of furnishings and collectibles seems to work together very nicely.

Just as the decor is unusual, so are the styles of guest rooms. The most traditional chambers are in the main inn, which is comprised of 25 bedrooms. However, these chambers are almost incidental, as those traveling with a dog will be staying in the "motel units." Fortunately the word motel is a misnomer, although the unassuming exterior doesn't alter one's initial impressions. However, as it turns out, this really is an ideal set up for those traveling with a dog. Each room has a small private patio with a table and chairs. Step inside the door, and guests will discover a rather small bedroom which is made visually into a larger one with a wall of mirrors and opposite a wall of windows. Beds are draped in simple white spreads, with color added through the use of vibrant throw pillows and interesting wall hangings. Mexican stretched leather chairs and a small television are set on an Oriental rug. The bathrooms are very modern, and actually quite spacious, offering a full array of toiletries, thick towels, and extra amenities. The first floor rooms allow easy access to the grounds for walking Bowser. What these units may lack in antique charm, they compensate for in amenities and personal touches. Rest assured though that nothing stays the same for very long at The Village Latch Inn. Marta, a former theater director, and Martin, a photographer, are always changing and adding to the furnishings, thus constantly recreating the inn.

Those not traveling with a four-legged friend should look into the accommodations to the rear of the property. Here, they will discover two grey-shingled buildings joined by a Victorian greenhouse. Inside the greenhouse is a wonderful spa (available to all human guests), and comfortable Mexican leather chairs with throw cushions grouped around a few tables. In the warm summer months, the swimming pool is a favorite gathering spot for guests. The attractive fence is mostly hidden by huge shrubs and trees, creating a sense of privacy for sunbathers and swimmers alike. Lawns surround the pool deck, which is set with chaise lounges and huge clay pots planted with flowers. For those who are interested in other diversions, the is also a tennis court and bicycles to explore the surrounding area.

The inn is only a few blocks from downtown Southampton, with its many boutiques and restaurants. This is a terrific place to walk with Bowser, as the route eventually leads to the water. Unfortunately, there is a town ordinance that does not allow dogs on the beaches or in the perfectly manicured parks. However, during the off-season these restrictions do not appear to be as stringently enforced. Otherwise, there is much to explore in the beautiful residential neighborhoods. Some of the state parks also allow dogs, although these are not located in Southampton, but in nearby Montauk.

AUDREY'S FARMHOUSE
BED AND BREAKFAST

2188 Brunswick Road
Wallkill, New York 12589
(914) 895-3440
Hosts: Audrey and Don Leff
Rooms: 5 doubles
Rates: $90-110
Payment: MC and Visa
Children: Older children are welcome, it might not be appropriate for small
     children as they have an in-ground swimming pool.
Dogs: Welcome in the first floor room and must get along with the Leff's
     two dogs
Open: All year

During our travels we have often found wonderful antique homes set in scenic countryside locations and thought they would make perfect B&Bs. However, thinking about opening a B&B, and then actually doing it, are two very different things. Fortunately Audrey and Don Leff are people of action; when they discovered this 1740 farmhouse six years ago, they knew it would be just the right spot for realizing Audrey's dream of operating a B&B. They bought it, renovated it, and filled it with a mix of traditional furnishings and antiques, along with some collectibles from the Southwest. Shortly thereafter, they opened the doors to Audrey's Farmhouse B&B. It wasn't just the antique quality of the farmhouse that initially attracted them, but it was also the beauty of the picturesque property surrounding it. Set at the foot of the Shawangunk Mountains, this B&B has thirty acres of meadows interspersed with formal and informal gardens, mature plantings, and shade trees. Some guests have been known to lie contentedly for hours in a hammock, while taking in the gorgeous mountain views. Others prefer to hike the trails that crisscross the mountains or walk along the country roads dotted with farms.

When guests and their canine companions arrive, they will undoubtedly be greeted by the Leff's Golden Retriever and Shih Tzu. The natural shingle farmhouse is their home as well, with its quaint farmer's porch and multiple chimneys. Although most of the post and beam construction is hidden behind smooth plastered walls, new arrivals will be able to see evidence of its classic architecture in the exposed beam ceilings. Hardwood floors are found throughout the house, both in the common room with its fireplace and in the library, brimming with books, magazines, and periodicals. Soft background music is often heard here as well, and occasionally one of the guests will feel inclined to play the piano.

The bedrooms are well appointed and are also decorated with an assortment of traditional period furnishings and antiques. Feather beds and down comforters top the four poster and hand-carved bedsteads in the winter months, and in the summer, guests will appreciate the lighter coverlets and cooling mountain breezes. There are four bedrooms upstairs; two of these are good-sized chambers and come with their own private baths. An added feature in one is the woodstove, while another is furnished with an extra bed. The other two guest bedrooms are located in a separate wing and share a bath. The best room choice for those traveling with a dog is located on the first floor near a private entrance. This room is also furnished with antiques, and has a queen-size bed and a private bath. All of the chambers are filled with Audrey's thoughtful touches, which include vases of fresh flowers, decanters of brandy set out in the bedrooms, and decoratively wrapped sweets found on the pillow each night.

In the morning, Audrey is up early in order to prepare the gourmet breakfast, served utilizing the family's fine china, silver, and glassware. In the cooler months, this hearty repast is usually enjoyed in front of a roaring fire; as the weather begins to warm, many guests are delighted to take this meal out to the flagstone patio near the pool. The meal commences with fresh fruits and granola, accompanied by warm breads and muffins served with homemade preserves. Some choose to supplement this Continental fare with Audrey's delicious omelettes, crepes, and waffles along with local meats and delicate smoked fish. Cross-country skiers and other outdoor enthusiasts will appreciate these delectable carbohydrates, which may help keep them energized throughout the morning. Upon returning in the late afternoon, guests will find wine set out with cheese and crackers — a sampling which will stave off the hunger pangs until dinner, when they can try any one of the excellent local restaurants.

Whether visitors come to the New Paltz area to enjoy the outdoors, visit historic sites, investigate art galleries and antique stores, or sample some of the wines available from the local wineries, they are certain to enjoy their stay at Audrey's Farmhouse B&B.

BENT FINIAL MANOR

194 Main Street
Warrensburg, New York 12885
(518) 623-3308
Innkeepers: Patricia and Paul Scully
Rooms: 5 doubles, 1 suite
Rates: Doubles $85-95, Suite $150
Payment: Personal checks
Children: Not appropriate for children, except in the suite with a separate outside entrance
Dogs: Welcome with advance notice in the suite
Open: All year

The elegant Bent Finial Manor is one of those places that prospective (and ambitious) B&B owners dream about finding. The 27 rooms are filled with more character and authentic details than most people could possibly imagine. The house was built in 1904 by a flamboyant cattle rancher who made his fortune selling beef to Union troops during the Civil War. He created a manor house that was meant to rival some of the great houses found both here and in Europe. Using only the finest and most unusual woods — 23 different kinds to be exact — and hiring only the best craftsmen, Thomson created gables, columned porches, turrets, and even a porte cochere to form this exquisite Queen Anne Victorian. And yes, one of the turrets does have a bent finial on top of it.

Unfortunately, he only lived a year or two after the house was built and left it in his will to his wife and daughter. These two women resided here until they were too old to care for it anymore. Because the house stayed within the same family for 70 years, all of the original features have remained intact. When Pat discovered the house, it had been boarded up for some time. Once the boards were removed, she was pleasantly surprised to learn that most of the work she needed to do would be cosmetic. She then embarked on the refurbishing which involved painting, wallpapering, and locating enough period antiques to fill the spacious rooms — no small task in a house of this magnitude.

Guests enter the Bent Finial Manor by way of a wraparound porch and, upon stepping over the threshold, begin to appreciate the immensity of Pat's project. There are 104 original stained, etched, and beveled glass windows in the house. Light streaming through these windows illuminates the detailed wainscotings, moldings, and cherrywood floors. The building's hallmarks are most apparent on the first floor, where Corinthian columns support some of the ceilings and the grand cherry staircase rises up to the second and third floors. The four queen-bedded guest rooms are located on these upper levels, and each forms an unusual and most inviting space. The Turret Chamber has a lovely sitting area in the rounded walls of the turret, while the Master Chamber offers the luxury of a fireplace and an outside balcony. The bedrooms' color schemes are centered around the coloration and design of the stained glass windows, with coordinating wallpapers and floral fabrics reflective of the Victorian era.

Pat prefers that guests traveling with a dog stay in the suite which has a separate outside entrance. She has had a couple experiences with guests who are either frightened of dogs or allergic to them, therefore she is extremely conscientious and tries to keep dogs (and children) in rooms where they would be less apt to disturb other people. The suite is the perfect choice in this regard. It has recently been renovated, and as of this writing Pat was just going out to purchase the sheets, bedspreads, and fabrics which will decorate the space. Families will especially appreciate this space because it **is not** filled with precious antiques and expensive breakables, and **is** spacious, offering a queen-bedded chamber, another room with twin beds, and a sitting room. The separate kitchen and private bathroom make the suite even more convenient for those traveling family-style. Anyone who might be apprehensive about coming to such a lovely B&B with children will be happy to learn that Pat has four children of her own and is very accommodating. The yard is also mostly fenced, which should ease the minds of both families and those traveling with their canine cohorts. Visitors traveling as a group might want to check out the original servants quarters which Pat recently converted into small guest rooms with a shared bath. These simple spaces have been enlivened by stenciling and a country decor.

In the morning, everyone convenes under the coffered ceilings in the dining room for a fabulous gourmet breakfast. Pat, who also lives in the house, is up as early as four or five in the morning to bake the muffins and breads she serves with the quiches, souffles, Belgian waffles, apple-walnut French toast, or omelettes brought to the table right in the pan. Fresh fruit, juice, and strong coffee always accompany this feast which is presented on fine china surrounded by equally exquisite linens. Pat says that depending upon her guests, the breakfast can be as leisurely or as timely as is required. Many downhill skiers like to rise early and get to the mountains as the lifts begin operating, whereas the cross-country skiers tend to wake up a little later, linger over their meal, and head out at a more reasonable hour.

Although Warrensburg is not necessarily a hub of activity, Pat says she is constantly amazed by the wide variety of things to do in the area. Some come for the summer craft shows or the lumberjack demonstrations, while others prefer to boat on Lake George or to hike the many mountain trails that dot the region. In the spring, white water river rafters often frequent the B&B, either before or after their adventure along the scenic waterways. If the day is cool, guests look forward to returning and warming themselves by the fireplace in the living room, passing the time at the Victorian-style game table or with one of the many other games to be found in the turret's game room.

APPLE ORCHARD INN

R.D. 2, Box 85
Old Fairhaven Road
Whitehall, New York 12887
(518) 499-0180
Innkeepers: Wayne and Judy Jones
Rooms: 5 doubles
Rates: $65-105
Payment: AE, MC, and Visa
Children: Welcome (cribs are available)
Dogs: Welcome with advance notice and prior approval
Open: All year except from April 15 to May 1

Although the Apple Orchard Inn technically lies in New York State, guests have the distinct impression that they are staying in the Green Mountains of Vermont. Perhaps, this is because of its proximity to the Vermont border, a mere five minute drive from the inn. The 1826 farmhouse rests on a hill with wonderful views of the 134 acres of pastures and woods and the majestic Adirondacks set off in the distance. With the farmhouse's westward positioning, guests are often attracted to the spectacular sunsets, which are best viewed from the front porch.

The Jones' renovated the farmhouse over ten years ago, although it has been so lovingly maintained since then, it could just as well have been yesterday. Most guests enter by way of the slate courtyard encircled by a picket fence. During the summer months it is awash with perennials and herbs. Most people instantly gravitate to the sun room, located just off the entry. This cozy spot has been painted a subtle pink and has huge paned windows which offer pretty views of the courtyard and orchards. Here, guests will find an assortment of games, puzzles, and books, along with a Hoosier cabinet, which is stocked with coffees, teas, and an array of baked cookies. One of our favorite bedrooms lies on the first floor just off this room. It is the most private of all the bedrooms and has its own bathroom. This good-sized chamber has been attractively decorated and furnished with country antiques. One particularly unusual piece is an antique Murphy bed housed in what looks like an oversized armoire. The wood paneled doors, fronted by mirrors, open to reveal a bed.

A staircase in the front foyer leads to the rest of the bedrooms on the second floor. While these are not as large as the one on the first floor, they offer just as much charm. The eaves in the ceilings create a sense of coziness and provide a nice backdrop for the assortment of informal antiques and collectibles. The bureaus are each topped with a carved wood mirror, while the double bed, or pairs of twin-size beds, are backed by interesting headboards. Judy has papered the bedroom walls with delicate country prints.

Even though the inn is quite cozy and very appealing, it is the hosts who make guests feel so comfortable and welcome. Judy is particularly bubbly and easy-going, willing to go with the flow when it comes to her guests. She and her husband, Wayne, live and sleep across the street from the inn and invite people to make themselves at home. In the morning, the first one downstairs usually turns on the coffee maker. Although Judy cooks breakfast for her guests, visitors always have access to the kitchen and are invited to store any extra drinks and snacks in the refrigerator.

People quickly learn to bring a hearty appetite to the table each morning, as there is always plenty to eat. A fresh fruit plate and homemade sweet rolls begin the meal, followed by pancakes, omelettes, French toast, or eggs, all of which are accompanied by bacon, home fries, and coffee, tea, and juice. The homemade maple syrup is produced by the Jones from the sugar maples on their property. Those who want a lesson in maple sugaring should visit in March and April when the trees are tapped; anyone interested in assisting in the sugaring will receive a pint of the freshly made syrup. After a hearty meal, most head off for a day of hiking in the mountains or swimming and boating on nearby Lake George. Others are perfectly content to just swim in the B&B's pool and relax in the sunshine. In the wintertime, guests can cross-country ski on the nearby pastures or head further afield for some terrific downhill skiing. Judy insists that those who go hiking sign the log book so that she knows where they are. She told us a story about a guest who went for a hike on nearby Bald mountain, got lost, and spent most of the night somewhere on the mountain (he ultimately returned to the B&B feeling tired but fine).

After a day of activity, some people retire to the living room. This bright space has off-white walls and red woodwork. The comfortable couches are great for watching television or just enjoying the warmth from the fire. On the weekends, Judy cooks a gourmet dinner. She usually offers her guests a choice of one of three entrees, chicken, shrimp, or lamb. They decide on one and then she creates a meal around it. For instance, some might be treated to the eggplant rolletini, baked clams, or fettuccine as an appetizer. This may be accompanied by a house salad and then a stuffed flank steak, butterflied leg of lamb, or shrimp scampi. The desserts are equally as enticing, with selections including a chocolate mousse, lemon Charlotte russe, or a strawberry Romanoff. At this point, most fall into bed, completely sated and ready for a good night's sleep.

POINT LOOKOUT MOUNTAIN INN

Route 23, Box 33
East Windham, New York 12439
(518) 734-3381
Innkeepers: Mariana DiToro and Rosemary Jensen
Rooms: 14 doubles
Rates: $65-95
Payment: AE, DC, DSC, MC, and Visa
Children: Welcome
Dogs: Welcome with a $10 fee and a $50 deposit
Open: All year

Driving mountain roads usually makes one's adrenalin start to flow, particularly when reaching the summit and the spectacular views begin to unfold. Entrepreneurs try to build restaurants or hotels in these locations, hoping to capitalize on the magnificent natural beauty of mother nature, but more often than not they encounter a great deal of difficulty making it succeed. This was the case with the Point Lookout Mountain Inn before Mariana and Rosemary bought it in 1979. With backgrounds in hotel management, they had just the right combination of qualities to imbue this rundown building with a sense of style.

The inn is virtually impossible to miss for those traveling along Route 23.

After climbing the road leading to Windham High Peak, visitors will discover the inn perched on the edge of a cliff. The structure is rather unassuming from the exterior, built to resemble a ski lodge with simple lines and covered walkways. The warm blueberry color that the partners chose for the exterior gives guests a glimpse of the unpretentious warmth and charm they will find inside. The first glimpses of the decor and furnishings inside the inn are of the dining room, with its huge fireplace, low-key atmosphere, and enormous plate glass windows offering spectacular views of the valley and farms below. On a clear day, of which there are many, we are told that guests can see five states, as well as the Berkshires, Green Mountains, and White Mountains.

The bedrooms are located on the second floor off a long corridor, with the most desirable being those situated on the side with commanding views of the valley. Each is decorated in a similar fashion utilizing earth tones and Native American themes. The furnishings are country reproductions that feature a pair of double beds, a bureau, and a rocking chair. The little extras include a remote controlled color television, fresh vases of flowers, and Gilchrist & Soames soaps, shampoos, conditioners, and lotions. As attractive as the rooms might be, the decor is secondary to the views of sunsets, rainbows, and magnificent foliage in the Fall. A Continental breakfast is included with the price of the room and includes yogurt, granola, and baked goodies. Although it is not formally served to the guests, it is made available to those who want to "raid the refrigerator."

Guests of the inn are offered a $5 credit toward their dinner meal. The fare is varied and quite good. Some might want to select an appetizer or one of the tapas, which are meant to "awaken the taste buds." The roasted eggplant in a balsamic vinegar, martini mushrooms, and Cajun shrimp are some additional choices. Quesadillas (grilled tortillas filled with delectables such as goat cheese and pinenuts, chorizo sausage, and new potatoes with cheese) are another interesting option. While it would be easy to make a meal of the appetizers and substantial salads, there are some entrees difficult to pass by. The Cajun catfish is served in a Southern tradition with hush puppies and black beans. Other selections include the mixed grill or the penne and sausage with roasted red peppers, tomato sauce, and fresh rosemary.

There are handwoven sweaters and other handmade items for sale, and books to peruse that provide interesting background on the region. A great activity (or non-activity) on sunny and warm days is to spend a little time on the outside deck just reading or sampling one of the many beers they have on hand.

There are plenty of things to do in the area with Bowser. While there is hiking in the hills surrounding the inn, those who want to venture slightly further afield will find the Catskill Forest Preserve. Here, there is fishing, hiking, and picnicking in the summer months and cross-country skiing in the winter. Ski Windham is a small family-oriented resort located just minutes from the inn. During the remainder of the year, there are trails for mountain biking and hiking as well.

We must stress that the Point Lookout Mountain Inn is comfortable and casual; there is nothing fancy about it. Mariana and Rosemary have taken basic motel rooms and have infused them with some warmth. Additionally, they have taken a nondescript dining room and imbued it with character and given it a terrific menu. Most importantly, they have capitalized on the inn's strongest asset — its panoramic views.

PENNSYLVANIA

COACHAUS

107-111 North Eighth Street
Allentown, Pennsylvania 18101
(800) 762-8680, (215) 821-4854
Owner: Barbara Kocher
Rooms: 10 doubles, 14 suites
Rates: Doubles $74-78, Suites $90-125, Townhouses $150-180
Payment: AE, CB, DC, MC, and Visa
Children: Welcome in certain guest rooms
Dogs: Welcome with advance notice in certain guest chambers, $10 fee
Open: All year except the week between Christmas and New Years Day

European cities have long been known for their intimate hotels. These usually provide a more personalized level of service and are less expensive than most of the huge city hotels. In the same European tradition, Barbara Kocher established the Coachaus in 1980. Over the years, she has purchased five traditional row houses, giving her the opportunity to offer a full range of accommodations to her guests.

On one side of the street, there are three simple brick buildings which are interconnected. Across the street there is a slightly more ornate pair of brick buildings with intricately detailed bay windows. One of the many unusual features in these particular buildings, is the spiral staircase that joins the top two floors. Barbara and her dalmatian, Abby, prefer that those traveling with a dog stay across the street in either the one or two bedroom suites. However, as Barbara is quick to point out, these rooms may not always be available and guests arriving with Bowser might end up staying in one of the other chambers. Barbara operates a relocation service and often has families using one of her suites for months at a time while they search for a home to buy in the area. Thus, guests who would like to stay for just a night or two will usually choose from the rooms that are not already reserved by the long term relocation guests.

Although the exteriors are relatively simple, inside the high ceilings, intricate woodworking, and paneled doors create a sense of sophistication. Guests' first impressions of the inn are usually of the sitting and dining rooms. The former is an intimate space, that appears substantially larger because of the long windows and outdoor courtyard. The latter is a warm, inviting space which has been decorated in deep green and burgundy. A Queen Anne dining room table and chairs dominate this chamber and chintz curtains frame the floor-to-ceiling windows. As with many of the other rooms in the house, fresh flower arrangements provide an additional splash of color. Each morning, guests place their breakfast order with Barbara and either chat with her or the other guests as she prepares a full breakfast for them. This hearty repast often consists of eggs and bacon, ham or sausage, cereals with fruit, muffins or pastries, and coffee or tea.

Many of the accommodations are also equipped with full kitchens and good-sized eating areas, giving guests the option of preparing many of their own meals and dining privately in their suites. The decor in most of the chambers mirrors that of the public areas, with Queen Anne reproductions interspersed with a few select antiques. Pencil post beds can be found in the bedrooms. Unusual collectibles and original works of art provide a personal touch. The bathrooms are all private and well-appointed. Barbara has put a good deal of effort into providing many of the same amenities traditionally offered by larger establishments. Same day laundry and dry cleaning, a fax machine, and 24-hour message services along with a daily newspaper are very much appreciated by all travelers, especially those in town on business.

While a tremendous amount of time and care has gone into creating a sophisticated environment, it is the personal attention given to each guest that is most memorable. Barbara has a wealth of knowledge to share, with suggestions on good, local restaurants, shopping, or entertaining things to do in the area. Bowser might want to walk over to the Lehigh Parkway with its large grassy areas and shade trees. Although people tend to think of Allentown as an industrial center, the outlying areas are primarily comprised of sprawling farmlands. Visitors will be surprised by the number of old stone barns, antique homes, and covered bridges they can find just outside the city. Others might be interested in investigating the Dorney Park/Wildwater Kingdom, which, aside from its wooden roller coaster, also has plenty of other great rides. The Trexler-Lehigh County Game Preserve is also a great place where visitors will discover many animals to observe and even a few for the children to pet. In the winter months, Bowser will probably enjoy a little cross-country skiing in the local hills or some downhill skiing at Blue Mountain.

While most of the Coachaus' clientele are often business people and transferees to the area, any short-term guests who are seeking a high level of comfort, self-sufficiency, and convenience to downtown Allentown should consider staying in these charming townhouses.

PONDA-ROWLAND BED & BREAKFAST

R1, Box 349
Beaumont, Pennsylvania 18612
(717) 639-3245 (also used as a fax line)
Hosts: Jeanette and Cliff Rowland
Rooms: 6 doubles
Rates: $55-75
Payment: MC and Visa
Children: Welcome (crib and cots are available)
Dogs: Well-behaved dogs are welcome in their outdoor run
Open: All year

Some people dream about living on a farm — Jeanette and Cliff Rowland actually did something about it. After residing in New Jersey for years, they decided it was time for a change so they bought an old dairy farm in western Pennsylvania. They brought with them their extensive collection of American country antiques and a lot of enthusiasm. Aside from the original 1850s farmhouse, there was also a huge barn and various other outbuildings situated on the 130 acres. They initially spent their time creating paths leading to the handful of ponds that dot the property, taming just a bit of the wilderness that surrounded the place. Soon, native wildlife began to congregate at the numerous feeding areas the Rowlands created. They also added their own domesticated creatures to the fold, including a turkey, a handful of ducks, sheep, a potbellied pig, a horse, and even a ferret. When we last spoke with Jeanette, she had just rescued the turkey, who had encroached on the pig's stall, creating a bit of a ruckus in the process.

With the ever present animal menagerie, new arrivals are certain to quickly feel a part of the farm-like environment. There are enough ponds on the property for guests to canoe, fish, or swim in. One particular pond offers a sandy beach, a slide, and a diving board. Hiking trails are scenic, both on the property and in the nearby mountains. In the winter months, people's thoughts turn toward ice skating, sledding, and cross-country skiing. No matter which season they visit, children always seem to love visiting the farm animals. Even if the weather isn't cooperating, guests find they thoroughly relish their time spent in the casual, country setting.

The actual farmhouse, where guests sleep and have breakfast, still contains many features from the past century. The Great Room is the centerpiece for the home with its open-beam, cathedral ceilings and massive stone fireplace, complete with an old yoke hanging above it. Braided area rugs are scattered among the Colonial antiques, comfortable sofas, and Windsor chairs. Wrought iron cooking utensils hang from a rack in one corner of the room, while an assortment of folk art and pewter provide decoration in many of the other alcoves. The living room is a more intimate space, with beamed ceilings supporting the exposed floor boards from the second floor. A massive, raised panel cupboard dominates this space, along with smaller hutches that contain still more collectibles.

The B&B houses three upstairs bed chambers, each containing a smattering of simple American country antiques and various king, double, and twin bed combinations. The largest of these is the king-bedded room (which can also be broken down into a pair of twin beds), with beds draped in simple heart pattern spreads and windows that are framed with plain swag curtains. Another room has an antique quilt on a four poster bed and a few country collectibles adorning the walls, side tables, and dressers. All of the guest rooms contain private bathrooms. Jeanette and Cliff have just finished renovating three additional guest quarters in a separate, ground floor wing of the farmhouse, creating the Swan, Eagle, and Mallard rooms. The Eagle can combine with the other two chambers to form a spacious suite, an ideal combination for larger families or couples traveling together; or, they may be rented separately. These carpeted bedrooms are furnished in the same manner as the other guest rooms in the house. The two bathrooms are shared among the three rooms.

In the morning, Jeanette offers a full, farm breakfast that should certainly satisfy everyone's morning appetites. This is served in the rather formal dining room, which is often illuminated by candle light emanating from both the pewter candle sticks and an overhead wrought iron chandelier. The standard fresh juices, fruit, and hot beverages are presented, along with some more unusual dishes such as stratas, and the ever-popular cornmeal pancakes. Afterward, guests can relax for awhile on the glassed-in sun porch and read the morning paper or make plans for the day's activities. If the morning should prove to be inclement, children can always watch television, or pop a tape into the VCR, giving their parents time to read one of the many periodicals the Rowlands have on hand. On such mornings, guests will probably meet the Rowlands' recently adopted greyhound, which often needs the heat of the fire to stay warm. This gentle creature is the only dog they allow in the house, their other two are strictly outside dogs. As might be surmised from their outside menagerie, both the Rowlands love animals, and will certainly welcome Bowser, as long as s/he is gentle, does not bother the farm animals, and gets along with other dogs. Guests have been bringing their dogs for years, leaving them outside in the kennel during the night, and then bringing them along on their various daytime outings and excursions. While this situation might not work for everyone, it is certainly a terrific option for those who want to introduce Bowser to a true farm vacation.

THE INN AT TURKEY HILL

991 Central Road
Bloomsburg, Pennsylvania 17815
(717) 387-1500
Innkeeper: Andrew B. Pruden
Rooms: 16 doubles, 3 suites
Rates: Doubles $50-90, Suites $110-130
Payment: AE, DSC, MC, and Visa
Children: Welcome
Dogs: Welcome with a $15 nightly fee
Open: All year

Usually when travelers hit the Interstate they can look forward to days of rather mundane motel lodgings; however, there is at least one exception to this rule in The Inn at Turkey Hill. It is a small oasis, literally a minute from Interstate 80 yet seemingly miles away. White-washed brick walls surround the property which contains the main house, built in 1839, the newer guest rooms, a gazebo and a pond. In the wintertime, a fire crackles in the intimate sitting room of the main house. With its wide pine floors, sophisticated yet comfortable wing chairs and sofas, and deep hunter green and rich burgundy color scheme, this is indeed a restful spot for the weary traveler — however, it is not the only one. The individual cottages provide many additional alternative spots in which to seek refuge.

In 1984, Andrew's mother made the decision to transform the family home into an inn. This was tricky because she wanted to make sure it was in keeping with the historic nature of the inn. After almost two years of work and over a million dollars, the Prudens have created a delightful retreat that inn-goers are sure to enjoy. Today, guests will find three bedrooms in the main house and the remainder located in a series of one-story clapboarded buildings that are joined by covered walkways. These outlying rooms encircle a lovely expanse of grass framed by flower gardens. The highlight of this setting is a small pond surrounded by rock walls, daylilies, and other perennials. A tavern and a glass-enclosed dining room were also added to the house. A greenhouse restaurant faces this bucolic scene.

Most guests can also enjoy this setting through their paned windows. Each of the oversized bedrooms offers two queen-size beds covered with down comforters (in the warmer months they switch to the lightweight variety). There is a sophisticated country charm to the rooms which have chair rails and ceiling moldings accented by Williamsburg blue and rust tones. Accents are provided by paintings of whimsical farmyard scenes. A wing chair with ottoman is a comfortable place for reading, with light illuminating from pottery and brass table lamps. There is no need to get up from the chair or bed, as the cable television is controlled by a remote. The pine tables and bureaus are reminiscent of the French countryside, as are the carved, natural wooden headboards. Thoughtful touches, such as live plants and baskets of toiletries, are a welcome addition. For anyone who might have forgotten something, the staff is happy to supply additional toothbrushes, toothpaste, razors, and any other personal care items. Reserve one of the country suites for the most luxurious experience. Here, guests will find king-size pencil post beds, small sitting areas, fireplaces, and Jacuzzi tubs.

One of the nicest features of The Inn at Turkey Hill is that there is no need to go anywhere in search of dinner. We have always enjoyed excellent meals at the inn. For casual dining there is the intimate tavern or sunny greenhouse. Of course, for those in search of fireside dining at candlelit tables, there is the formal dining room. The walls here have been stenciled, with crystal and china laid out on mahogany tables surrounded by Chippendale chairs. The menu changes seasonally, but guests might want to start their meals with a salmon bisque flavored with dill, smoked trout, or the escargot sauteed with garlic, artichoke, lemon, tomato, and various fresh herbs. The multi-course evening meal is complemented with sorbet, served just before the entree. The apricot glazed duck, pan-blackened prime rib, or crab meat baked in a mushroom bechamel sauce and topped with bread crumbs and Parmesan cheese are just three of the entrees served. The pasta dishes are light, a favorite being the fettuccine tossed with sauteed shrimp, asparagus, tomatoes, and artichokes in a garlic clam broth. Desserts change daily and are always decadent, including a frozen raspberry and chocolate brownie creation.

The Inn at Turkey Hill is so pleasant, that it seems a shame to just use it as an overnight stop when en route to a nearby destination or visiting a student at Bloomsburg State College. For those who want to stay awhile, there is plenty to do in the area. Local hiking can be found at the Rickets Glen State Park, and fishing is an option in some of the streams and tributaries flowing into the scenic Susquehanna River. For anyone interested in indulging in a bit of luxury, there is a special package deal which combines a stay at the inn with therapeutic massages, whirlpools, and biofeedback at the Gentle Dove Relaxation Center— without a doubt, all the ingredients needed for a thoroughly enjoyable sojourn.

Finally, for those who are wondering about the origins of the inn's name, there once was a large turkey farm on the site. Today, with the exception of the big red barn in the far corner of the property, there are certainly no indications that turkeys once inhabited this delightful spot.

INDIAN MOUNTAIN INN

Tripp Lake Road
Brackney, Pennsylvania 18812
(800) 435-3362, (717) 663-2645
Innkeepers: Dan and Nancy Strnatka
Rooms: 10 doubles
Rates: Doubles $65-75
Payment: Personal checks
Children: Welcome
Dogs: Welcome
Open: All year

We discovered Nancy at the Indian Mountain Inn quite by accident. She used to own another B&B called Linger Longer at Quaker Lake; however, just before our visit she had sold it and bought the Indian Mountain Inn. She told us she was initially drawn to this mountain setting because of its unspoiled beauty and sense of seclusion. However, she later discovered something which solidified her interest in the area. It turns out that William Penn granted her great-grandfather 400 acres of land in an adjacent valley. Although this was many years ago, there remains a sense of timelessness about this region that is most intriguing. With the exception of a few more homesteads and a fairly modern dirt road, today most guests can enjoy the same sense of solitude in this secluded mountainous setting that Nancy's great-grandfather must have experienced.

When Nancy bought the Indian Mountain Inn, it had a reputation for its fine food. Nancy wanted to expand upon that theme and update the bedrooms as well. Her chef, Michael Lusk, graduated from the Culinary College of Washington D.C. Locals and inn-goers alike rave about his creations which emphasize fresh, local ingredients in the summer months. Patrons will find the dining room has been broken up into large yet intimate seating areas, our favorite being the converted summer porch, with walls of windows offering the best views of the meadows below. Fresh flowers adorn the tables. Appetizers include vegetable ravioli with a ginger and carrot puree, baked brie with almonds and apples, and escargot served with a thyme and hazelnut butter. The seasonally changing menu offers such entrees as salmon Dijonaise, lamb tenderloin served with a spearmint and garlic demi-glace, and shrimp and scallops prepared with white wine, tomatoes, mushrooms and whole butter.

Afterwards, many guests often choose to congregate in the living room, where they may read or just cozy up to the woodstove. There is also a Jack Russell terrier and a variety of house cats to keep everyone occupied. Upstairs, a small sitting room equipped with a television and VCR provides some of the guests with the more modern electronic diversions.

Guests will find their bedrooms by climbing the stairs and wending their way along the top floor. Although none of the accommodations are over-whelmingly spacious, each is bright and attractive. Naturally finished wood paneled walls create the backdrop for some of the country antique furnishings and crisp Swiss dotted wallpaper lends charm to others. Finial bedposts support antique double beds in some rooms, while pencil post, brass, and sleigh beds can be found in many of the other chambers. Most of these are covered with simple white Bates bedspreads. Nancy has also added her creative touch to many of the rooms, such as placing Amish plain-faced dolls on guest beds, displaying assorted family heirlooms and paintings in other chambers, and ensuring there are vases of fresh flowers on each of the bureaus. These personal touches serve as beautiful accents to the lovely views of the surrounding woods and meadows seen through the windows. Although guests will often share a bathroom, they are sure to find plenty of soaps, shampoos, and toiletries conveniently located in baskets in their rooms.

Bowser is a most welcome addition to the inn, although it is important that s/he like cats, as they are definitely a part of the household. There is plenty to do for master and canine companion alike. There are five miles of hiking trails on the over 500 acres of property. Nearby Salt Springs State Park offers guests the opportunity to fish in the morning, have a picnic (Michael is happy to provide a lunch), and then explore the gorge and waterfalls in the afternoon. Quaker Lake is also a short drive away and offers swimming and boating opportunities. This is a beautiful part of Pennsylvania, particularly in the summer months. After a busy day, most enjoy returning to the inn to spend the quiet hours of the day sitting out on the expansive deck, enjoying the serenity that is so abundant here.

GATEWAY LODGE

Route 36, Box 125
Cooksburg, Pennsylvania 16217
(814) 744-8017, (800) 843-6862 (in PA)
Owners: Joseph and Linda Burney
Rooms: 8 doubles, 8 cabins
Rates: Doubles $104 double occupancy (B&B), $154 double occupancy
    (MAP), Cabins $80-120 (EP), $52-143 per person (MAP)
Payment: AE, MC, and Visa
Children: Over the age of 8 are welcome at the inn, all ages are welcome in the
    cabins
Dogs: Welcome in the cabins with a $15 daily fee and a refundable deposit of
    $25
Open: All year except Wednesday and Thursday of Thanksgiving and Decem-
    ber 24th and 25th

In 1681, King Charles II of England gave a piece of land to William Penn. This land, which later came to be known as the Black Forest, occupied a corner of western Pennsylvania. Cook Forest is the name now given to the remaining 60,000 acres of the original land grant, and in the heart of it lies the Gateway Lodge.

The historic lodge, found in a clearing at the top of a hill, is the focal point for the resort. Newcomers will soon discover there are also a small grouping of cabins located across the road and down the hill. The lodge's charming front porch, one of the few additions over the years, is a favorite place for guests to relax during the warm summer months. This is a comfortable spot that has been furnished with wicker tables and chairs along with an inviting hammock swing for two. From here, guests have a panoramic view of the surrounding hills covered with dense stands of pine trees that cast shadows over the forest floor.

Step inside the rustic lodge and follow the narrow hallway leading to the sitting room, which is dominated by a large fieldstone fireplace flanked by comfortable plaid sofas and armchairs. Even though we visited on a late summer's morning, there was still a hot fire crackling and popping in the fireplace. Both the walls and low beamed ceilings are hewn from large pine and hemlock logs. The character of the room is further enhanced by braided rugs covering the hardwood floors, throws draped on well-worn couches and leather chairs, and an assortment of collectibles and paraphernalia hanging from the walls. A bench situated on one side of the room looks all the more inviting with an antique quilt draped over its back. We noticed that most guests enjoyed lingering in the sitting room, both before and after their meals.

Continuing in the same rustic theme, is the dining room, with its wonderful antique wagon wheel chandelier. Dinner guests will find tables draped with simple gingham tablecloths, illuminated with kerosene lamps, and set with vases of flowers and pewter tableware. Plates come filled with good, home-made cooking — the kind one's grandmother might have offered. Chicken and dumplings smothered in gravy, barbecued spareribs, and rolled veal stuffed with mushrooms and spinach are just a few of the traditional choices. The baked trout, prime rib, and seafood Newburg are also favorites among the guests. One of the unusual things about dinner at the Gateway Lodge is that the first caller to make their reservation sets the entree selection for the night (such a responsibility!). However, what the locals and guests all are certain to turn out for are the breakfasts — a specialty of the lodge. Some choose to start the day with Eggs Benedict or Belgian waffles, but more often they opt for even heartier fare. This could include creamed chipped beef served over homemade biscuits, steak and eggs accompanied by home fries, or the lemon-pepper catfish. Omelette fans will be in heaven with a list of 15 different ingredients from which they may create their own masterpiece.

Those who want a little exercise will find it by just meandering to and fro from the cabins to the lodge. While the lodge is located on top of a hill, the cabins can be found down the drive and across the road. These are quite rustic, yet clean and very comfortable. Even though the natural wood exteriors are stained a matching dark brown, the interiors are each different. Most cabins are two bedroom affairs with small porches. Others are larger, offering three bedrooms (guests provide their own linens) and more ample living quarters. Some of our favorite features were the fieldstone fireplaces, oversized sofas and chairs, and windows overlooking the surrounding forest. While the natural wood walls and abundance of trees make these lodgings a little on the dark side, these aspects also add a lot of character to each of the dwellings. Those who want to do their own cooking will appreciate the kitchenette, although guests will want to bring their own cooking utensils, flatware, garbage bags, and even some extra matches. For those who opt to cook outside, there are stone-rimmed fire pits and tables for barbecuing and picnicking. Finally, for guests who want nothing at all to do with cooking, there is the option of paying the Cottage Rates, which include breakfast and lunch at the lodge, the use of the indoor pool (which is heated to 92 degrees in the winter months), and other amenities usually reserved for guests of the lodge.

There are plenty of activities in the area to keep everyone happy, including Bowser. The local river is a favorite in the summertime for tubing, canoeing, and swimming. Of course there are also miles of hiking and horseback riding trails both in the mountains and along the river. While the beauty of nature here is abundant, there are also more commercial ventures such as putt-putt golf, bumper cars and boats, and deer and petting farms. While in many areas these may seem a little on the tacky side, here they almost border on quaint. The lodge's gift shop offers crafts, country collectibles, and Amish-made rope swings and quilts, along with other notable items. Visitors to the area will certainly feel removed from the sophistication of Bucks County and instead feel free to bask in the beautiful surroundings of the Cook Forest and the rustic and unpretentious setting of the Gateway Lodge.

THE SMITHTON INN

900 West Main Street
Ephrata, Pennsylvania 17522
(717) 733-6094
Innkeeper: Dorothy Graybill
Rooms: 7 doubles, 1 suite
Rates: Doubles $65-145, Suite $140-175
Payment: AE, MC, and Visa
Children: Well-behaved children are welcome in all of the chambers except the
        Gold Room (cribs and cots are available)
Dogs: Well-behaved dogs are welcome, but they must stay off all the furniture
        and beds and cannot be left alone in the room
Open: All year

Ephrata is a small, but thriving town, located in the heart of Pennsylvania where the Mennonite, Amish, and Brethren people still conduct their lives according to strict and simple codes. Travelers will certainly see them out in the fields, tilling the soil with their rudimentary tools and using horses to pull their wagons. By today's standards their lifestyle might seem antiquated, but upon closer observation there is something to this simplicity. Vegetables are grown without pesticides, handmade crafts and quilts are made to last a lifetime, and family life is of paramount importance. These enduring qualities are also reflected in the history of the Smithton Country Inn. Built of stone in 1763, the thick walls still provide travelers with a sense of privacy and comfort after more than 230 years.

Dorothy Graybill, a lifetime resident of the area, has meticulously restored the inn with her partner Allan Smith. Since 1979, they have devoted most of their energies to repointing the building's walls, creating intimate and elegant gardens, and rebuilding the stone walls that surround the property. They have produced an enclave that feels very private, even though the inn is located at the junction of two well-traveled roads in Ephrata.

Step inside the front door and any thoughts of the Twentieth Century dissipate. Hand-planed and pegged hardwood floors lead into a formal living room and library. Elegant sofas and a leather chair are all focused on the fireplace. Original oil paintings direct one's attention to the walls and the windows framed in full length swags of rich fabrics. There is a wonderful mixture of antiques and handcrafted furnishings throughout the inn, all with lustrous finishes resulting from natural patina or from many hours of hand-rubbing and waxing. Fortunately, both Dorothy and Allan are extremely gifted artisans. While many of the antique reproductions have been locally made, Allan has used his talents to design some of the furnishings and restore much of the flooring and detailed woodworking throughout the inn.

Many of the bedrooms in this historic building are filled with charming nooks and crannies. The second floor houses the majority of these chambers, with the exception of the Gold Room on the first floor and the suite found on the back of the inn. Although each room has a distinct personality, there are certain features that all guests can expect to find. A boxed canopy bed, four poster bed, or trundle bed all sit high above the floor and are covered with hand-crafted quilts. Stenciling, hand-painted furnishings, and a number of decorative influences copied from the adjacent Cloister make the chambers even more authentic. One of the standouts is a white quilt artfully appliqued with a hand-stitched gold and red bird. Black leather covered sofas are set adjacent to lamps with parchment shades and Chippendale chairs footed by small stools. A Queen Anne mirror reflects many of the American folk art collectibles that Dorothy has utilized as accent pieces. The large chests at the ends of the beds are filled with feather beds and down quilts that envelope guests with their exquisite softness. At the end of the day, when the candles are lit and the fireplace casts an amber glow over the bedrooms, many guests turn on the soft chamber music and easily drift off to sleep. In the morning, an invigorating shower or bath is a good way to start the day. The bathrooms are all updated and fitted in porcelain and Allan's hand-crafted tiles. One additional modern convenience is the small refrigerator subtly occupying an inconspicuous corner of each bedroom.

While all of the accommodations at The Smithton Country Inn are superb, the one space that deserves special comment is the suite. A separate outside entrance leads guests into a dramatic two-story chamber. While the furnishings and decor in the suite are just as appealing as in the other rooms, the addition of this separate, fireplaced parlor truly seems luxurious. Additionally, the convenience of a refrigerator has been expanded to include an entire nook where guests can prepare snacks and beverages to be enjoyed on the private screened-in porch. At the end of the day, guests can opt for a rejuvenating bath in the whirlpool tub or separate shower before climbing into their canopied bed for a good night's sleep.

Each morning breakfast is served in the dining room. The brick fireplace is the focal point for this intimate space, with its small tables draped in red tablecloths. The four course gourmet breakfast varies, with a choice of beverages and juice followed by a fruit plate, and perhaps the cinnamon bread French toast, blueberry waffles, or pancakes. A delicate pastry always marks the end of this lovely meal. Afterwards, many look forward to visiting the Ephrata Cloister, located just a short walk from the inn. Here lies a monastery that was founded in 1732 by a German priest and died out in the 1880s. Today, the dark, damp medieval-looking stone buildings are visited by tourists who quickly gain insight into the sacrifices this small order of monks made to live here. Also, within walking distance is a town park where Bowser can romp in the grass for awhile. Down the hill a bit further is Ephrata's town center with a few local art galleries, craft's shops, and restaurants. Dorothy can direct her guests to some of the less well known sights and attractions, as well as open green spaces for Bowser. She is also very well acquainted with the local customs of the "plain people" and can explain how to best interact with them without being offensive. On the premises, guests will find a family of lop-eared bunnies and a pond full of Koi, although it would be best to keep Bowser leashed so he won't go swimming with the fish.

Finally, Dorothy does have just a few rules about dogs. She requests that they never be left alone in the room. During breakfast, guests can either leave Bowser in the car or on a chain outside in the garden, provided s/he does not bark. These requests seem small indeed, and certainly worthwhile to honor for the pleasure of a stay at Smithton, a treasure to be found in the heart of Amish country.

DULING-KURTZ HOUSE AND COUNTRY INN

146 South Whitford Road
Exton, Pennsylvania 19341
(215) 524-1830
Manager: John Faller
Rooms: 8 doubles, 4 suites
Rates: Doubles $50-100, Suites $75-120
Payment: AE, DC, MC, and Visa
Children: Not appropriate for small children. Cots are available.
Dogs: Welcome, but guests must call in advance and consult with the
    manager.
Open: All year

When visiting a community rich in history, it is always nice to choose accommodations which reflect this sense of antiquity. Exton is in the heart of

Chester County, with its rolling hills, antique farmhouses, and national historic sites. The Duling-Kurtz House was erected in the mid-1830s. Built of stone, it was home to a man who owned several local limestone quarries, a sawmill, and a gristmill. Today, the remnants of these businesses can be found by following a path over Valley Creek to the ruins of the lime kiln and grist mill. These were discovered in 1982 during the initial stages of the stone house and barn renovation.

Raymond H. Carr and David J. Knauer were the two men responsible for converting what was formerly known as the Meadows House to the Duling-Kurtz House. Named for their respective mothers, the project took over a year to complete. The original home became a formal restaurant, complete with an authentic beehive oven as the centerpiece for the entry way. A covered bridge walkway links the restaurant to the original barn. The barn was completely redesigned to accommodate the guest rooms and intimate parlors.

In keeping with the historical nature of the property, each bed chamber was named after a famous historical figure. For instance, there is a Mary Todd Lincoln suite where guests will find an intimate sitting room where the sofa and chairs rest upon an Oriental rug. The bedroom houses a king-size pencil post bed and green velvet wing chairs. Televisions can be found in both rooms. The well-appointed bathroom has brass fixtures and an array of Gilchrist and Soames personal care products. The color scheme for this suite includes rust, burgundy, and dark green. Fabrics covering the bedsteads are also used in place of the louvers on the window shutters, providing a coordinated look. One of the nicest features about this guest room, for those traveling with Bowser, is the private patio with an iron table and chairs.

The Benjamin Franklin Suite also has an intimate sitting room and adjacent double-bedded chamber. Here, rich blue and burgundy are the predominant colors found in the delicately patterned wallpaper. Brass lamps offer good light for reading. Those who want to enjoy the warmth of a fire, might opt for the Thomas Jefferson Room. The guest rooms on the top floor offer the most architectural interest in the way of charming nooks and crannies. Guests should be aware that all the chambers at the inn are not as spacious as the suites — in fact, some are rather small. Several also have tiny and authentic windows, which are endearing, but do not allow much sunlight to filter into the rooms. One of our favorite common areas in the barn is the second floor sitting room. This is a intimate space created from brick and glass, with comfortable sofas for reading and relaxing.

Each morning, guests may decide to eat their Continental breakfast in the bedroom or in the first or second floor parlors. Cereals, fresh fruit, and croissants are some of the standard features. There is also coffee and a selection of teas available. The cookie jar is always filled with a batch of homemade cookies that will more than satisfy a sweet tooth. Dinner at the inn is an entirely different type of experience. Appetizers run the gamut, from the delicious crab cakes and shrimp Dijon to the sampler of smoked sausages, assorted cheeses, and fish. Those who enjoy soups should consider sampling the Duling-Kurtz snapper soup. When selecting an entree, many people are intrigued with the seafood offerings. A modified version of bouillabaisse is served over pasta, and the soft shell crab (when in season) is dressed with an herbed lemon butter sauce. Those who can't seem to choose between seafood or meat might want to compromise and try the veal scallop with artichokes. Finally, there is the breast of duck roasted with apricots and oranges and covered with a brandy port wine sauce.

After dinner, guests may choose to take a leisurely walk about the grounds. These are quite beautiful in the summer months with the colorful perennial gardens leading the way to a footbridge that crosses a babbling brook before ending at the gazebo. Others may want to take Bowser for a little romp in the field. Those who are so inclined, settle into the wicker chairs that are well-situated to take advantage of the evening quiet. During the daylight hours, visitors to the area might be interested in exploring Chadds Ford and the Brandywine Battlefield Park which encompass 50 acres and offer glimpses into some of the historic buildings of the era and give an insightful perspective into the Battle of Brandywine, fought in 1777. In nearby Valley Forge, there is the Valley Forge National Historical Park with its various buildings and monuments commemorating George Washington and those men who served under him. For those who have an interest in American history, the Duling-Kurtz House is an ideal starting point for a thorough investigation of this historic region.

SWEETWATER FARM

50 Sweetwater Road
Glen Mills, Pennsylvania 19342
(215) 459-4711, Fax: (215) 358-4959
Innkeeper: Barbara Pietsch
Rooms: 9 doubles, 4 cottages
Rates: Doubles $135-185, Cottages $175-225
Payment: AE, MC, and Visa
Children: Welcome in the cottages
Dogs: Welcome in the cottages
Open: All year except for January and February

Sweetwater Farm is just the place one would envision for a perfect weekend in the Brandywine Valley. Although it is less than an hour's drive from Philadelphia, guests have the feeling they are tucked away in a remote country enclave. Travelers wend their way to the inn along narrow lanes, eventually arriving at a sign, printed simply with the words *Sweetwater Farm, Est. 1734*. A tree-lined circular drive leads a short distance to the lovely stone Georgian mansion, framed by large shade trees and an assortment of flowering shrubs. As guests look around the expansive homestead, the sight of small outbuildings, a distant barn, and numerous horses grazing in the rolling fields behind split rail fences, give the impression that this is indeed a lovely old gentlemen's farm.

Upon entering the house, new arrivals will discover a long front to back foyer that is flanked by a pair of dining rooms, a living room, and a library. A staircase winds to the upper floors and a door at the end leads to an expansive veranda. The rooms reflect a sense of history, not so much by what they contain as by how they are detailed. Wainscotings and bullet moldings add interest to the high ceilinged chambers, while fireplaces with intricately carved mantels supply warmth. The splayed windows mask the thickness of the walls and are finished with raised panel trim. Each room has important English antiques in them, but without any sense of clutter. Chippendale wing chairs and a sofa grace the living room, but our favorite room to retreat to on a cold winter day is the informal library whose built-in shelves are bulging with books. Additionally, a concealed television awaits interested viewers, although guests are more likely to find classical music softly playing and a fire crackling in the fireplace.

Surprisingly, in the main house there are nine good-sized bedrooms. The four most elegant ones feature fireplaces, canopied pencil post beds, Queen Anne highboys, and Chippendale-style tables set with cut glass lamps. Many of the bedsteads are graced with exquisite antique or Laura Ashley linens. Handmade antique quilts, dried flower arrangements, and a collection of primitive pieces, as well as a lovely assortment of botanical prints and original artwork are all displayed about the house. A secret door in one chamber leads to a wing with three bedrooms tucked into the corners and eaves. Each is reminiscent of a fairy tale, being a bit magical and somewhat surreal. Little extras include the cut flowers resting on bedside tables, alarm clocks, and Sweetwater Farm glycerin soaps and shampoos.

Although the antiques are not as prevalent here, each cottage has been furnished beautifully. Our favorite is the Green House, which offers a unique living room that once was literally an old-fashioned greenhouse and still contains the original glass windows in the eaves. This room acts as the centerpiece for the cottage, with French doors opening to a small patio set with a table and chairs. Just beyond this is a large shade tree, from which hangs a wooden swing, and beyond are the rolling fields. Back inside, the fieldstone fireplace is framed by comfortable sofas and chairs, which is particularly inviting on a cold night. Hardwood floors are covered with dhurrie rugs and plastered walls are stenciled with tiny ivy leaves. For those who are so inclined, a fully-equipped kitchen is available for cooking and storing food.

Each bedroom has a brass plaque with the room's name upon it. One of the bedrooms has a wicker sleigh bed, detailed around the edges with blue paint. Pink roses are stenciled on the walls and even the adjacent modern bathroom is done in pink. Just off the living room is a second, smaller bedroom, furnished with a white iron and brass double bed and still more stenciling.

Barbara offers quite an array of foods at breakfast time. There is granola with dollops of yogurt, fresh fruit cups, tiny muffins, and coffee or a variety of teas. She also cooks a hot dish for those who are interested. During our visit, she was offering eggs cooked with chives or cinnamon French toast, both accompanied by bacon. Cottage guests are usually on their own for this meal; however, we are sure Barbara would be happy to work something out for those who don't want to cook.

Afterwards, guests might want to sit out on the stone porch or go for a walk. There is an inviting swimming pool available in the summer months. Nearby, the Longwood Gardens are truly magnificent, as is the world-renowned Winterthur. Those who have a fondness for animals will surely want to visit with the resident horses, goats, and sheep who are always busy keeping the fields in order.

Barbara had only been on board for a short time when we visited. However, she seems like a natural with her love of people, cooking, and tending to flowers and plants. In the back of the house, she has an entire room dedicated to flower arranging. Her goal is to do silk flower arrangements in the important areas, with fresh flowers in the guest rooms. Her background is as a set designer for photographic shoots and we are sure it will take her little time to place her personal touch on all the rooms at Sweetwater Farm.

THE HISTORIC GENERAL SUTTER INN

14 East Main Street
Lititz, Pennsylvania 17543
(717) 626-2115
Innkeepers: Joan and Richard Vetter
Rooms: 12 doubles, 2 suites
Rates: Doubles $70-90, Suites $90
Payment: AE, MC, and Visa
Children: Welcome (cribs are available)
Dogs: Well-behaved dogs are welcome with advance notice
Open: All year except Christmas Eve, Christmas Day, and New Year's Day

Lititz is a beautiful, rural farming community located in the heart of the Pennsylvania Dutch country. Its roots go back to 1756 when it was founded as a Moravian community. Today, the heart of this village has been carefully preserved. Housed in many of the antique buildings are specialty stores, along with a girl's school, a museum, the local historical society, and even pretzel and chocolate factories. One of the standouts though is the three-story brick building located on the square which houses the Historic General Sutter Inn and the adjacent gardens.

The inn was established in 1764 by the Moravian Church and was then known as Zum Anker (the sign of the anchor). Additions were made to it in the early- and mid-1800s, and what guests see today remains relatively unchanged from 1848. The exception to this is the name, which was changed to honor General John Augustus Sutter, the California Gold Rush pioneer who later moved to Lititz. Today, the Victorian decor of the lobby sets the theme for the rest of the hotel. This cozy chamber is warmed by a small fireplace and illuminated by Victorian crystal and gas parlor lamps set on marble tabletops. Assorted antique chairs, medallion backed sofas, and an antique organ complete the effect. Adjacent to the lobby is a coffee shop, with more formal and intriguing meals served in the Zum Anker Room. The varied menu is Continental in flavor. Traditional samplings include steak Diane, shrimp scampi, veal cordon bleu, and roast duckling with a peach brandy sauce. Each entree is accompanied by soup or salad, a potato or pasta dish, vegetable, and homemade breads. After a hearty meal, many find it is easy to just slip off to bed.

Hardwood floor hallways lined with Oriental rug runners lead to the bedrooms. Each of the guest rooms is decorated and furnished in a somewhat different manner. Some are larger than others, with the most spacious being the two-bedroom family suites. All have Victorian and early American antiques, with a preponderance of oak and a smattering of mahogany. Walls have been papered with old fashioned floral prints and windows are framed by lace curtains. In each room on the bureaus, there are antique nail care kits alongside brushes and combs. There is also a preponderance of colorful handmade quilts. One bedroom might have a pink and blue star quilt and another a multi-hued blue quilt. There are small black and white televisions in each of the bedrooms, along with air conditioning and telephones.

Those who are in search of a common room that is set off from the rest will enjoy paying a visit to the cozy library on the second floor. This is the only room that truly seems to belong to a more modern era with its leather armchairs, an Oriental rug, and decoy-patterned wallpaper. Little extras, such as a nice selection of books and periodicals, a television, and an assortment of candies make guests feel quite at home.

After a good night's rest, many like to explore the downtown area. Bowser might enjoy a little window shopping. The streets are most conducive to leisurely walks, as is the Lititz Springs Park. History buffs will surely enjoy taking the tour of the town's National Historic District, which includes such sites as the Moravian Church Square, the Johannes Mueller House built in 1792, or the Brothers House, which was used as a hospital after the Battle of Brandywine. Many can hardly wander through Lititz without the aroma from the Wilbur Chocolate Factory drawing them in for a closer look. The Amish farms found throughout the area are also a source of interest for most people. Most visitors to the Pennsylvania Dutch Country would agree that Lititz is centrally located for all of their wanderings. The Historic General Sutter Inn provides a good base and a warm and inviting atmosphere from which to make some great day trips.

BLACK BASS HOTEL

Route 32
Lumberville, Pennsylvania 18933
(215) 297-5815 or 297-5770
Innkeeper: Herbert Ward
Rooms: 7 doubles, 2 suites
Rates: Doubles $80, Suites $150
Payment: AE, MC, and Visa
Children: Welcome
Dogs: Welcome with prior approval
Open: All year except December 25

Although it is possible to reach the Black Bass Hotel from various locations in New Jersey, the most scenic route is driving up from New Hope on the River Road to Lumberville. Along the way lie quaint antique stone houses perched on the banks of the Delaware River. Huge trees offer shade from the summer sun and refuge from the heat. Driving along the narrow winding road, it is easy to imagine what life might have been like hundreds of years ago when Washington crossed the Delaware, not far from this spot. The Black Bass Hotel was a part of this heritage. Having been constructed in 1745, its original use was that of a temporary safe haven for Colonial travelers, providing them with food and lodging along the river. Then President, Grover Cleveland, even spent some time here while on a fishing vacation.

Today, behind the thick stone walls, there remains a strong sense of this history. There are obviously the modern conveniences, such as hot and cold running water and electricity, but guests have the distinct feeling they have stepped back in time. An entry way leads off into a variety of directions. Step into one room and visitors will be greeted by the sounds of the finches and parakeets which occupy the half-dozen cages artfully arranged against one wall. It is a space that has been painted a pale blue and filled with an eclectic assortment of antique furnishings. Guests cannot help but notice the artistic touches throughout the inn. Wooden window shades have been hand painted with wildlife, one with a monkey and the other with a bird. The stairway leading upstairs has a lovely mural of a mother and child.

The bedrooms are all located on the second floor off a long hallway, whose sloping floors lend much to the authenticity of the inn's antiquity. Shuttered doors allow the cool breezes to blow in from the river and through the inn to the bedrooms on the street side. With the exception of the two suites, all of the guest rooms are rather small. Most provide enough room for an antique bureau and either a double or a pair of twin-size beds, the latter are often covered with white Bates spreads or handmade quilts. The walls are sponge painted in pink or orange and often are adorned with an original painting as well. The most desirable rooms are those on the river side, as each has a door leading to a small iron porch. There is one especially nice room with a green velvet quarter-canopied bed and a decorative fireplace. For those who are looking for a little more space, the suites at either end of the hall are the best choices. The largest of the two offers a small, eclectically furnished sitting area. This opens up into another expansive room dominated by windows that overlook the river. A charming sleigh bed is tucked into an alcove. The smaller suite offers two rooms, one on the street side with a wonderful canopied bed, whose headboard had been artfully decorated with a painting of a bird. The adjoining riverside room is quite narrow and is furnished with a couch and a few side tables. With the exception of the suites, the bedrooms all share two bathrooms, which are equipped with an abundance of towels and soaps.

Much of the inn's business comes from their restaurant. In the summer months, the screened verandah is a coveted resting spot, with its ornate iron railing and picturesque views of the river. Whether enjoying lunch or dinner, guests are treated to a frequently changing menu. During our visit the appetizers included a zucchini and watercress soup, chilled shrimp gazpacho with avocado, and a salad created from smoked duck, fresh thyme, Jicama, oranges, and pecans. Entrees are equally as tantalizing, with the Charleston Meeting Street crab and the grilled lamb chops with an orange Guiness sauce and minted crumb topping as particular highlights. There is also the fettucine with bay scallops, salmon, and trout, the twin tournedos of beef in an herbed brie crust, and the roast duck with a gruyere mustard and bread crumbs. Those who have any room left for dessert will enjoy a number of the homemade selections. The Grand Marnier chocolate torte with orange sherbert and cream and a frozen lemon souffle each are as delectable as they sound.

In the cooler months, most people like to retreat to the small tavern with its intimate table settings, natural rock walls, and roaring fireplace. Just beyond this is the actual bar, a wonderful pewter creation that was originally in Maxim's, a Paris institution. Glass bookcases are literally filled with collectible plates and tins bearing the likenesses of the British Royals. This is truly just the right spot for enjoying a hot toddy, while the snow falls outside.

During the day there is plenty to do in the area. A small general store offers all sorts of gourmet goodies to take on a picnic. A footbridge next to the inn crosses the Delaware to Bull's Island State Park. This is a nature preserve, and is also a delightful place to enjoy some quiet time. Along the road leading to the inn there are also plenty of great places to picnic and fish, each offering solitude for those wishing to escape the hustle and bustle of nearby New Hope. Those who prefer to get out on the river should look into the Point Pleasant Canoe and Tube, where they may rent canoes, rafts, and inner tubes for the day or the week. There are also some quiet roads in and around Lumberville, which are perfect for long walks with Bowser.

What the Black Bass Hotel does not offer in fine antiques and elaborate amenities, it more than makes up for in character, charm, and excellent food. Those who want a true taste of the Colonial era, should contemplate spending a night or two at this historic hotel.

THE GREAT VALLEY HOUSE
BED AND BREAKFAST

RD 3, Box 110
Malvern, Pennsylvania 19355
(215) 644-6759
Host: Pattye Benson
Rooms: 3 doubles
Rates: $75-85
Payment: Personal checks
Children: Welcome
Dogs: Welcome as long as they are not left alone in the room
Open: All year

Malvern is a pretty town, located just outside of Philadelphia, but seemingly hundreds of miles away. The winding roads and rural feeling have not been disrupted with the huge growth seen in many neighboring communities. Ten years ago, Pattye and her husband Jeff bought the second oldest house in the town, filled it with antiques they had collected while abroad, and opened a charming Bed and Breakfast. Those who have stayed here over the years couldn't be happier, and those who haven't don't know what they are missing.

Staying at the Great Valley House is like taking a step back in time — way back, as the stone farmhouse was built in 1720. Actually, some contend that the original Welsh squatters, who probably occupied this land, built rudimentary structures on the farm as early as 1681. This is premised upon an unusual stone sink that was part of the stone wall in the Old Kitchen. Thomas James was the first person known to take legal residence of the land in 1720 and he is responsible for building most of the house. Over the years, other owners have left their respective marks. For instance, according to the historical information on the house, "a date stone in the west peak of the house is inscribed "FREDRICK HOUSEMAN 1791." Those who stay here would better know this section as the living room and center hallway. William Thomas also carved his initials and the date of 1812 into the mantel of the original kitchen fireplace. Many guests take it as a challenge to try and find his inscription.

Today, there are almost three hundred years of history contained within these walls. Flagstone steps lead up through ancient boxwood hedges to the veranda, where guests have wonderful views of the undisturbed acreage surrounding them. Each one of the 15 rooms is an historic treasure, with random-width hardwood floors, hand-hewn nails, and hand-forged iron hinges on the doors. Three of the chambers can accommodate guests and are aptly named the Peaches and Cream Room, the Rose and Grey Room, and the Piano Room. The first two bedrooms are located on the third floor of the house, and both contain queen-size and twin beds. One is canopied and the other an antique

116

brass bedstead. The Piano Room is the largest chamber and is located on the second floor. Here, the antique brass double bed fills one corner of the room, leaving enough space for a small sitting area and a piano. While each guest bedroom has its own distinct personality, the walls in all have been hand stenciled, the beds adorned with colorful handmade quilts, and each is furnished with wonderful antiques. When guests head upstairs at night, their beds are turned down and if the night is cold, a down comforter is provided to keep them warm.

In the morning, early risers often make use of the microwave oven, sample some freshly brewed coffee and choose from one of the delectables in the refrigerator. This Continental fare is all conveniently located in the central hallway. A little later a full breakfast is served in the kitchen on a table set close to the huge, walk-in fireplace. Here, guests are treated to wonderful quiches, French toast, and light pancakes along with freshly baked muffins and breads. This is accompanied by fresh fruit, preserves, and either tea or strong coffee.

After breakfast, guests are free to explore the three acres of land that surround the house. Many will certainly stumble across the old smoke house in their wanderings, along with the original cold storage keep. The shrubs and plantings on the property are quite old, piquing the curiosity of anyone with a green thumb. One of the more popular features of the B&B, in the summer months, is the good sized swimming pool located to the rear of the property. Others will enjoy exploring this rural area, which offers great back roads for leisurely walks with Bowser. Those who would like to take a short drive will find the Valley Forge Historical Park, Audubon Wildlife Sanctuary, and Longwood Gardens easily accessible.

We feel fortunate to have discovered the Great Valley House, not only for its historical ambiance but for the true spirit of hospitality that permeates the place.

THE CARRIAGE HOUSE AT STONEGATE

RD 1, Box 11A
Montoursville, Pennsylvania 17754
(717) 433-4340, Fax: (717) 433-4563
Hosts: Dena and Harold Mesaris
Rooms: 2 doubles
Rates: $50-70
Payment: Personal checks
Children: Welcome (cribs and cots are available)
Dogs: Welcome
Open: All year

Most people are often intent to bypass central Pennsylvania, as they rush to reach their final destination — the Poconos, Pittsburgh, or New York City. Those who decide to stop, and spend some time investigating this beautiful hilly countryside, will be surprised by the abundance of wildlife, the lush state parks, and the number of hiking trails. We discovered the region some years ago when we first visited The Carriage House at Stonegate. As we drove along the country road leading to the B&B, we were so taken with the beauty of the Loyalsock Creek Valley, that we drove right by the stone pillars that marked the entrance to The Carriage House at Stonegate! After turning around, we entered the gates and drove a short distance to main house. As soon as we arrived, the Mesaris' friendly Newfoundland came bounding out to greet us. We later discovered the full array of furry and feathered creatures who live on the property, ranging from ducks and chickens to cats and even a sheep. These creatures are a fortunate lot, having over 30 acres of woodlands, informal gardens, and even a creek to explore.

While the Mesaris family occupies the main house, guests enjoy the privacy of the carriage house tucked some 30 yards away at the edge of the woods. According to Harold, the actual carriage house was part of one of the "oldest farms, dating from the early 1800s, in the lower Loyalsock Valley." During our visit, some flowers that Dena had planted in her summer flower garden were just beginning to bloom. Once inside, we felt as though we were standing in a Maine summer cottage. On the first floor, there was an open-air living room furnished with comfortable couches and chairs, an ideal place for playing board games and watching television. Just beyond this, and within the same space, was the breakfast area. To the rear of The Carriage House lay the fully-equipped kitchen, which included a refrigerator stocked with some munchies. This is a welcoming, homey place, where we easily could have spent just a night or stayed for a full week's vacation.

The two upstairs chambers share this same comfortable feeling with wide board floors leading into the two bedrooms. Each has been decorated in bright country colors and a smattering of antiques. Our favorite bedroom is at the front of the house, with a four poster queen-size bed and sunshine that pours in through the windows. The second bedroom is somewhat larger and has a double bed. The shared bathroom has been updated as well, with contemporary tiles and a great shower. As the carriage house is only rented to one couple or group at a time, guests always have as much privacy as they need.

Although the kitchen is well outfitted for preparing meals, guests are pampered in the morning when Harold brings cottage guests their breakfast. He prepares a terrific Continental fare, with warm muffins or breads, fruit in season, juices, and coffee or tea. After breakfast, Bowser might be interested in taking a walk down to Mill Creek. The creek is fun to follow, leading adventurers on either a short or long trek, depending upon their mood. Early risers, who just want to enjoy their secluded surroundings, sip their coffee, and gaze out the windows, are certain see their fair share of local wildlife.

Harold is usually around to provide suggestions for additional things to do, and will sometimes even act as a tour guide or local historian. Some of the area's popular activities include hiking in the nearby state parks, where rivers and waterfalls merely add to the incredible scenery. Fishing is another favorite pursuit in the nearby streams. In the Fall, some come to hunt, while others prefer to do their "hunting" year round by taking pictures of the wildlife with a camera. In the wintertime, the logging roads that were great for summer walks with Bowser, become fine cross-country ski paths. Visitors and their canine companions will certainly have a great time exploring this mountainous portion of Pennsylvania, replete with rural charm.

AARON BURR HOUSE

80 West Bridge Street
New Hope, Pennsylvania 18938
(215) 862-2343
Innkeepers: Mary Gerdes and Larry Weber
Rooms: 4 doubles, 2 suites
Rates: Doubles $80-125, Suites $125-160
Payment: AE
Children: Welcome depending upon availability of the crib and/or cot.
　　　　(Babysitting services are available)
Dogs: Welcome with advance notice and prior approval. No puppies please.
Open: All year

The Aaron Burr House is actually part of the Wedgwood Collection of Inns which are owned and operated by Nadine ("Dinie" to her friends and customers) Silnutzer and Carl Glassman. While two of their inns can be found side by side, the Aaron Burr House is two blocks away and is their most recent acquisition, purchased just three years ago. The house was built in 1854 and reflects the Victorian period of architecture with its deep sofits, Dutch-lap clapboards, and ornate woodwork. Painted a bright yellow, with blue shutters and white trim, it is difficult to miss this gracious building when walking along Bridge Street.

Those with a love of antique homes are sure to enjoy their stay at the inn. Hand-worked moldings and baseboards frame the high ceilings and rounded windows. The floors are particularly noteworthy, having been made of native black walnut. Interestingly, the doctor who owned the house was given a grove of these trees. After cutting them down, he had them made into floor planking, but waited twenty years before laying them down in the house. Linseed oil is applied four times a year to keep the floors glowing.

Of the six guest rooms available, three have fireplaces and two have king-size beds. Soft comforters cover four-poster beds and separate sitting areas provide nice places to read. Although the rooms in this house have fewer antiques than the Umplebe House and Wedgwood House, the ambiance is still cozy and intimate. Those who want a room with a great deal of character should request those on the third floor as they are tucked under the eaves. After coming back from an evening in the village, guests will find their beds turned down and usually a small sweet treat awaiting them.

In the morning, freshly baked muffins and breads along with fresh juice and coffee or tea is laid out for guests. The innkeepers are always available to help with making plans for the day's adventures. One of the nice things about the Aaron Burr House is the private parking available to guests as there are a limited number of spots this close to town. Bowser will truly enjoy his/her walks through New Hope and perhaps down to the river. Further afield, and within an easy drive, is the spot where George Washington crossed the Delaware. Here, there are acres of grass, allowing Bowser an opportunity to kick up his/her heels and have a fine time while you explore the more historic aspects of the park-like setting.

WEDGWOOD COLLECTION OF HISTORIC INNS

111 West Bridge Street
New Hope, Pennsylvania 18938
(215) 862-2570
Innkeepers: Nadine (Dinie) Silnutzer and Carl Glassman
Rooms: 5 doubles, 5 suites, 1 cottage
Rates: Doubles $60-130, Suites $130-155, Cottage $150-170
Payment: AE
Children: Welcome (cribs, cots, and babysitting are available)
Dogs: Welcome with prior approval in specific rooms
Open: All year

When we first learned about the Wedgwood Inn years ago it consisted of an antique Victorian home and a small cottage. Guests raved about the charm of the rooms, the great food, and the warmth of their hosts, Dinie Silnutzer, Carl Glassman, and their friendly dog, Jasper. As with any fine wine or piece of furniture, age has beautifully mellowed the inn. Today, aside from the Wedgwood House, there are the Umplebe and Aaron Burr Houses (see under separate listing) each offering their own unique antique charm which delights new and returning guests. Together, the group forms the Wedgwood Collection of Historic Inns.

The original Victorian and its neighbor, the Umplebe House, are still the centerpieces for the group. A huge porte-cochere protects one side of the house, and it is under this that guests will find the door that leads them into the inn and a small sitting room. It has been painted a Wedgwood blue with white trim, and just in case one missed the connection, there is a full array of Wedgwood china collectibles tucked into hutches and resting on bookshelves. A handsome woodstove warms the room, and on top is a cast iron dog that bears a strong resemblance to the inn's dog, Jasper. Also tucked away in this room are an assortment of board games, brochures covering just about any activity available to visitors, and a small television. Upstairs, guests will find the bedrooms, each one unique as much for the alcoves and bay windows as for the decor. Victorian antiques predominate in this house, with complementary old-fashioned floral wallpapers setting the tone.

Next door to the Wedgwood House is the Umplebe House, an 1833 Classic Revival stone manor. The house is cheery, even from the exterior, with its yellow walls and colorful flower gardens. Guests pass by an intimate brick courtyard set with a few white iron tables and chairs, and by beds of azaleas to reach the front door. A long hallway leads to the two floors of accommodations. Some might stay in a downstairs room complete with an antique bed covered with a handmade Wedgwood blue comforter and floral pillows. An antique bureau rests off to the side with a window seat that is just right for a lazy afternoon of reading. One of our favorite rooms lies upstairs to the rear of the house, which gives it a particularly nice sense of privacy. This is a corner room with double hung windows on all sides, giving the feeling of being in a tree house. The brightness of this bedroom is further enhanced by the floral comforter covering the white iron and brass bed. The large, private bathroom is stocked, as are all of the bathrooms, with an assortment of English-made shampoos and soaps.

Those who want even more luxury will appreciate the upstairs suite. This huge room is dominated by a mahogany sleigh bed. A wall of built-in shelves is filled with books and original artwork adorns the walls. One of the many delightful things about this room is the woodstove which warms it. In the summer months, freshly cut flowers from the garden are thoughtful touches, although throughout the year guests can expect to find mints set next to their turned down beds, along with a decanter of sherry and glasses in which to enjoy it. We have mentioned some of the more noteworthy rooms, although each one, both large and small, offer a great deal of character and antique charm. Those who stay in the more intimate rooms, without the luxury of a sofa or armchairs, will appreciate the large first floor parlor with its woodstove and comfortable sofas. At the end of the room is a long table where they will find a Continental breakfast laid out each morning.

Breakfast at the Wedgwood Collection of Inns is an expanded version of the usual coffee, tea, and muffins. Breads are always homemade, and often feature such exotic choices as Cappuccino chip muffins, orange tea muffins, and pineapple muffins or maybe some of Dinie's grandmother's apple cake. The jams are often ones found at the local farmer's market, as is any of the fresh fruit and produce. It is sometimes difficult to decide where to dine, whether outside in the gazebo, on the sun porch, or simply, in bed. Breakfast is not the only time to enjoy the goodies created at the inn. Often there are things set out when guests arrive in the afternoon, along with a special afternoon tea on Saturday.

There are an assortment of things to do in the area, ranging from playing croquet and badminton, to relaxing on a hammock in the shade or taking a horse drawn buggy ride. Some people opt to play a little tennis or just explore some of the many historical attractions available in the vicinity.

As with any successful inn, there is usually more to it than just a beautiful room and good food. A caring innkeeper or two are always working hard behind the scenes to make sure guests have a relaxing stay. Dinie and Carl have owned the inns since 1982. They put as much energy into their guests' today as they did twelve years ago. They have been so successful that Carl now offers classes to teach those who want to be innkeepers just how to do it and how to avoid some of the usual pitfalls. In the meantime, they keep practicing and perfecting their own technique, although to those who have stayed with them there is little they could do to improve upon virtual perfection.

THE RITTENHOUSE

210 Rittenhouse Square
Philadelphia, Pennsylvania 19103
(800) 635-1042, (215) 546-9000, Fax: (215) 732-3364
General Manager: David G. Benton
Rooms: 88 doubles, 11 suites, 20 long-term apartments
Rates: Doubles $220-270, Suites $300-1,300, Apartments-inquire
Payment: AE, CB, DC, MC, and Visa
Children: Welcome (cribs, cots, and babysitters are available)
Dogs: Well-behaved dogs are welcome with advance notice
Open: All year

From the exterior, there is nothing old or traditional about The Rittenhouse Hotel, which resides in a modern, geometrical high-rise overlooking the residential and scenic Rittenhouse Square. This young upstart might disturb the sensibilities of those used to the traditional brownstones of Philadelphia which surround the square; however, once inside, guests are immediately surrounded by an elegance that would make even the most conservative Philadelphians feel at ease.

The lobby is a mixture of the Art Deco period and the traditional, with coffered ceilings illuminated by large, domed brass and frosted glass lights. Enormous pillars, resting on a half wall, form a natural break between the lounge and tea room. Rather than being imposing, the entire effect is quite intimate with its small seating arrangements, tailored sofas, and Queen Anne style armchairs resting on plush Chinese carpets. The taupe, ecru, and cream colors of the fabrics, the walls, and the natural woods that have been used create a comfortable serenity in these surroundings. This soothing effect is accented by the splash of color from fresh flowers that spill from huge urns and vases. A few steps down into the Cassat Tea Room, guests will find comfortable sofas set next to French chairs covered in blue and pink tapestry fabrics surrounding small tables. On a sunny day, the light streams in here through a wall of French doors and windows. Potted palms reach almost to the full height of the 20-foot ceilings. A formal tea is served in the afternoon accompanied by soft piano music. Of course, in the evening, this makes an equally delightful spot for cocktails or after-dinner liqueurs.

The hotel offers two restaurants for the enjoyment of most palates. The informal Treetops is the hotel's cafe — similar in style to the lounge with its muted colors and its views of the Square through skylights and windows. The cafe offers a full menu of delectable items virtually 24-hours a day. One of the favorites is the Pacific coast spicy crab cake served over a smoked tomato fume. However, it is the hotel's Restaurant 210 that deserves most of the culinary accolades. This chamber is reminiscent of a supper club with its sleek lines, mahogany trim, and brass accents. Under the guidance of chef David Derfel, patrons are treated to an ever-changing menu that features innovative entrees. During our visit, the offerings included a sweet Jersey corn and blue crab chowder with baked polenta croutons, the mixed shellfish gazpacho with snow crab claw and jumbo shrimp, and the foie gras with a crisp potato, seasonal fruit chutney, and a citrus infused port oil (even the condiments are made at the hotel). The Dover sole was unusual, as it was prepared with a spinach coulis, lobster, and asparagus fleuron. Other interesting selections included the medallions of Texas antelope with a rosemary marinade accompanied by a pearl onion, sweet corn and fresh sage strudel and the fresh mint and honey mustard crusted lamb loin with a ratatouille-potato tart. Desserts are all creations of the chef, and are equally delectable.

After dinner, one can either head for the clubby Boathouse Row Bar, with its preponderance of mahogany setting off an assortment of rowing memorabilia, or grab Bowser and go for a walk in Rittenhouse Square. This six-acre park in the center of Philadelphia is perhaps the best known of the city's scenic squares. Residential buildings surround it and Bowser is certain to meet some of the full-time doggie residents during his meanderings. During the day, there is plenty of window shopping available within a block or two of the hotel. For additional ideas, contact the concierge before visiting or talk to some of the residents of The Rittenhouse, who can usually be found walking their four-legged friends early in the morning or in the evening.

These same residents occupy the top twenty or so floors of the Rittenhouse building, while hotel guests have access to the fifth through ninth floors. Because of the hotel's architectural design, with its wave of glass outcroppings, all accommodations enjoy unique views and have unusual interior configurations that may contain small sitting areas or writing desks. Bedroom decors vary, although navy blue and camel tones predominate in the tailored bedspreads and upholstered Queen Anne style armchairs, lending a residential quality to these rooms. Mahogany is used for most of the furniture, including the bedside tables, Chippendale chairs, writing desks, or armoires. There is certainly no shortage of amenities as each chamber is furnished with a 25" television, a VCR (the hotel has a large library of videotapes), a mini-bar and refrigerator, three telephones, and a television in the bathroom. The other bathroom details were not overlooked during the design process. Marble, marble, and more marble creates an inviting and opulent bathroom, with separate walk-in showers, bathtubs that are oversized, and a full array of toiletries to use during and after bathing. Extra-large terry cloth robes are available, along with hair dryers and a separate dressing area.

Those whose plans call for a longer stay in the city, will be pleased to know about the studios and apartments that are available at The Rittenhouse. These are more sophisticated and better appointed than the standard guest rooms, offering formal living rooms decorated with very traditional furnishings such as finial secretaries, leather-backed chairs, and Oriental rugs. There is a very masculine ambiance to these apartments with their rust accents set against a neutral background. As with the hotel rooms, guests are often drawn to the views of the Square and of the city through the expanse of windows.

The Rittenhouse it truly a self-contained oasis for those visiting Philadelphia with excellent restaurants, fabulous rooms, a few exclusive boutiques, and Toppers Spa. The latter offers all the traditional services of a spa, as well as a sky-lit swimming pool, an outdoor terrace, and a full complement of exercise equipment. Guests will soon discover that very little escapes the attention of the staff at the hotel, and if it does, just ask, and the request will surely be honored. It isn't surprising that the five-star Rittenhouse has consistently earned accolades from every guidebook and reviewer since its opening in 1989.

FOUR SEASONS HOTEL

One Logan Square
Philadelphia, Pennsylvania   19103
(800) 332-3442, (215) 963-1500, Fax: (215) 963-9507
General Manager: Tom Kelly
Rooms: 262 doubles, 100 suites
Rates: Doubles $155-280, Suites $210-1,185
Payment: AE, CB, DC, DSC, MC, and Visa
Children: Welcome (cribs, cots, and babysitters are available)
Dogs: Welcome with advance notice
Open: All year

The Four Seasons Hotels consistently offer guests the ultimate in luxury, service, and amenities — their hotel in Philadelphia being no exception. Located in the heart of the museum and "New North Side" business districts, there are plenty of interesting sights and attractions for guests to see within walking distance of the hotel. Just across the way is the arresting Swan Fountain and beyond are the St. Peter and St. Paul basilicas. The entire area has been strikingly refurbished, making it all the more appealing to its visitors.

Walking into the lobby of the Four Seasons, guests are immediately struck by its sense of serenity. This is due in part to the combination of richly hued woods and marble, which have been chosen for the walls and floors. Enormous live palms and ferns create subtle backdrops for the private sitting areas that can be found on various tiers. If arriving in the afternoon, guests might want to unwind during high tea in the Swann Lounge. Of course, the premier restaurant in the hotel, and perhaps in the city, is The Fountain Restaurant. Fine china and crystal table settings are merely the finishing touch to the already intimate setting created by the use of French doors, handfinished moldings and paneling, and massive fresh flower arrangements. This all provides the necessary backdrop for the meal which follows. Some choose to start with the stuffed jumbo sea scallops accompanied by a potato compote and sevruga caviar or the

125

marinated quail with an artichoke heart. Entree selections range from such tantalizing choices as a sauteed venison medallion wrapped in pasta and covered with a light black peppercorn and currant sauce, the Virginian squab in a honey and red wine sauce, or the roasted rabbit saddle with a fennel vavioletti, tomato concasse and thyme jus. Without exception, the lovely atmosphere, excellent service, and fine food combine to make for a memorable dining experience.

The attention to detail that guests enjoy during their meals also extends to the guest rooms. While the king-bedded chambers are quite luxurious, our first choice remains the executive suites. Here, a sitting room is separated from the master bedroom by a pair of French doors. All the rooms have been furnished in the style of the Federal period with the finest reproductions. Mahogany writing tables and drum tables are embellished with wood inlays and brass pulls. Tasteful fabrics and wallpapers, reminiscent of Philadelphia's Federal period, add an additional sense of authenticity. Televisions and fully stocked mini-bars are inconspicuously concealed in armoires. Bedside tables hold one of the room's three telephones, a clock radio, and porcelain lamps. The bathrooms are equally well appointed with hair dryers, terry cloth robes, an assortment of personal care items, and an additional telephone. We certainly appreciated the fact that windows open, allowing for a bit of fresh air. Traveling families will also like the little extras such as cookies and milk for the children, "pint-size" terry cloth bathrobes, and a variety of video games, stuffed animals, and children's books. In the morning, breakfast can be delivered complete with the daily newspaper.

While many hotels now offer spas and swimming pools, the facilities at the Four Seasons are exceptional. The pool has enough space for two lanes dedicated to lap swimming and a shallow area for children to frolic around. The decks around the pool are broken up by indoor gardens filled with live plants and colorful flowers, making it all the more appealing. Additionally, there is a full array of Stairmasters, Lifecycles, and treadmills along with a rowing machine and additional weight lifting equipment. Those who are in search of a little pampering will want to have a massage, whirlpool, and/or sauna. Freshly squeezed orange juice, teas, and coffee along with spring water and fresh fruit are usually set out in the sitting area alongside the spa for guests to enjoy after their workout.

As far as things to do with one's canine cohort, there are plenty of walking areas for Bowser to explore. The hotel is just off Logan Circle and close to several lovely grassy areas. Jogging maps are available for those who are so inclined. Longer walks will take guests to the scenic Rittenhouse Square and Philadelphia's historic district. Day trips from the city can lead visitors southwest to Lancaster County, Westchester County, and the Longwood Gardens or north to scenic Bucks County. Of course, there are so many things to see and do in the city that most people and their canine companions will have no problem keeping themselves occupied.

SIGN OF THE SORREL HORSE

243 Old Bethlehem Road
Quakertown, Pennsylvania 18951
(215) 536-4651
Innkeepers: Monique Gaumont and Jon Atkin
Rooms: 5 doubles
Rates: $85-125
Payment: AE, CB, DC, MC, and Visa
Children: Over 12 years of age are welcome, exceptions are sometimes
made for small children
Dogs: Welcome with advance notice, provided permission is granted by the
inn owners
Open: All year except for the first two weeks in March and most Mondays
and Tuesdays

We are always pleased to discover an inn whose ambiance is matched by the food it serves. If the idea of eating gourmet foods and staying overnight in a 1749 tavern set in the rolling hills of Bucks County sounds appealing, then read on. The Sign of the Sorrel Horse was bought by Monique and Jon nine years ago. Their French and British backgrounds combined with their culinary expertise has turned this historic stagecoach stop into something right out of the French countryside.

Set on eight acres, the stone house is surrounded by mature shade trees, ivy lined brick walkways, and open fields. Sitting on the patio, people can see the extensive herb and vegetable gardens, that are as pretty to look at as they are useful. Toward the rear of the property guests can find the swimming pool, which looks more like a pond surrounded by natural rocks. Beyond this there are more gardens and a small archery range. The birds that congregate at the redwood bird feeders can be viewed from benches placed about the grounds.

While the outside patio is a wonderful spot for summer dining, it is the ambiance of the two intimate beamed-ceiling dining rooms that most patrons remember. Each room holds just four or five tables — all of them covered with white tablecloths and set with fine china and crystal. The subdued colors and candlelight create just the right atmosphere for a quiet and leisurely dinner. The meal is always a multi-course affair, with sorbet served at intervals to cleanse the palate. Because the herbs and vegetables are grown at the inn, Jon is most innovative when it comes to planning his evening menu as he doesn't have to depend on what may or may not have been delivered that day.

For those who want to sample the full range of offerings, there is the a la carte menu; however, this can become an expensive proposition. A less expensive alternative is the fixed price menu which changes daily. The following is just a sampling of some past menus, giving gourmands a sense of what they may expect. A fresh lobster bisque, chestnut soup, or Nasturtium flower soup are always appropriate beginnings. Of course there are also the house specialties; the French Belons Oysters on the half shell, Beluga and salmon caviar for two, or the goose liver pate served with a Gewurztraminer aspic and black truffles.

Although guests often comment on the amount of time between courses, it is always worth the wait as each dish is truly a work of art, both visually and gastronomically. Entrees are often built around exotic cuts of meat such as wild boar, elk, caribou, or bear. The elk is imported from Sweden and might have a huckleberry and cassis sauce, while the venison is often served with a veal mousseline, Enoki mushrooms, and a juniper berry sauce. Some of the more classic choices are the roast quail with a red currant and Armagnac sauce or the rainbow trout stuffed with salmon mousse and covered with a crayfish sauce. Desserts are no less inspired, including such selections as the three layer cappuccino terrine, a peach and white chocolate souffle with a peach and ginger sauce, and a baked white chocolate and raspberry cheesecake.

After dinner, some choose to retreat to the tiny Hunter's Bar for their brandy, cognac, or port. Another favorite nook, warmed by a woodstove in the winter months, is a glassed-in porch framed by French doors. Here, two white doves reside in a white iron cage, listening in on late evening conversations. Afterwards, a small passage guides overnight guests up to their bedrooms.

These are each individually furnished with a collection of French antiques Jon and Monique have carefully selected. While some of the rooms are a little on the cozy side, we expect that the lovely antiques and decor coupled with the exquisite meals will more than compensate for the somewhat close quarters. As a matter of fact, the hosts just returned from another European buying spree in March, where they picked up an assortment of additional furnishings. Guests will find a chandelier provides soft light for an intimate sitting area. Another room offers an exposed stone wall as the backdrop for a lovely antique bedstead. All feature private bathrooms and air-conditioning. Each morning a light breakfast of fresh croissants, strong coffee, and juice is served. This is a pleasant way to ease the palate back into service after its indulgences from the night before. For those who are going to spend the day away from the inn, Jon will pack a picnic lunch.

Locally, there is the Nockamixon State Park, which offers fishing, hiking, bicycling, and boating opportunities. While Bowser is welcome to enjoy the outdoors, it is requested that he remain leashed at all times and stay away from the designated swimming and camping areas. Others may choose to hike up Haycock Mountain, the second highest point in Bucks County. There is also tennis and golf, as well as a sporting clay pigeon range nearby. Today, finding one's way back to the inn at the end of the day is rarely a problem. In the 1700s, however, when illiteracy was high, it was a more difficult proposition. Then, rather than looking for the inn's sign, guests would search for the horses already tied up outside. Hence, looking for the "Sign of the Sorrel Horse" became the preferred way to find, what today has become, a most unusual inn.

HISTORIC STRASBURG INN

Route 898, Historic Drive
Strasburg, Pennsylvania   17579
(800) 872-0201, (717) 687-7691
Manager: Denny Pierce
Rooms: 102 doubles
Rates: $85-120
Payment: AE, DC, DSC, MC, and Visa
Children: Welcome, children under 16 years of age are free when staying in
        same room with parents
Dogs: Welcome in all rooms
Open: All year

Driving along the back roads of Lancaster County, visitors feel transported into another place and time. For a good portion of the year, the "Plain" (Amish, Mennonite, and Brethren) people can be seen tilling the soil or harvesting their crops using only their horse or mule drawn plows. The traditional open black buggies or closed family carriages travel these back roads as well, and cars seem quite out of place in this unchanged rural setting.

While there are many towns worth visiting in Lancaster County, one of our favorites is Strasburg. Those with an interest in trains will find this area to be a mecca of sorts. Traintown U.S.A. has a myriad of miniature working trains and animated figures along with a detailed 1,700 square foot display of the area. Those who want to ride on a train should visit the Strasburg Railroad Co., which has steam locomotives pulling wooden passenger cars through the rolling countryside. Another noteworthy option is the Railroad Museum of Pennsylvania, where railroad engines and cars, dating as far back as the 1800s, are on display. Those with interests focusing more on the local people will gain some insight into their lifestyle by visiting The Amish Village. Here, a short tour guides visitors through an historic 1800s farmhouse that has been furnished and decorated as a typical contemporary Amish household.

A good base for these expeditions is the Historic Strasburg Inn. Since it is more of a contemporary building, historic is not the first word that comes to mind when describing the inn, although it does exude a sense of tradition. Two story brick-buildings, trimmed in Williamsburg blue, dot a portion of the 58 acres. Surrounding the inn are huge Amish farms and rolling hills of corn and wheat. If no one else is impressed by all this beautiful open space, Bowser sure will be as he will undoubtedly find plenty of things to explore while visiting here.

The actual guest rooms at the inn are quite simple, dressed up by an occasional wainscotting and Colonial wallpapers. Most are simply furnished with bedsteads covered by white cotton spreads, a writing desk, and a rocking or wing chair. The bathrooms are exceptionally clean and have been stocked with a basket of soaps and shampoos. While the first floor rooms offer direct access to the outside, the second floor accommodations are more architecturally interesting with their vaulted ceilings and windows situated under the eaves. Although the rooms are rather plain, the amenities are varied. Guests are free to check out bicycles for exploring the local back roads. The outdoor pool is a great spot for children in the summer months, as are the playground, volleyball court, and horseshoe pits. Should the weather take a turn for the worse, there are indoor activities for the children as well, ranging from Ping-Pong to a game room.

For those who just cannot wait to get a start on the day, there are coffee and muffins awaiting them in the lobby. This is the most intimate of all the inn's public rooms with its warm Williamsburg blue walls, hardwood floors, and wing chairs set before a fireplace. Guests of the inn are treated to a full breakfast each morning, which is served in the Washington House Restaurant. This is a reproduction of the original Strasburg Hotel, which was built in 1793. Most mornings there is a large buffet that is loaded with everything from scrambled eggs, pancakes and waffles, to fresh fruit, home-baked breads, and cereals. Lunches can be of the picnic variety, with choices ranging from fried chicken to either ham and cheese or roast beef sandwiches. The dinner menu is reasonably priced with entrees that include Maryland crab cakes, veal marsala, filet mignon, and prime rib. We would also recommend trying some of the other restaurants in town for a nice change of pace.

Guests will find the Historic Strasburg Inn to be a good combination between a quaint motor lodge and a small resort, offering clean, comfortable rooms, a variety of amenities, and a good restaurant. It serves as a fine central base from which to explore this historic and intriguing part of the country.

NEW JERSEY

MARQUIS DE LAFAYETTE
On The Beach

501 Beach Drive
Cape May, New Jersey 08204
(800) 257-0432, (609) 884-3500
Innkeeper: Beth Menz
Rooms: 73 doubles and suites
Rates: Doubles $106-234, Suites $116-250 (AP packages are available)
Payment: AE, CB, DC, DSC, MC, and Visa
Children: Welcome, children under 8 years of age are free
Dogs: Welcome in all but the Marquis Suite for a $20 nightly fee
Open: All year

Cape May is reputedly the oldest resort by the sea in the United States, and it also happens to have the largest collection of authentic Victorian "cottages". Captain Cornelius Mey first happened upon this peninsula in 1620 and subsequently christened it with his name. He was soon followed by fishermen and whalers who began to establish these waters as their fishing grounds. By the mid-1700s, Cape May was in its tourism infancy with a few cottages to accommodate those who traveled here by steamer. These were later dwarfed by the massive wooden hotels that sprung up during the early 1800s to serve the growing influx of wealthy and influential visitors who were arriving from Philadelphia, Baltimore, and even Washington D.C.

Unfortunately, Cape May's growth was marred by a series of disastrous fires that occurred in the 1800s, the worst being the devastating fire of 1878. While some cottages remained standing, the majority were lost. This prompted many of the families, who had grown accustomed to summering here, to send in their personal architects and builders to recreate and improve upon this tiny enclave. What emerged were Victorian and Italianate homes, each vying for attention on the narrow streets that wound through the village. Soon Cape May was thriving again, entertaining some of the most influential people of the time. With the arrival of the automobile, many tourists were drawn to other, more convenient vacation destinations and the town returned to its old sleepy self.

Sadly, during the early part of this century an assortment of natural and economic calamities befell Cape May, including a huge flood in 1962 when most of the great wooden beach front hotels were destroyed and subsequently, many of the once magnificent cottages fell into disrepair or were abandoned. It was not until the late 1960s and early 1970s that entrepreneurs saw the opportunity to revitalize this decaying community into something truly unique. They bought the Victorian cottages, renovated the interiors and dressed the elaborately shingled exteriors in rich hues of color. They filled their historic cottages with period antiques and started B&Bs. During this time, an eclectic pedestrian shopping district also sprung up, where visitors could leisurely explore the many boutiques and dine in some of the finest restaurants in the region. Today's Cape May is a wonderful combination of the old and the new, allowing visitors a peek at the past while they take advantage of the many modern amenities instituted by the town.

Unfortunately, those traveling with dogs or children have a good deal of difficulty finding lodging in Cape May. One exception to this is the Marquis de Lafayette hotel, which stands directly across from the main beach. As we mentioned, most of the huge original hotels were either destroyed by fire or flood over the last century, paving the way for some of the newer structures that now line the beach front drive. From the exterior, the Marquis de Lafayette is a contemporary hotel; a six-story, crescent shaped structure connected to a three-story wing. What the hotel may lack in Victorian character, it more than makes up for in magnificent unobstructed views of the Atlantic.

All of the guest rooms, with the exception of those on the first floor, offer balconies which overlook the water. The units are actually part of a condominium association, where individuals own the rooms; however, there is a management company that handles all the details and reservations. The most basic of the accommodations is the small motel room offering a double bed. Those who are interested in a few more amenities and space will enjoy the more deluxe chambers with a pair of double beds or a king-size bed. These rooms have been furnished with white or naturally stained wicker, reflecting an informal cottage theme that has its roots in seaside communities like Cape May. Given the option, most people prefer the suites, as much for their sense of space as for the additional features. Guests actually enter the suite through the bedroom, which is situated toward the rear of the building, and then walk along a short hallway which has a kitchenette on one side and a bathroom on the other. This leads into the cozy sitting area, or in some cases, a large living room with a wall of windows and a door that open directly onto the balconies. The Queen Anne reproductions of dark cherrywood lend a sense of formality to the suites, but this is softened by the floral Victorian wallpapers. The bathrooms are all updated and offer the usual selection of soaps and shampoos. While guests are welcome to prepare their own meals, most find it far easier to try one of the many unusual restaurants within walking distance of the hotel.

Breakfast is included in the rates and can be enjoyed in either the Gold Whale Restaurant on the premises or across the street at Altheas. Often, during the high season, an elaborate buffet is set out with a wide array of offerings. Afterwards, some choose to sit by the pool or grab their beach paraphernalia and beach tags (all summer visitors must have a tag to gain access to the beaches) and meander across the street to the main beach. There are also many other beaches around Cape May, each one different from the other. There is the Surfing Beach and Poverty Beach, both of which attract the surfer set. The latter is also known for their supply of perfectly weighted clam shells, which are often used in the yearly clam pitching contest held in town. Windsor Beach seems to be the classic family favorite.

Bowser might enjoy the fine birding opportunities on Cape May. South of the historic district travelers will find the Cape May Bird Observatory, which is operated by the New Jersey Audubon Society. Two of the other popular options are the Cape May State Park and Higbee Beach. On Cape May Point, Bowser can nose around the pebbles and rocks, while his two legged friends go in search of the famous Cape May "diamonds." These are actually pieces of quartz that wash up on the beach and resemble diamonds when wet. Their varying hues have captivated visitors, both young and old, for years.

In the evening, some choose to go to the Top of the Marq for dinner, dancing, and fabulous views of the ocean. Others prefer to walk through town, perusing the many restaurant menus until they find something that interests them. At night, a quietness often falls over Cape May that allows visitors, even during the busy summer season, to gain a sense of life as it might have been during the Victorian times.

NASSAU INN

10 Palmer Square
Princeton, New Jersey 08542
(800) 243-1166, (609) 921-7500, Fax: (609) 921-9385
Manager: Mark Flaherty
Rooms: 199 doubles, 18 suites
Rates: Doubles $155, Suites $245
Payment: AE, CB, DC, MC, and Visa
Children: Welcome
Dogs: Welcome
Open: All year

The Nassau Inn has been a part of Princeton hospitality for over 200 years, with little in the original building changing in all that time. The distinguished Palmer's Restaurant resides here, with an assortment of antiques, richly hewn pine-paneled walls, and random-width wide pine flooring. As guests enter the original section of the inn, they will see a large mahogany sideboard bedecked with fresh flowers. During the cold winter months this beamed-ceiling chamber is usually aglow with candles and a crackling fire in the fireplace. Queen Anne coffee tables and armchairs rest on Oriental rugs, while Sheraton end tables hold brass lamps and picture frames. There is a sense of graciousness about this part of the inn that is quite appealing.

While the rest of the Nassau Inn does not reflect the same sense of antiquity, there is a similar feeling of tradition. Some of the guest rooms have a modern feeling with clean, crisp lines and soft pastel colors. The peaches, greens, and yellows are a part of everything, from the handmade floral country quilts adorning the beds to the decorative prints that dot the walls. Side chairs and bedside tables are good quality reproductions of traditional English pieces. Many of the more recently updated guest chambers are more formal with deep shades of cranberry predominating. Here, guests will often see matching chintz fabrics adorning bedsteads and framing the windows. For those who find it hard to break with tradition, there are still some bedrooms which offer celadon green walls from years past. All spaces have tiled bathrooms which are very clean and well appointed with a full assortment of soaps and shampoos found in small decorative baskets. Unfortunately, we found many of the bathrooms to be on the small side. One of the many thoughtful touches are the chocolate chip cookies left out for the guests in their bedrooms each day.

Something which some people may wish to consider before making a reservation, is that each of the standard rooms is the same price. Therefore, if the overall decor and size of the accommodation is of concern, we suggest being as specific as possible when making reservations. For instance, although each bedroom is delightful in its own way, those in the Nassau Wing are somewhat smaller, but offer more character than the larger ones in the Wilson Wing.

Breakfast each morning is served in The Greenhouse, which overlooks Palmer Square. This affair can be as simple or as deluxe as guests require. For dinner fare, although there is an assortment of fine restaurants in the Princeton area, many people thoroughly enjoy sampling the delicious entrees presented at Palmer's. The seasonally changing menu concentrates on classic American cuisine. Appetizer selections might include smoked catfish cakes, the chilled Catskill foie gras, or a grilled vegetable soup with lobster ravioli and saffron aioli. Entrees are often simple meats and fish combined with interesting sauces and side dishes, making for delicious gourmet meals. For instance, pan-seared pork tenderloin is served with a preserved kumquat sauce; cinnamon-smoked lamb is accompanied by a red onion and thyme potato tart and ancho chilli sauce; and the steamed sea scallops are served with a Vidalia onion relish and herb whipped potatoes. Finally, a grilled, marinated T-bone steak is complemented by a wild mushroom pudding and the grilled filet of beef has a sun-dried tomato and lemon grass sauce that spices things up a bit.

Another special tradition at the Nassau Inn is the Yankee Doodle Tap Room, named for the large Norman Rockwell mural which hangs here. This was painted specifically for the inn by Rockwell and remains, amid other Princeton University memorabilia, the centerpiece for this room.

One of the many terrific things about the Nassau Inn is the amount of open space for Bowser to explore in the nearby area. The small, grassy park in the middle of Palmer Square is easily accessible, but most enjoy just meandering across the street to the Princeton University campus. In addition to investigating the miles of paths and open grassy fields, there are several parks nearby. The perennial favorite, Lake Carnegie, is the place to watch oars men and women during the warm months and ice skaters in the winter months. The Nassau Inn is in the heart of old Princeton, flanked by the University on one side and a wonderful old residential neighborhood on the other, providing guests of the inn a first-hand glimpse into this intimate college town.

PEACOCK INN

20 Bayard Lane
Princeton, New Jersey 08540
(609) 924-1707
Manager: Michael Walker
Rooms: 17 doubles
Rates: $80-125
Payment: AE, MC, and Visa
Children: Welcome
Dogs: Welcome with a $15 fee
Open: All year

One would think that with Princeton being the busy college town that it is, there would be more inns and Bed and Breakfasts. Strangely enough, one of the only places in town offering intimate B&B accommodations is The Peacock Inn. The house was built on the Princeton campus in 1775; however, in the late 1800s it was moved to its current location on Bayard Lane. Today, the gambrel-roofed building, with its dormers and pillared porch, looks as though it has always been here. Huge shade trees, mature plantings, and well-established perennial gardens frame the brick walk that leads to the double French doors which mark the entrance to the inn.

The inn has a loyal clientele, who enjoy it as much for the fine food as for the individual character of the bedrooms. Over the years, noteworthy guests have included Albert Einstein, F. Scott Fitzgerald, and Bertrand Russell. Today, guests are more likely to encounter visiting professors to the University, alumnae, or parents of Princeton students, who are appreciative of the homey atmosphere and personalized attention during their stay.

The first floor contains an old-fashioned bar, a large common area, and a lovely French restaurant called Le Plumet Royal (after the Peacock's Plume). A fairly formal atmosphere prevails in the latter, with cloth covered tables, fine silver and china, green carpeting, and Queen-Anne style chairs and tables. Paneled walls have been painted in peach tones that further soften the atmosphere. Guests of the inn are treated to an ample breakfast every morning, commencing with homemade muffins or coffee cake and followed by fresh fruit and a variety of egg dishes. Of course, there is also the more elaborate, and quite popular, Sunday Brunch. During our visit, patrons could choose between such appetizers as smoked breast of duck with a sweet onion compote and a raspberry leek aioli, sliced fresh fruit with an orange glaze, or the mixed seasonal greens with a Balsamic vinaigrette. The main course was more reflective of a dinner menu, with grilled tournedos of beef stuffed with boursin cheese, grilled salmon served with a roasted garlic butter, or an omelette filled with smoked salmon and dill. As one would expect, dinner is also a multi-course gourmet affair, with a menu that changes seasonally.

Three different stairways lead to the two floors of bedrooms. The main staircase contains a series of landings, the largest of which holds an antique armoire, a few side chairs, and an assortment of collectibles. Most of the bedrooms that are accessible off these landings are sunny and cozy and filled with Victorian and more formal English or French furnishings. The carved oak or mahogany beds, covered in white Bates bedspreads, usually dominate these carpeted chambers. Upholstered armchairs rest beside small draped tables adorned with vases of flowers and rather unusual lamps. Peacock paraphernalia can be found in most nooks and crannies, including one particularly colorful peacock, that had been painted on a decorative fireplace fan. Those who are looking for a little extra architectural character in their bedroom, should request a chamber on the third floor. These are not only set under the eaves but also offer gently sloping floor boards and detailed moldings. While the majority of the accommodations have private bathrooms, six bedrooms do share a bath. Though these are modern in many respects, some of the bathrooms still contain vestiges of the past, with four-legged bathtubs and porcelain sinks. Thoughtful extra touches such as live plants, hand-milled soaps, ice buckets, and glasses further personalize each bedroom.

The inn is situated just off a busy road, although it seems to be fairly well insulated from any street noise. Downtown Princeton is just two blocks away, as is the University. Long walks on campus and along quiet residential streets are terrific activities for Bowser and his two-legged friends. Palmer Square has a number of nice shops, as well as a few grassy areas for Bowser to explore. Although Princeton is no longer a sleepy little college town, the residential atmosphere of The Peacock Inn along with its proximity to town, create the feeling among many guests that they are visiting the Princeton that existed many years ago.

PRINCETON MARRIOTT HOTEL

201 Village Blvd.
Princeton Forestal Village
Princeton, New Jersey 08540
(800) 228-9290, (609) 452-7900
General Manager: John Moore, Jr.
Rooms: 300 doubles
Rates: Doubles $125-145
Payment: AE, CB, DC, MC, and VISA
Children: Welcome
Dogs: Well-behaved dogs are welcome
Open: All year

Princeton is an ideal place to stop, whether visiting Princeton University, traveling west toward picturesque Bucks County, or taking a brief break en route to Philadelphia or New York City. While this is a Marriott Hotel, it is a moderately upscale version of what most would expect and offers many of the amenities not found in a motel, including a concierge floor. Moreover, the hotel is part of a small village complex that houses shops and restaurants.

Within the hotel's six-story brick facade, the light and airy reception area and lounge are spacious and inviting due to both the vaulted glass ceilings and the extensive indoor planting arrangements. Just outside, an intimate terrace with dark green chairs and tables set under white umbrellas, creates a festive atmosphere. Also located on the ground floor are a variety of dining and entertainment options ranging from the casual Village Green Restaurant to a Japanese restaurant, Mikado. The latter has several Teppan Yaki chefs who prepare a full array of authentic entrees.

The guest bedrooms are quite similar to one another in both layout and in their decor, which boasts Sheraton-style reproduction furnishings and brass accents. Subtle earth tones, ranging from rust to muted forest greens, make up the color scheme. Bathrooms are good sized, with separate dressing areas, and offer a full complement of toiletries. Those who are searching for chambers with a more sophisticated look and who want a slightly higher level of services and amenities may request a room on the concierge floor. This semi-private floor is available through key access only. In the morning, a complimentary Continental breakfast is available to concierge level guests in the sitting area, a convenience for those who do not want to eat in the restaurant. In the afternoon, there are a variety of hors d'oeuvres available here, as well as an honor bar.

Regardless of room choice, everyone is invited to use the health club facilities. An indoor/outdoor swimming pool and whirlpool are situated just off the reception area. In addition to its ability to accommodate swimmers in any season, the structure for the pool has also won several architectural awards for its unique design. A fitness center is located adjacent to this facility for those who want to workout before or after their swim.

Guests will enjoy taking their canine cohorts for walks around the Forrestal Village, as well as through any one of the lovely parks in Princeton. Others may want to explore the beautiful Princeton University campus, or take advantage of any of the entertainment options. This could include a live performance at the McCarter Theater or a sporting event at Baker Rink or Jadwin Gymnasium. The Princeton Marriott is well situated to allow visitors easy access to just about anything Princeton has to offer.

DELAWARE

TEMBO BED AND BREAKFAST

100 Laurel Street
Rehoboth Beach, Delaware 19971
(302) 227-3360
Host: Gerry Cooper
Rooms: 6 doubles
Rates: $55-110
Payment: Personal checks
Children: Over twelve years of age are welcome
Dogs: Welcome with prior notice from November through March provided the
    dog is not left alone in the bedroom
Open: All year

Those who know anything about Rehobeth, usually associate it with the summertime. While many enjoy basking on the beach, in the warmth of the sun, others know that the time to truly enjoy this charming coastal community is during the off-season. Visitors like meandering through the picturesque parks, wandering along the sandy beaches, and exploring the interesting shops, which remain relatively uncrowded throughout the fall, winter, and spring months. For those whose travel plans bring them to Rehoboth, or for those who think it might be an ideal retreat, we highly recommend a stay at the Tembo Bed & Breakfast. Situated just a block or so from the beach, this charming two-story, white shingled "beach cottage" rests under a canopy of shade trees in a quiet residential neighborhood. It was originally built in 1935 as a summer cottage for a railroad conductor and his family. Today, this lovely home has been thoughtfully updated and refurbished, which is one of the many reasons guests are certain to enjoy their stay.

A walkway leads to the cozy enclosed front porch set with rocking chairs and a porch swing. Just beyond the front door new arrivals will emerge into the living room, one of the more inviting chambers in the house. Setting the tone for the rest of the B&B, the lower portions of the walls in this room are defined by vertical boards, which encircle the central brick fireplace. The early American furnishings are often draped with calico blankets and rest upon the braided area rugs. A wonderful collection of waterfowl carvings and elephant (tembo) memorabilia is scattered throughout the room. To the rear of the B&B is the kitchen, where Gerry prepares a Continental breakfast for her guests each morning. Starting with orange juice and a fresh fruit salad, guests are also treated to homemade scones, muffins, toasted bagels and cream cheese along with an assortment of healthy cereals. Should there be an unseasonably warm day, Gerry often suggests that this meal be taken out on the sunny front porch.

Of the six bedrooms available, two are located on the first floor, and the rest on the second. Most of them are quite light and decorated with plush wall-to-wall carpeting. Family heirlooms coupled with antique furnishings fill the rooms, and often include inviting rocking chairs and comfortable armchairs. The wood-paneled Tembo Room is perhaps the nicest of the accommodations, as it is also filled with antiques and has a private bathroom. The king-size bed, found here and in many of the other bedrooms, was designed by a local craftsman to easily break down into twin beds should an overnight guest request it. Upstairs, the Blue and Aqua rooms are similarly furnished but offer pretty views of the old stone church just across the way. The remaining Yellow, Green, and Simba Rooms each provide equally comfortable accommodations. Gerry's special touches are what make this B&B especially appealing for most guests. Her bed linens are hand-ironed, 200-count cotton percale, the bedrooms all have small refrigerators for storing snacks and drinks, and she provides electric heating blankets for her guests in the cooler months. The only potential drawback for some, is that five of the bedrooms share one bathroom.

After enjoying a good night's sleep, many people opt for an early morning stroll on the beach. The main beach in town does not allow dogs on it from April to October; however, there are a number of beaches in the nearby state parks that have recently lifted their dog restrictions, after being petitioned by the year-round residents. Upon returning from their jaunt, guests are bound to notice the small paths along either side of the house that lead to a charming back yard and an enclosed beach-shower annex. In addition to investigating the seaside community, visitors will also find there are such diversions as miniature golf, water slides, amusement parks, and great areas to bicycle, fish, walk, and swim (weather permitting).

In talking with Gerry, it is clear she has a true love for animals and expects them to treat her home like their own. She encourages guests to bring their dog to breakfast or enjoy a fire in the living room during the afternoon or evening hours. Because the B&B is small, this becomes a little difficult when Gerry has a full house, which is why she requests that those traveling with a dog visit during the off-season. Dogs are also restricted from the boardwalk and on the main beach "in season" making it far more enjoyable for everyone involved if they pay a visit to Rehoboth and the Tembo B&B during the quieter months of the year.

MARYLAND

LOEWS ANNAPOLIS HOTEL

126 West Street
Annapolis, Maryland 21401
(800) 23-LOEWS, (410) 263-7777, Fax: (410) 263-0084
General Manager: Thomas A. Negri
Rooms: 217 doubles, 111 suites
Rates: Doubles $110-165, Suites $300
Payment: AE, CB, DC, MC, and Visa
Children: Welcome, those under 17 years of age are free of charge when staying
     in their parents' room
Dogs: Small dogs are welcome with prior approval
Open: All year

The name Annapolis has long been synonymous with the distinguished U.S. Naval Academy. Newcomers will also be surprised by the city's strong historical flavor, found along cobblestone streets that are lined with lovely pre-revolutionary Georgian-style homes. Additionally, the scenic harbor area is rimmed by quaint shops, restaurants, and an interesting historic neighborhood. Situated in the midst of this Capitol city, is the Loews Annapolis Hotel.

Tucked behind black iron gates, the hotel's entrance is dominated by a sprawling brick courtyard softened by lacy trees and dense ground cover. The expansive lobby features the reception area which opens into the nautically decorated Weather Rail Lounge and Oyster Bar situated across the way. A glimpse into the room reveals a long, richly glowing teak bar lined with bentwood stools and colorful signal flags hanging from the ceiling. The strong nautical theme is present throughout the hotel, and is particularly evident in the atrium lobby where a dozen or so large glass cases contain assorted ship's models. The charming and excellent Corinthian Restaurant is also situated just off this atrium. Here, subtle earth-tones are not only used for the wall treatments, but also for the comfortable armchairs and intimate booths. Linen covered tables adorned with fresh flowers are visually separated from one another by arrangements of potted trees and plants. The extensive Continental cuisine is highlighted by fresh seafood. Some of the delectable appetizers are the lobster spring rolls, Creole seafood gumbo, or the braised calamari with crab meat, basil, spinach, and tomato. The lemon-baked crab cakes top the dinner menu, as do specials that often include the Annapolis-style bouillabaisse. Of course, the pan-seared duck breast with a merlot cherry sauce, the roasted rack of lamb with a port wine and rosemary sauce, or the salmon en papiotte with a basil butter are other favorite classic selections for many patrons.

After a filling meal, the short trip upstairs to the guest rooms is very appealing. Grass-papered walls line the hallways that wend along the central atrium to the bedrooms. Although the hotel is a contemporary structure, the guest chambers vary in size, amenities, and the views that they afford. The good-sized standard rooms are furnished in the style of many fine hotels, including comfortable sofas and wing chairs, covered in a variety of soft, earth-tone fabrics. Armoires conceal both the television and the honor bar. The large modern bathrooms have not been overlooked and offer a complete selection of toiletries. Those who are searching for a little additional sense of security and luxury, may be interested in reserving a specialty room on the Concierge floors, where the bedrooms and suites are even more elegantly decorated and appointed. Guests can expect the same traditional decor in these accommodations, which are furnished with attractive reproductions along with brass accent pieces, and a variety of nautical prints and knickknacks.

While there is much to recommend about the Loews Annapolis Hotel, from the standpoint of service and facilities, much of its appeal also lies in its convenient location. Those unfamiliar with the area, might start their explorations by taking a stroll past Church Circle and the State House, and then head down toward Market Square and the harbor. In addition to an assortment of shops, boutiques, and eateries, most visitors will discover a host of interesting historical attractions along the waterfront. The Visitor Information Center is also located here, providing detailed maps of the Naval Academy, the historic district, and other notable points of interest in the nearby area. Bowser will thoroughly enjoy his trek along the waterfront, as well. A trip to Annapolis would not be complete without a visit to the Naval Academy, and the Loews Annapolis Hotel provides an ideal basis from which to enjoy this landmark and all the other noteworthy sights offered in this wonderful old city.

THE INN AT GOVERNMENT HOUSE

1129 North Calvert Street
Baltimore, Maryland 21202
(410) 539-0566, Fax: (410) 539-0567
Innkeeper: Mariana Palacios
Rooms: 20 doubles
Rates: $125-150
Payment: AE, MC, and Visa
Children: Welcome
Dogs: Small, well-behaved dogs are welcome with prior approval
Open: All year

Baltimore has undergone quite a resurgence over the last few decades, much to the delight of long time residents. In a city that was fast succumbing to urban decay and gentrification, a group of insightful individuals began creating their own bit of history. It was a painstaking process that involved restoring the decaying docks and warehouses of the Inner Harbor and rebuilding downtown Baltimore's charming row houses. In the Otterbein neighborhood, which lay decrepit and abandoned, houses were sold for $1 with the restriction that the purchaser must restore the row house in keeping with its historic integrity. The Inner Harbor, once a scene of decay and vacant sites, is now a bustling hub of activity and a proud reflection of a wonderfully revitalized Baltimore. Today, these projects and the refurbishing of the the downtown area stand as a model for many other cities to follow, one in which history was preserved from certain destruction.

The Inn at Government House, situated in the historic Mount Vernon district, typifies the city's interest in preserving its heritage. The Victorian home was originally constructed in 1889 by a prominent architect for John S. Gilman, the president and director of several banks and companies in the area. In 1897, the house was sold to William Painter, who made his fortune by forming the successful Crown Cork and Seal Company and inventing the bottle cap. Over the years, the house exchanged hands several times until it was finally taken over by the Baltimore Department of Public Recreation, which then moved their offices into the building. They stayed here until 1983, leaving their North Calvert Street location for larger quarters in another part of town. At this point, the city government stepped in and renovated the buildings using 100 trainees from a program for the economically disadvantaged under supervision by those skilled in restoration work. When all was completed, The Society Hill Hotel group took over, thus beginning an innkeeping tradition. Today, the Baltimore International Culinary College oversees the Government House, continuing the tradition of innkeeping, as well as housing one of their two culinary colleges within its confines.

While there is a host of sparkling new inns and hotels in Baltimore which reflect the city's renaissance, those who want a true taste of its history should reserve a room at The Inn at Government House. The carefully refurbished inn is actually comprised of three adjoining townhouses whose centerpiece is John Gilman's original 1889 house, a commanding structure dominated by a three-story turret. The effort that went into uncovering the oak woodwork and inlaid floors is apparent from the moment guests enter this Victorian masterpiece. Intricate wainscotings and paneling are complemented by the William Morris wallpapers in the entry way and a lovely silver and gold leaf chandelier. Additional Victorian chandeliers and sconces illuminate the way as guests are escorted from one sitting room or parlor to the inn's spectacular dining room. Here, new arrivals will undoubtedly be impressed by the magnificent chandelier and the thirteen patterns of wallpaper adorning the dining room walls. For post-dining pursuits, there is the elegant music room. As with all other public rooms in the inn, period antiques rest on handwoven rugs and original lithographs, on loan from the Walters Art Gallery, adorn the walls. The focal point, however, is the carefully restored 140-year old Knobe piano.

Guests find their way to the bedrooms by either ascending an atrium staircase or by taking the elevator, crafted of finely carved wood. The 20 guest chambers vary in size and architectural detail, some even offering original marble fireplaces and stained glass windows. Fine reproductions and original Victorian antiques are accented by period wallpapers outlining the original woodwork. Most of the chambers are bright, with their richly detailed windows framed by fine fabrics. Sleeping arrangements vary, with four poster king-size beds placed in some bedrooms or a pair of double beds and sleep sofas in others. While all of the guest bedrooms are inviting, most people, if given the option, would choose one of the two rooms located in the turret. These offer ample amounts of natural light, as well as interesting architectural detail. Although the inn nicely reflects its Victorian heritage, the bathrooms are more modern affairs, offering hair dryers, cosmetic mirrors, and a fine selection of toiletries. Additional amenities that twentieth century guests appreciate are color televisions, clock radios, and telephones. There are also two suites at the inn which, unfortunately, most guests will never get to see as they are permanently reserved as an official residence for the mayor.

While meals are not served at the inn, guests should expect a rather substantial Continental breakfast to be delivered to their room each morning. The students of the Baltimore International Culinary College prepare a variety of delectable danishes, muffins, and breads that are accompanied by fresh fruit, juice, and coffee or tea. For those who are interested, the inn's dining room can be reserved in advance for elegant private meals or functions. The staff is always eager to be of service as they polish and hone their culinary skills. Along with providing knowledgeable tours of the inn, they are also particularly well-versed in the culinary arts.

Guests and their canine cohorts will undoubtedly want to find out what the new Baltimore has to offer. Expeditions may include visits to the Inner Harbor, the restored downtown area, Johns Hopkins University, or Camden Yards (the home of the Baltimore Orioles). Within walking distance of the inn is the historic Mt. Vernon residential district with its churches and restored row houses. Finally, a visit to Baltimore would not be complete without a sampling of crab cakes found in many of the eateries in the city.

INN AT THE COLONNADE

4 West University Parkway
Baltimore, Maryland 21218
(800) 222-TREE, (410) 235-5400, Fax: (410) 235-5572
Reservations Manager: Bruce Wagner
Rooms: 94 doubles, 31 suites
Rates: Doubles $109-125, Suites $190-500
Payment: AE, DC, DSC, MC, and Visa
Children: Welcome (cribs are available)
Dogs: Welcome with prior notice provided guests sign a waiver and provide a $25 deposit
Open: All year

Some people may be familiar with Baltimore's incredible urban revitalization that has taken place over the last few decades. What was once a great historic city had fallen into decay until the town fathers took matters into their own hands. They began to resurrect the dilapidated row houses and constructed new, attractive office buildings. Perhaps, one of their finest achievements was the complete restoration of the Inner Harbor, an area that was composed of crumbling factories and warehouses, but now has sleek, contemporary buildings and even a yacht basin.

Located just four miles from the Inner Harbor, and right across the street from the famous Johns Hopkins University, visitors will find The Inn at the Colonnade. Opened in 1990, the inn is an attractive modern brick building which is conveniently located by the University's athletic fields. As guests drive up to the rather impressive columned port-cochere, they will be greeted by one of the staff members. Although the facade is impressive, the common rooms are even more so. The main lobby is highlighted by the octagonal rotunda, which is supported by huge maple-hued pillars and richly paneled walls. The Biedermeier-inspired furnishings look especially appropriate under the domed, coffered ceiling that has been hand painted with a stunning mural. The subtle recessed lighting, coupled with the sunlight streaming in through the floor-to-ceiling windows, makes this room a most enjoyable place to relax. Original artwork by 18th-century masters occupy several places on the walls.

After check-in, guests are escorted to their spacious bedrooms. Soft ecru painted walls are adorned with original works of art. The caramel and chocolate brown color scheme is reflected in the patterned carpets, the sleek Biedermeier-inspired headboards, and the tailored bedspreads and pleated dust ruffles. Even the lamps and sofas have clean deliberate lines. The beds, by the way, are all triple sheeted. The hotel offers a video library full of the classics, which can be enjoyed on the cable televisions and VCRs contained in the armoires. The large marble bathrooms have brass fixtures, sometimes a whirlpool, and always offer fine, French milled soaps and shampoos. The separate vanity outside the bathroom is one pleasing aspect, as is the convenience of having three telephones in the chamber. Most guests are impressed with the high level of service they find at the hotel. In the evening, maids come in to replenish room supplies, turn-down the bed, and place gourmet chocolates on the pillows. Arriving guests are also offered home-made chocolate chip cookies. The staff has been known to satisfy unusual requests over the last four years, including satisfying a guest's pang for gourmet jelly beans or providing a meal or special blanket for Bowser.

The hotel's Polo Grill, and the people who staff it, is also exceptional. Patrons may expect a varied appetizer selection, which includes Blue Point oysters, soft shell crab tempura fried with a Chinese black bean sauce, and an American woodland mushroom tartlette that is glazed with fontina cheese and a Madeira wine sauce. The equally tantalizing entrees may include an aged filet mignon with steak mushrooms and shoestring potatoes, venison chops with braised red cabbage, mountain hedge mushrooms, and glazed pears, or sauteed red snapper glazed in a corn crust on Mescalin greens tossed in a raspberry walnut oil vinaigrette. After a "light" dinner, many guests like to indulge in such specialities as the warm peanut butter chocolate chip cheesecake with glazed bananas, a lemon almond tart with almond marange and raspberry coulis, or the unusual butternut squash, blueberry, and toasted almond turnovers with cinnamon raisin ice cream and a caramel sauce.

Guests will find that while there are a myriad of sights and attractions in the Baltimore area, they will probably be quite happy relaxing by the inn's swimming pool. Situated in a rear courtyard, the pool is set under the domed glass roof, which is adjacent to a lounging area bedecked with Italian marble walls, picture windows, and Tivoli lights. The fitness room is well-equipped with a host of exercise machines. For those who are interested in investigating the surrounding area, we can recommend such attractions as the Maritime Museum, National Aquarium, Science Center, Market Center, Washington Monument, Baltimore Zoo, and Fort McHenry. Bowser can certainly accompany his family on many of the expeditions throughout the city or just go for a leisurely walk through Johns Hopkins University campus.

SARKE PLANTATION BED AND BREAKFAST

6033 Todd Point Road
Cambridge, Maryland 21613
(410) 228-7020
Host: Genevieve Finley
Rooms: 3 doubles, 1 suite
Rates: Doubles $50-90, Suite $110
Payment: AE, MC, and Visa
Children: Those over 10 years of age are welcome
Dogs: Welcome with advance notice and prior approval
Open: All year except New Year's Eve

Those travelers who are interested in staying at a waterside B&B, in a sprawling country setting, will find The Sarke Plantation to be a good choice. Situated off a meandering country lane, newly arriving guests will follow a long driveway, lined by a split-rail fence and mature trees, to the sprawling house which is set behind flowering trees and shrubs. This bucolic setting is made even more picturesque by the huge red barn set off to the right, which stands on the banks of the Choptank River.

A sprawling grey wraparound porch fronts the traditional white clapboard and green shuttered home. Step inside the foyer and guests will come upon the small billiards room. Toward the rear of the first floor, is a cavernous beamed-ceiling living room with comfortable furnishings and some elegant pieces that include a grand piano and tall clock. The brick fireplace is usually ablaze in the winter months, creating the perfect atmosphere for either reading a good book, listening to the stereo, or watching a little television. French doors lead from the living room to the expansive lawn, where many often congregate on warm summer evenings.

The guest bedrooms can all be found on the second floor of the house. The most popular and charming of these chambers is the master bedroom, which lies just above the living room and is nearly as large as its first floor counterpart. This light and airy pastel yellow chamber has a hardwood floor adorned with an Oriental rug, and offers guests the comfort of a queen-size bed and the charm of a working fireplace. Lovely views of the grounds and river can be seen through the handful of windows that grace the room. There are two other bedrooms just around the corner from this chamber, which are furnished with country antiques, family collectibles, and pairs of single beds. While these are smaller than the master bedroom, they are equally as comfortable and inviting. Another option for families is the suite of two adjoining bedrooms. One of these chambers has a double bed and a love seat that folds out to a couch bed, while the other is furnished with a pair of twin-size beds. While this might sound spacious, the combination of wood paneled walls and wall-to-wall carpeting creates the illusion that it is really smaller than the other accommodations. Some B&B travelers may also find that the rather plain decor and Spartan furnishings make this suite a slightly less appealing choice than the other three accommodations.

Each morning, guests are served an expanded Continental breakfast in the breakfast room, which has been painted a cheerful yellow with royal blue accents. The setting is made all the more interesting by the lovely views of the grounds and river and by the local artwork that Mrs. Finley has displayed on the walls. Afterwards, many people choose to take a leisurely walk through the 27 acres of property that surround the B&B. Here, there is an abundance of waterfowl and small animal life waiting to be discovered. A large swimming pool is also available to B&B guests, although many opt to wait until the afternoon for taking a dip and instead use their morning to recline on one of the porches to read the paper.

We should make it clear that the Sarke Plantation B&B is an unpretentious casual place, where guests come to enjoy the rural atmosphere and pleasant surroundings. It also offers an affordable weekend getaway for anyone wanting to escape a busy work week. We know that Bowser will certainly enjoy a change of venue as well, appreciating the chance to romp around the countryside with his/her human counterpart.

THE COLUMBIA INN

Wincopin Circle
Columbia, Maryland 21044
(800) 638-2817, (410) 730-3900, Fax: (410) 730-1290
General Manager: Ken Pinchak
Rooms: 300 rooms
Rates: Doubles $69-125, Suites $225
Payment: AE, DC, MC, and Visa
Children: Welcome (cribs and cots are available)
Dogs: Welcome in the three-story section of the hotel
Open: All year

The term "inn" has become somewhat of a misnomer over the years, used by both the traditional Bed and Breakfast accommodations, and the larger chain hotels. Somewhere in the middle of this spectrum lies the Columbia Inn, ideally situated between Baltimore, Maryland and Washington, D.C., providing travelers with a myriad of recreational and cultural diversions from which to choose. Although this is a fairly standard, mid-sized hotel in an executive park, it has the additional appeal of its surrounding woodlands and beautiful lake.

The ten-story main building and its adjoining three-story structure are located on the banks of Lake Kittamaqundi, thereby providing many of the common areas and guest rooms with wonderful lakeside views. Upon entering the hotel, guests will find a lush, sun-splashed open-air atrium rising ten floors and encircled by guest chambers. Just off the atrium, on the ground floor, are the hotel's two restaurants, Peppers and the Waterside. The latter is the more formal of the two, with its white tablecloths, fine china, pretty views, and Continental menu. Entree selections range from Chateaubriand and filet mignon bernaise to blackened redfish or duck with a Grand Marnier sauce. Waterside is also convenient, because after a wonderful meal it is a short walk back to the room.

Those traveling with Bowser are asked to stay in the rooms located in the three-story building adjacent to the tower. While this section of the hotel does not offer suites, the individual bedrooms are nonetheless decorated in the same manner as those in the main building. The decor is dominated by Scandinavian style furnishings, earth tone fabrics, and brass accents. Aside from the somewhat Spartan surroundings, each bedroom is extremely clean, appointed with color televisions and clock radios, and offers individual thermostats and good-sized bathrooms. While the Tower Rooms have a somewhat crisper decor and more panoramic view of the lake and woodlands, the chambers in the three-story inn section also provide scenic vistas. There are also subtle touches that guests appreciate, such as chocolates left by the bed in the evenings and a Continental breakfast brought to the room in the mornings. Laundry, valet, and concierge services are also available to guests, services that people usually associate with luxury hotels.

While guests will surely be most comfortable lounging around in their own rooms, many might also choose to sample some of the multitude of athletic diversions made available through the Columbia Inn. While there are plenty of areas for Bowser to explore, there are even more human-oriented activities available to guests. There is an outdoor swimming pool on the premises, as well as the 18-hole Hobbitt's Glen Golf Course, two tennis clubs, an indoor swim center, a racquetball club, and a full-service athletic club within easy driving distance of the hotel. The ice skating and roller skating rink provide additional distractions. Guests and their canine cohorts will appreciate the green spaces around the hotel, and might even choose to visit nearby Wilde Lake, which offers one and a half miles of paths for running and walking. This is a very dog-friendly area, making an overnight stay as easy on Bowser as it is on his/her two-legged friends.

GROSS' COATE 1658

11300 Gross' Coate Road
Easton, Maryland 21601
(800) 580-0802, (410) 819-0802, Fax: (410) 819-0803
Hosts: Jonathan and Molly Ginn
Rooms: 6 suites
Rates: $295 ($395 with gourmet brunch)
Payment: AE, MC, and Visa
Children: Welcome
Dogs: Welcome
Open: All year

Situated on the eastern shore of Maryland, the charming town of Easton is one of the quaint country villages lining the more than 600 miles of shoreline that runs through Talbot County. Small, charming cottages and gracious old manor houses mix comfortably here, in much the same way that they did in the 18th-century. In 1760, William Tilghman built a brick Georgian manor on a peninsula situated at the confluence of the Wye River, Gross Creek, and the Lloyd Creek. The name Gross' Coate goes back even further in time to 1658, when Roger Gross had the property patented to him by Lord Baltimore. The term "coate," loosely translated, means cottage and refers to the original cottage that was built on the property. One of the many endearing characteristics about the Gross' Coate 1658 of today is that only a few additions have been made to this expansive 28-room manor house over the years, allowing guests the luxury of stepping back in time with the subtleties of a few modern conveniences. Since Molly and Jonathan Ginn purchased the property ten years ago, they have seen to it that the historical integrity of the estate has remained intact.

Guests have been known to arrive at Gross' Coate 1658 by many means, motor yacht, helicopter, and yes, even by automobile. It is nearly impossible not to be immediately impressed by the magnificence of this 63-acre waterfront estate and at the same time be enveloped by its sense of solitude and intimacy. The manor house, the centerpiece of the property, is an elegant structure highlighted by a large white wraparound porch that is accented by double-columned supports and a veranda set up with green rocking chairs. While the cavernous foyer is dramatic, guests are usually drawn through this space to the airy sitting rooms and common areas, which hold a smattering of English antiques and reproductions. The dining room is equally refined, with the exquisite furnishings set on black walnut hardwood floors crafted from trees salvaged after a hurricane. Each of these spaces is dominated by floor-to-ceiling windows — windows unadorned by draperies as the Ginns felt they would merely provide a distraction to the unparalleled views of the grounds and water. There is a large, gracefully curved staircase that ascends two floors to the upstairs parlors and library. The furnishings and decor in these spaces is lovely and gracious, while, at the same time, maintaining a true sense of comfort.

The guest chambers range from an elegant suite with a charming sitting area to a sprawling six-bedroom suite with two bathrooms. Deviating ever so slightly from the decorative theme on the main floors, the suites are nicely furnished with a combination of traditional reproductions and a few antique accent pieces resting on wall-to-wall carpeting. Fresh flower arrangements, picked from the extensive gardens that surround the B&B, add both color and a welcome personal touch to each of the chambers. There are 16 fireplaces at Gross' Coate, with many of these found in the bed chambers, further adding a romantic element to this most distinctive retreat. In many ways, an abundance of ornate furnishings would detract from the suites' inherent appeal, namely the incredible views of the water and gardens.

While the main house offers just about every comfort one could imagine, including a summer kitchen that has been converted into a tavern, the outbuildings on the property are also worth investigating. One brick building is a garden house (where guests can create an herbal wreath or a jar of potpourri), another a smokehouse, and a third a carriage house. The latter is occupied by the Ginns, who refurbished it by utilizing lumber from some of the old barns on the estate. They approached many of the other renovations to the buildings in the same manner, often using salvaged materials from older structures, which, thankfully, has helped to preserve the overall historic ambiance of the property. One prime example is the latticed pool house, which was formerly the dairy for the property, but today guests would be hard pressed to ascertain its origin.

One of the many wonderful things about staying at Gross' Coate is that guests never feel overwhelmed by their surroundings or their hosts. They are free to use the house as their own, and the grounds as they were intended. A quiet walk through the estate will reveal grazing horses, waterfowl taking flight over each of the four ponds, and lovely flower and herb gardens resplendent in full summer bloom. Some choose to sit at the end of the inn's dock and try crabbing or just spend their time daydreaming as the boats glide by the peninsula. Those who are yearning for a more energetic pace, might consider a swim in the pool or a challenging game of golf on the 18-hole pitch and putt course (a converted 20-acre pasture). An array of lawn sports including croquet, volleyball, and badminton are also available to guests. Equestrians will be interested to learn that Molly breeds and trains thoroughbred race horses on the premises. In the fall, many horse enthusiasts bring their own horses and join the Wye River Hunt Club for their autumn fox hunts.

With so much to do, many like to get a jump on the day by getting up early. Awaiting these eager souls is a wonderful Continental breakfast. Several hours later, there is the often anticipated brunch, which is truly exquisite. Molly likes to serve dishes that are representative of the Chesapeake Bay area, creating gourmet treats around staples such as salmon, rock fish, soft shell crab, jumbo shrimp, and backfin crab. Those whose tastes lean away from seafood, can let Molly know in advance and she will be more than happy to create something equally as tantalizing for the landlubbers. In addition to using fresh, seasonal, and exotic fruits to create some of the salads, Molly also combines a variety of delicate greens for her tossed salads. During the early evening hours, many are drawn to the charming, old-fashioned tavern. Here, a fire is often blazing and a bar is well-stocked with libations to ease guests into the dinner hour or off to bed.

There are many reasons to visit the remarkable Chesapeake Bay region, and there are no accommodations that offer as magnificent a setting, as wonderful an old-world ambiance, and such a thoroughly unpretentious and yet most welcoming atmosphere as Gross' Coate 1658.

THE GARDEN COTTAGE
And Sinking Springs Herb Farm

234 Blair Shore Road
Elkton, Maryland 21921
(410) 398-5566
Hosts: Ann and Bill Stubbs
Rooms: 1 cottage
Rates: $85
Payment: MC and Visa
Children: Welcome
Dogs: Welcome with advance notice and prior approval
Open: All year

The Garden Cottage and Sinking Springs Herb Farm is set in the Maryland countryside, amidst winding country roads that pass by corn fields and rolling meadows. A long gravel driveway leads to the 280-year old grey clapboard main house shaded by a massive sycamore. Guests are often surprised to discover that the homestead has always been in Bill's family. It was originally a two-room log cabin surrounded by 150 acres, but over the years a number of additions took place and some of the acreage was sold. Today, the circular driveway brings guests to the rear of the house, where there is a small parking area. This is, in many ways, the most picturesque part of the property with a pair of old barns, a pond teaming with ducks and geese, a lovely herb garden, and a charming cottage. The expansive herb garden is the focal point of the grounds, with fragrant flower beds and assorted herb gardens that are bisected by slate pathways. To the rear of this botanical showplace is a red barn, where guests will find Ann's charming gift shop and Mux'n Room, a spacious chamber, where she creates beautiful arrangements and other collectibles from her dried flowers and herbs. Ann can usually be found here, or in her gardens, checking on the many varieties of plants she grows.

As busy as Ann might be with her horticultural projects, she loves visitors and enjoys showing them to the natural barn board cottage, which is surrounded by rock and perennial gardens. As guests ascend the stairs to the small front porch, Ann will probably want to give them a brief history about the cottage and how it came to this farm. It was lifted onto two steel beams and transported by truck from their old home to its current location. The cottage survived the move intact, except for some crumbling at the base of the chimney. Once guests step inside this cozy abode, it becomes easy to understand why Ann felt so strongly about moving the cottage. The sitting room's walls are made up of rough hewn wood trimmed in cream, creating a rustic ambiance. The rebuilt brick fireplace is enhanced by the wall behind it which has been painted a dark, cherry red. The eclectic furnishings are comfortable, and include a pair of side chairs set around the breakfast table, along with a scattering of antiques. Guests are free to create meals and snacks using the microwave oven found on top of the small refrigerator. A high shelf holds a handful of decorative plates. The tiled floors lead from this space directly into the tiny bedroom, which is dominated by a brass bed. The staircase, in one corner of the room, is filled with a family of teddy bears. The equally diminutive bathroom is very clean and offers soft cotton towels.

Each morning, guests may choose from one of the four menu items that Ann offers for breakfast or, with a little advance notice, they may request something all together different. Some of the standard options are whole wheat pancakes with blueberry, peach, or raspberry sauces, seven grain French toast, or the Bristol Farm oatmeal that is actually a combination of grains sweetened with apple juice and cooked with diced pear or apple. The eggs can be served poached, scrambled, or as an omelet. This meal may be enjoyed inside, on the front porch, or in the gazebo by the herb garden.

Afterwards, some people might want to explore the 130 acres of land surrounding the B&B, finding the assorted herbal and perennial treasures in the gardens, or visiting the other animals on the property. Many people also express an interest in touring the 275 year old home and learning a little more about its history. As we mentioned in the beginning, there is an enormous Bristoll Sycamore tree, which shades the main house. With a circumference of 20 feet and branches that spread out some 80 feet, experts knew it must be old. Just how old was always in question until it was discovered the tree dates back to 1578, or roughly to the time of Queen Elizabeth I.

History aside, guests are certain to find that the cozy accommodations, abundance of space, and picture postcard gardens will undoubtedly make their stay at the Garden Cottage & Sinking Springs Herb Farm a most enjoyable and rewarding one.

KEMP HOUSE INN

Box 638
412 Talbot Street
St. Michaels, Maryland 21663
(410) 745-2243
Innkeepers: Diane and Steve Cooper
Rooms: 7 doubles, 1 cottage
Rates: Doubles $65-90, Cottage $110
Payment: DSC, MC, and Visa
Children: Welcome (no cribs or cots are available)
Dogs: Dogs are welcome in the first floor rooms and in the cottage
Open: All year

St. Michaels is a charming village located on the banks of Mile River, with captivating views of the Chesapeake Bay. Traveling along the shore, visitors are apt to become enamored with the quaint harbors dotted with small boats and ships navigating their way up and down the bay. The scenic village centers and pastoral farm settings merely add to the overall tranquil ambiance of the region.

The Kemp House Inn can be found in the heart of St. Michaels' town center behind a white split-rail fence. Dating back to 1805, this attractive brick house has been painted white and the windows framed with contrasting black shutters. Guests enter the parking area, situated behind the inn, and will notice the crunching sound of the car tires running over the crushed shells that cover the driveway. A flower-lined path leads to the front porch, where a handful of white wicker rockers and chairs tempt weary travelers. Most new arrivals like to get settled before exploring the inn or making themselves comfortable on the outdoor porch. Thus, after checking in, guests and their canine cohorts will be escorted to either one of the first floor rooms or out to the private cottage. Along the way, some might notice the attractive brick flooring found throughout the first level. It has been covered with braided throw rugs, making it all the more inviting.

In keeping with the house's historical nature, the guest rooms are decorated with many period furnishings. Double- and queen-size handmade four poster beds are adorned with down pillows and covered by handmade quilts, and many are high enough to accommodate a trundle bed underneath. In one first floor bedroom, wing chairs are placed within close proximity to the fireplace. Dried wreaths decorate many of the fireplace mantles, antique sconces provide subdued lighting, and tab curtains frame some of the original windows. The second and third floor chambers offer wide-board floors, many of these have been painted or stenciled and then covered with braided rugs. In several of the chambers, the sinks have been retro-fitted into wooden tables and chests to further create an air of authenticity. The two third floor chambers are set into the eaves of the house and are the most historic in terms of their overall decor and furnishings. To the rear of the property is the intimate cottage set in the midst of a small yard. This is perhaps the best place to stay with Bowser. Cathedral ceilings in the cottage create a sense of spaciousness, and in fact there is enough room here for a pineapple finial two poster bed, a love seat, and an assortment of collectibles. One of the many thoughtful touches in the bedrooms is the nightshirts, which guests are welcome to use during their stay.

Guests look forward to the Continental breakfast of fresh muffins, cheese, and fruit which they may take in their bedroom or on the private, outdoor brick patio, surrounded by a garden and hedge. After a delightful repast, some choose to walk a few blocks to the water's edge and watch the fishing boats head out for the day. Others decide to explore the town center or just meander through this residential neighborhood. The Kemp House is a charming B&B and provides a terrific central location for exploring much of the Chesapeake Bay, whether by traveling the back roads on bicycle or by car, or chartering a boat and seeing these majestic waterways up close.

WASHINGTON D.C.

FOUR SEASONS HOTEL

2800 Pennsylvania Ave N.W.
(Georgetown) Washington, D.C. 20007
(800) 332-3442, (202) 342-0444; Fax: (202) 944-2076
General Manager: Stan Bromley
Rooms: 167 doubles, 30 suites
Rates: Doubles $295-345, Suites $575-2,000
Payment: AE, CB, DC, ENR, JCB, MC, and VISA
Children: Welcome, children under 18 years of age are free of charge
Dogs: Welcome, but must be leashed in the public areas
Open: All year

Washington D.C., aside from being the seat of our national government, has always been a terrific vacation destination offering visitors a plethora of historic and cultural sights. What some people seek when visiting this bustling political hub, is an intimate hotel, close to the major attractions but insulated from the congestion and noise of the city. The Four Seasons Hotel is not only situated just minutes from the White House, Smithsonian Museums, Lincoln Memorial, and National Gallery of Art, but is also right on the edge of Georgetown. An unobtrusive brick facade and small courtyard mark the entrance to the hotel. Just inside the front door, guests will walk along thick carpets that line the elongated wood paneled entry until they reach the reception desk. Inside the lobby is a mix of the contemporary and the traditional, with modern recessed light fixtures and sleek lines accented by formal French armchairs, elegant writing desks, and antique secretaries displaying collections of fine china. The Garden Terrace can be found to the rear of the hotel, where guests may relax in tranquil surroundings overlooking the rock gardens and the Chesapeake & Ohio Canal. Many people, guests and locals alike, spend quiet Sunday afternoons here, reclining on the soft chintz-covered sofas, listening to the pianist, and enjoying the high tea. Others prefer having a cocktail here before heading downstairs to Au Beaux Champs, which specializes in French cuisine and fine service. Late evenings are often spent in the hotel's private nightclub, Club Desiree, where guests are extended privileges during their stay.

At the end of a long day, the bedrooms are particularly inviting. This hotel stresses service, truly going out of its way to satisfy any request, no matter how offbeat it might be. The usual nightly turndown and valet services are appreciated, as is the morning paper that can be delivered to the room. The furnishings are understated, although reflecting a good deal of sophistication. Pale greens and peaches might be the color scheme for one chamber, while another is decorated with bright floral chintzes. The furnishings are traditional, but with sleek, almost contemporary lines. Writing desks are outfitted with an assortment of stationery and the armoires open to reveal color televisions and honor bars. The various bedsteads range from one with a Biedermeier-inspired headboard to another that has a canopy with fabrics draped from the corners of the faux four-posters. The bathrooms are also noteworthy, offering ample space and appointed with terry cloth robes, hair dryers, a secondary telephone, and a host of toiletries. The windows all open, revealing varying views of the Chesapeake & Ohio Canal, Rock Creek Park, Georgetown, or the brick courtyard (illuminated in the evenings by small white lights laced through the trees).

Guests of the Four Seasons, as well as some local residents, appreciate the extensive services of the hotel's fitness club. Here, three floors of Nautilus, StairMaster, LifeCycle, and other electronic workout equipment will definitely keep people in shape. The lap pool is naturally lit by skylights and afterwards the whirlpool, sauna, and steam facilities are most rejuvenating. Bowser should appreciate his/her leisurely strolls through the picturesque Georgetown neighborhoods and window shopping in the various stores and boutiques that are found throughout the area. There is even a wonderful boutique pet store within a block or two of the hotel. The Four Seasons Hotel also provides a jogging map which outlines different scenic routes through Georgetown and beyond to the Washington Monument, Lady Bird Johnson Park, and Key Bridge.

ANA HOTEL

2401 M Street, N.W.
Washington, D.C. 20037
(800) ANA-HOTELS, (202) 429-2400, Fax: (202) 457-5010
General Manager: Hans Bruland
Rooms: 405 doubles, 10 suites
Rates: Doubles $205-355, Suites $600-1,400
Payment: AE, CB, DC, ENR, JCB, MC, and Visa
Children: Welcome (cribs, cots, and babysitters are available)
Dogs: Small, well-trained dogs are welcome
Open: All year

Those who are visiting Washington, D.C. and want to be close to many of the major attractions without being situated in the midst of the traffic and congestion, should consider the Ana Hotel. The nine-story building is located in the city's fashionable West End, on the other side of the Potomac River from the quaint Georgetown area and just a short distance from The White House, the Smithsonian Institute, Washington Monument, National Gallery, and National Air and Space Museum. This is a first class, luxury hotel, which offers guests as much in the way of amenities as it does in its prime location.

Residing on the corner of M and 24th Streets, the building has crisp, clean lines and is rather contemporary in design, built of stone and topped with a verdigris roof. Arriving guests drive under a port-cochere, lined with potted flowers and small trees, to unload their belongings. Once inside the expansive reception area, guests' eyes are not drawn to either the main desk or adjacent lounge, but instead to the impressive two-story glass loggia. Italian marble floors, inlaid with black tile lead into this inviting gallery, which overlooks the lovely garden courtyard through a floor-to-ceiling combination of paned and picture windows. Intimate seating arrangements are interspersed with huge, potted ficus trees set alongside brass tables topped with plants and pottery lamps. The soft colors in the patterned carpet reflect the teal green and pastel yellow used in the delicate floral fabrics of the Biedermeier-inspired sofas. New arrivals are also drawn out to the brick courtyard, particularly in the warmer months, when it is outfitted with hunter green umbrella tables that look out over the boxwood hedges and flower gardens surrounding the central fountain. The courtyard is a great spot for a light lunch, or for sipping a cool beverage.

The lovely Colonnade Restaurant, however, is the place to go for dinner. This is truly an opulent space — its Doric columns and walls of paned windows support the white coffered ceilings. An elevated center seating area, accented in coral pink, is set under an airy atrium. Service is clearly a priority here, and even with intimate alcoves situated on two levels, the attentive staff easily manages to meet each patron's needs. The ever-changing menu offers tantalizing dishes with asparagus Napoleon in a roasted red pepper coulis, a crab and corn cake in a vermouth tomato sauce, or the smoked shrimp with a spicy peanut sauce and pineapple chutney comprising just a few of the many appetizer selections. These might be followed by entrees such as the grilled swordfish accompanied with a mango, cucumber, melon and lime relish, the grilled filet of beef with a Roquefort butter and fried red onions, or the marinated lamb with a banana almond chutney. After dinner drinks can be enjoyed in the formal lounge, where a pianist often entertains the guests.

At the end of the evening, guests will return to their room to find the beds turned down and their linens and towels replenished. The decor is subdued, with camel color tones serving as the primary backdrop for the floral fabrics. Bedsteads have quilted spreads that match the draperies and swags which frame the wall of windows. Some of our favorite chambers were those which faced the central courtyard, where the view of the gardens and the sound of the cascading fountain were especially appealing. A Chippendale armchair might be outfitted with an ottoman, while an oversized writing desk is an ideal location for those with some work to wrap up. The bedrooms are softly illuminated by brass lamps, whose light reflects off the lustrous finish of the reproduction furnishings. A centrally-located armoire holds the television and well-stocked mini bar. Three telephones are available for added convenience, including one in the bathroom. The modern bathrooms, as one would expect, are bathed in marble and feature brass accents. The terry cloth robes and fine array of toiletries are welcome bathing additions.

Those who prefer an aerobic workout before their bath, might want to investigate the huge fitness center on the premises. This 16,000 square-foot facility, is situated on the Mezzanine level and offers guests everything from squash and racquet ball courts to a lap pool, saunas, massages, and fully-equipped weight rooms. Those who are interested in a more relaxed diversion may prefer a stroll through Georgetown or a visit to any one of the countless museums and monuments in the Washington D.C. area. In addition to providing guests with detailed information about the city, the Concierge also has up-to-date information about any special events or seasonal attractions that might be of interest to visitors and their canine companions.

THE HAY-ADAMS HOTEL

One Lafayette Square
Washington, DC 20006
(800) 424-5054, (202) 638-6600, Fax: (202) 638-2716
Manager: Erst Aedy
Rooms: 134 doubles, 21 suites
Rates: Doubles $175-390, Suites $495-1,200
Payment: AE, DC, MC, DSC, and Visa
Children: Welcome (cribs, cots, and babysitters are available)
Dogs: Small and medium size well-behaved dogs are welcome with prior
    notification.
Open: All year

In 1883, good friends John Hay and Henry Adams purchased adjoining lots across from Lafayette Square, The White House, and St. John's Church. They decided to build two homes here and asked architect Henry Hobson Richardson, who was renowned for his Romanesque style of architecture, to design them. Some time after their respective deaths, the buildings were leased to Harry Wardman, a developer in Washington. His firm, the Wardman Company, spent a year-and-a-half and some $900,000 to create the eight story, "U" shaped limestone building. In designing the space, the architect utilized many of the elements found in the original Hay and Adams homes, such as the Tudor detailing, coffered paneling, and the semi-circular entrance drive.

In the spring of 1928 the hotel was ready to open for business. From the beginning, this is where Washington's power brokers and notables congregated. The elegantly decorated and furnished guest rooms had a residential quality to them, with amenities such as kitchens, marble baths, circulating ice water, and huge windows offering magnificent views of the surrounding sights. Over the years, this landmark hosted such notables as Sinclair Lewis, Amelia Earhart, Charles Lindberg, and Ethel Barrymore, as well as countless political figures. Unfortunately, when the Great Depression hit, the numbers of guests dropped off considerably, eventually causing the hotel to fall into disrepair. Over the next 50 years, the property changed hands a number of times until David H. Murdock finally purchased it in 1983 and completely restored it.

What today's guests will discover is a place steeped in tradition, where the architectural details are numerous and the accommodations luxurious. When the literature for the hotel calls itself "an island of civility in a sea of power," they are right on the mark. Upon entering the grandly appointed foyer, guests are immediately impressed with the mix of textures and colors. Beautiful English antiques are set amid richly polished walnut paneling and brass fixtures coupled with intricately plastered ceilings and massive arches. A 17th-century Medici tapestry hangs on one wall and original oil paintings on others.

Upstairs, the bedrooms expand upon the decorative elements found in the public areas. Some of the oversized chambers also have high ceilings, many of which have intricate details set into plaster and French doors leading into sitting rooms outfitted with fireplaces. All are decorated with English chintzes that are coordinated between the bedspreads and draperies. Crystal chandeliers illuminate the individually decorated chambers, which are furnished with elegant reproduction sofas and side chairs. Patrons will also enjoy the lovely bathrooms complete with marble top sinks, long and deep bathtubs, marble walls, and an assortment of lotions and soaps. While many things have changed over the years, the original concept of natural light and interesting views continues to be a hallmark for these bedroom spaces. One local periodical has noted that the rooms at the Hay Adams are "as close as one can get to staying at the White House, short of being invited by the President." With the Hay-Adams Hotel having such unobstructed views of the White House, it seems natural that the Secret Service keep an eye on it. One evening, the Secret Service agents stationed atop the White House noticed, with their infra-red equipment, that there was a questionable object lying on a table in front of a guest's window pointing directly at the White House. Having trouble identifying it, they sent some agents over to investigate. Much to everyone's amusement, with the exception of the Secret Service, the mystery object turned out to be a simple camera with a telephoto lens.

At the end of the day, guests can easily find something to their liking at any of the intimate restaurants in the hotel. The English Grill offers authentic British fare, all within the cozy atmosphere of a traditional English pub. Those who prefer a proper English tea, will find it served each afternoon in one of the hotel's intimate, wood paneled alcoves. Here, a pianist plays soft background music, a fire is lit in the fireplace, and guests are grouped in intimate sitting areas, enjoying the exotic teas accompanied by the traditional scones, crumpets, and tea sandwiches. Many power breakfasts and lunches have been enjoyed over the years in the bright and cheery Adams Room. This elegant, sun-filled space has crisp, yellow wall treatments accented by bright floral chintzes and lovely flower arrangements. The more formal John Hay Room is reminiscent of an "English country estate setting" with walnut paneled walls, leaded glass windows, brass chandeliers, Oriental carpets on the floors, and French tapestries adorning the walls. The menu is equally Continental, with entrees including a whole guinea fowl with thyme, herbs, and foie gras, a breast of Long Island duckling with a cushion of sliced apple in puff pastry and a juniper berry sauce, and Atlantic sea scallops accompanied by a walnut sauce. The service and atmosphere provide the perfect complement to the beautifully presented meals.

The hotel is certainly within walking distance of just about every major attraction Washington has to offer. Bowser is certain to love the hotel's proximity to the many open, green spaces that can be found in this section of the city, where he will encounter the locals using the sidewalks for their walking, jogging, or "power strolling."

THE JEFFERSON

Sixteenth and M Streets, N.W.
Washington, D.C. 20036-3295
(800) 368-5966, (202) 347-2200, Fax: (202) 331-7982
Managing Director: Elmer Coppoolse
Rooms: 66 doubles, 34 suites
Rates: Doubles $145-250, Suites $180-750
Payment: AE, CB, DC, DSC, ENR, JCB, MC, and Visa
Children: Welcome
Dogs: Smaller dogs welcome with prior notification and a $15 nightly fee
Open: All year

Originally built in 1923 as a private residence, The Jefferson has recently undergone a substantial renovation that lifts the stature of this boutique hotel to even greater heights. Situated just four blocks from the White House, and surrounded by such landmarks as the Supreme Court, the Smithsonian Museums, the Lincoln Memorial, and the National Geographic Society, this eight story U-shaped building lies unobtrusively on the corner of M and 16th streets. Guests enter the hotel by way of an ornately detailed, marble portico topped by a Palladian window that has THE JEFFERSON chiseled above it. Once inside, the breezeway, with its long, domed ceiling, is flanked by a pair of small atriums. The pale marble floors covered with Oriental carpets coupled with the intricate detailing along the cornices and arches create a lovely backdrop for the three intimate sitting areas set in this elongated chamber. The unobtrusive reception area is situated off to the side of the last sitting area, which houses an original portrait of the Marquis de Lafayette resting above its marble fireplace mantel.

The subdued and gracious feeling in the public areas is also reflected in the bedrooms, which all share traditional architectural details such as crown moldings and paneled doors. Each chamber is uniquely designed though, and furnished with a mix of English antiques from the Louis XVth period combined with more traditional Colonial pieces. As newly arriving guests are escorted down the halls leading to their rooms, they will find impressive architectural drawings, lithographs, and portraits lining the walls. Once inside, the fine antiques and reproductions, along with original works of art, lend a residential quality to the bedrooms. Oriental carpets are often found resting on the plush wall-to-wall carpets. Four poster beds are covered with chintz fabrics, while silks and damasks can be found on the upholstered sofas and club chairs. Armoires conceal the televisions and VCRs, along with stereos and CD players. The minibars are well stocked with an intriguing mix of chocolates, snacks, and drinks. Multiple telephone and fax lines allow business to be conducted from just about any corner of the room. The modern bathrooms are crafted from marble and have either porcelain or brass accents, along with a hair dryer, soft terry cloth robes, and an assortment of luxurious toiletries.

Guests who enjoy the clubby atmosphere of the hotel, may wish to pay a visit to the subtly lit Jefferson Restaurant and Lounge for a drink and some intimate dining. The Lounge is a warm, inviting chamber with leather chairs set around small circular tables. The deep crimson walls hold numerous portraits and original works of art, but the primary focus is on the fireplace with the oil painting of a clipper ship hanging above its mantel. The restaurant is headed by executive chef, Will Greenwood, whose constantly changing menu focuses on New Virginia Cuisine. Appetizer selections might include marinated smoked quail with wilted Swiss chard, sweet potatoes, and spiced pecans or spicy pan-fired Chincoteague oysters on braised greens. The entrees range from herb crusted striped bass with shrimp dumplings in a red wine sauce to smoked filet mignon with a dark beer onion sauce and blue cheese walnut butter. The food is delectable, but it is the service that is truly beyond compare, both in the restaurant and throughout the hotel, the staff are exceedingly gracious and hospitable, without being intrusive.

While Bowser will certainly relish the luxurious accommodations at The Jefferson, he/she will undoubtedly prefer meandering through the countless parks, dipping his/her nose in the fountains, and visiting some of the many landmarks that are within walking distance from the hotel. There is also a host of terrific shops to explore along Connecticut Avenue, ranging from Cartier and Polo in addition to the charming cafes and boutiques. Those visitors who are in search of warm, traditional surroundings, attentive staff members, and a central location will find all they need during their stay at The Jefferson.

LOEWS L'ENFANT PLAZA

480 L'Enfant Plaza, SW
Washington, D.C. 20024
(800) 23-LOEWS, (202) 484-1000, Fax: (202) 646-4456
Manager: Ha Skip Hartman
Rooms: 370 doubles and suites
Rates: Doubles $205-235, Suites $370-750
Payment: AE, CB, DC, MC, and Visa
Children: Welcome, those under the age of 18 are free of charge when staying
          with their parents
Dogs: Small, well-behaved dogs are welcome with advance notice and must be
      leashed in the public areas
Open: All year

Washington has long been a bustling political mecca, also housing some of the finest museums found anywhere in the world. Not surprisingly, visitors to the city often have distinct preferences among the diverse quarters to be found here; some choose to stay in Georgetown, others on the outskirts of the city, and still others want to be within walking distance of attractions such as the Museum of Natural History, The National Gallery, the National Air and Space Museum, The Smithsonian, the Capitol Buildings, and the Washington Monument. Loews L'Enfant Plaza Hotel is well situated for visits to any of these attractions. Located just a block from the banks of the Potomac, this enormous hotel somehow manages to create an intimate overall feeling. The lobby has low ceilings and the recessed lighting casts a soft glow over the light marble floors and deep peach colored walls. Neutral fabrics cover the formal French furnishings, which are set in a profusion of cut flowers and potted plants. French doors add a sense of graceful openness to this space.

The same French-influenced furnishings and decor are found throughout the hotel. Each of the spacious guest bedrooms has traditional sofas and club chairs upholstered with floral fabrics or subdued cotton prints. A French writing desk is as lovely to look at as it is functional. Attractive architectural and botanical prints set amid an abundance of potted plants and flower arrangements make these chambers very inviting. Although it is not surprising to discover the television, VCR, and refrigerator concealed in an armoire, the telephone, television, and radio found in the bathrooms are unusual and appreciated extras. Even though the exterior of the hotel is not necessarily architecturally significant, the interior spaces offer commanding views of the Potomac River, the Capitol, and the Washington Monument. For those who are interested in deluxe accommodations with a few additional features, there are the Club 480 junior suites. These are set on one floor, similar to a Concierge Level in other hotels, and offer a myriad of additional amenities such as pre-registration, nightly turndown, a complimentary full breakfast, newspaper delivery, a terry cloth robe, and a platter of assorted cheeses and fruit. As one would expect, the most luxurious and spacious chambers are these expansive suites.

Guests will discover that there are a few additional features about the hotel that make it very appealing, other than its proximity to nearby landmarks. There is a wonderful all-season swimming pool situated on the hotel's rooftop, as well as a comprehensive fitness center offering a variety of equipment and classes. There is also an array of dining options available, ranging from the elegant Terrace to the more casual Cafe Pierre. The former offers intimate seating arrangements along walls painted with pastoral landscapes. The entree selection includes such dishes as beef tenderloin, mustard crusted rack of lamb, Pacific coast salmon, and lobster, shrimp, and scallops en croute. Guests may also want to investigate the assorted boutiques and shops, as well as the subterranean shopping mall adjacent to the hotel.

Whatever pastime suits your fancy, the lovely decor, attentive staff, sumptuous accommodations, and the abundance of sights and attractions situated nearby will undoubtedly make your stay at the Loews L'Enfant Plaza Hotel a most memorable one.

THE WATERGATE HOTEL

2650 Virginia Ave, NW
Washington, D.C. 20037
(800) 424-2736, (202) 965-2300, Fax: (202) 337-7915
General Manager: Ibrahim Sahmy
Rooms: 137 doubles, 98 suites
Rates: Doubles $285-410, Suites $560-1,885
Payment: AE, DC, DSC, MC, and Visa
Children: Welcome, no charge for children under 14 years of age sharing a
         room with their parents
Dogs: Welcome with advance notice, guests must be responsible for any
        damage and dogs must be leashed in all public areas of the hotel
Open: All year

The Watergate Hotel is situated in the midst of the Watergate Complex, which rests on the banks of the Potomoc River in the heart of Washington D.C. The hotel is not only centrally located, but it is also within walking distance of the White House, Georgetown, and the Kennedy Center for the Performing Arts. Its elongated reception area is visually enhanced by the black and white inlaid marble floors, fashioned with formal English and French mahogany antiques. Gold trimmed, ornately carved mirrors and original oil paintings create a museum-like setting for the intimate seating arrangements. Impressive cut flower arrangements are interspersed with blooming plants and potted palms.

A central elevator takes guests to one of the 16 floors, where a variety of guest room configurations await them. Even the simplest chamber is rich in bright chintzes and subtle stripes, from the tailored bedspreads and draperies to the coverings adorning the walls. Finial and four poster beds are usually king-size, and the oversized writing desks and coffee tables are high quality reproductions from the Queen Anne period. The Deluxe and Georgetown Rooms are notable for their sitting areas, and the Executive Suites have a bedroom separated from the living room by French doors. Standard amenities include fully-stocked minibars, clock radios, and services that range from the complimentary shoeshine to the twice-daily maid service. More deluxe rooms feature balconies, separate bar areas, kitchenettes, stereos, and VCRs. The Diplomat Suites not only offer wonderful views of the river or the lovely gardens from their wraparound patios, but are also equipped with a master and a half bath, full kitchen, and an elegantly appointed living room and dining room.

On the premises is a newly expanded and updated Health Club, offering a good-sized lap pool along with a full complement of Nautilus athletic equipment. The saunas and whirlpools are terrific ways to unwind after a workout, as is a massage from the resident masseuse. In other parts of the hotel, there are a number of areas where guests can also congregate. In the lounge, the gently curved interior and exterior walls are accented by Doric columns. French blues and whites, with gold accents, have been chosen for the sophisticated fabrics on the upholstered French furnishings. Every table offers wonderful views of the river, whether situated at one end of the room by the piano, or at the other end adjacent to the intimate bar. The Riverview Restaurant is located on the ground level, just below the reception area. This angular room, also privy to lovely water views through its walls of windows, has been decorated in a warm and inviting manner. The menu is interesting, with a spiced Mediterranean seafood risotto, comprised of shrimp, calamari, scallops, and clams; a grilled Kasu salmon served with a hoison and pickled ginger beurre blanc; and a peppered beef tenderloin with marsala, sultanas, juniper berry sauce sprinkled with pine nuts topping the menu.

The elegant Jean-Louis restaurant has won the highest accolades, ranging from the coveted Michelein two-star to the Mobil five-star awards. Others have rated it as one of the ten best restaurants in the entire country. The exquisite menu changes nightly, and is a curious mix of printed English descriptions along with the chef's handwritten French additions. The few patrons who dine here each evening may choose from two menus, one at $85 and the other at $95. Appetizers include a terrine of wild mushrooms with foie gras and red wine emulsion, the corn soup with Maine mussels and quenelle, or the terrine of woodcock with foie gras and brioche. Or perhaps the fricassee of snails with mushrooms, sweetbreads and garlic butter, croustillant of Maine crab with a coulis of smelt roe, or scallops with squid in noodles and Parmesan tuile sound tantalizing. This is exotic fare, where medallions of venison, roasted wild squab, and roasted wild partridge frequently grace the menu. For dessert, there is often a "symphony of pears," sauteed exotic fruits with almonds, coulis of rum, fruit confit and coconut sorbet, or the croustillant of chocolate and blackberries, coulis of coffee, and gianduja ice cream.

After an exquisite dining experience, it is nice to know that Washington is a great walking town, and visitors can easily stroll from one scenic site to another. Bowser would love to take invigorating walks around the charming Georgetown area, investigate the countless historic landmarks situated within the immediate vicinity, or help you find some of the picturesque gardens, parks, and magnificent fountains that abound in the Washington area.

VIRGINIA

MILTON HALL BED & BREAKFAST

207 Thorny Lane
Covington, Virginia 24426
(703) 965-0196
Hosts: Vera and John Eckert
Rooms: 5 doubles, 1 suite
Rates: Doubles $75-95, Suite $140
Payment: MC and Visa
Children: Welcome, those under ten years of age are free of charge
Dogs: Very well-behaved dogs are welcome with prior approval (they must
    get along with other dogs)
Open: All year

This part of Virginia has long drawn visitors, who come as much for the famous hot springs as for the beauty of the Blue Ridge and Allegheny Mountain ranges. The appeal of the area, and its rejuvenating properties, is not just limited to the present. In 1874, the Honorable Laura Marie Theresa Fitzwilliam, Viscountess Milton built an English country manor house for her ailing husband, Lord Milton. She was hoping that the tranquility and serene mountain setting would aid in his recovery. The serenity guests feel when walking the grounds is sure to ease any pressures they may have brought with them, with 44 acres of sweeping lawns, lovely gardens, and woodlands that are reputedly unchanged from the 1800s.

Presiding over this picturesque scene is the historic manor house, which also remains true to its heritage. With buttressed porch towers, Gothic trimmings, and assorted gables, the home is considered to be European in design. In stark contrast, the interior is rather Spartan because Lady Milton was concerned about overwhelming the local residents with the architectural details traditionally found in a house of this type. Today's guests will be pleased to see that Vera and John have maintained much of the historical integrity of the home and created an ambiance that reflects the 1800s. As a result of their efforts, the 17-room house has been selected to be on the National Register of Historic Places.

The Milton Hall B&B is built of brick, with rooms that are as spacious as they are quiet. One foot thick brick walls, with plaster overlays, support the eleven-foot ceilings that span each of the chambers. The spacious living room is furnished with many period antiques and some nice reproductions. Fresh flowers grace some of the tables and add welcome color to each of the rooms. If the day is cool, a fire is usually warming the space and one of the guests is certain to be tickling the ivories of the antique player piano. A television is the one modern concession. Those who wish to bring a little of the outdoors inside may open the French doors that look out toward the lovely gardens and lawn.

Another welcoming place, particularly in the morning, is the dining room where a full English breakfast is served. The Eckerts have traveled the world during their tenure with the Navy, and one of the many traditions they brought back to the United States was the hearty English breakfast. Beginning with fresh fruit, juice and coffee or tea, guests may expect a meal that consists of rainbow trout, grits, and bacon or herbed eggs, scones, and country sausage. Vera also bakes wonderful muffins that are often brimming with one of the fresh seasonal fruits, such as peaches or blackberries. The fireplace in this chamber is a nice feature on raw mornings, although when the day is warm the French doors are often opened to let in the fragrant breezes.

Sometime during their stay, guests are certain to encounter the Eckerts' 9-year old Brittany Spaniel and their daughter's rambunctious English Cocker Spaniel. They are most friendly and get along famously with other dogs their own size and temperament. One of the dogs might even accompany guests to their room. One of our favorite guest chambers is located on the first floor. This spacious suite is comprised of a large bedroom with a fireplace and queen-size four poster bed. A separate sitting room offers a sofa (which can become a bed) facing the intimate fireplace. French doors lead directly to the gardens. This chamber, and the one at the top of the stairs, are often preferred by those traveling with their canine companions. The latter is furnished with a queen-size four poster bed facing the fireplace, and the bathroom has one of the two old-fashioned claw-footed bathtubs found in the house. Those who prefer a more luxurious and modern bath might opt for the chamber with a Jacuzzi, which is adjacent to one of the smaller queen-bedded rooms. Vera has not overlooked the little extras, such as soft flannel sheets that grace the four poster beds and nightly turndown services. Coupled with the modern conveniences of air conditioning, private bathrooms, and even television on occasion, guests are certain to feel quite pampered.

These extra touches extend to other areas of the B&B. For instance, Vera will pack a gourmet box lunch for those who want to explore the countryside. Some may be interested in visiting the hot springs or heading to Lake Moomaw for other water oriented activities. Guests can also borrow a bicycle and explore the area closer to home, or opt to take the short walk on the path that leads into the nearby woods. Bowser will undoubtedly dictate how the day should be spent, but at the end of it, many look forward to returning to Milton Hall for the afternoon tea, which should leave them feeling pleasantly sated, relaxed, and rejuvenated.

FREDERICKSBURG COLONIAL INN

1707 Princess Anne Street
Fredericksburg, Virginia 22401
(703) 371-5666
Innkeeper: A.C. Echols
Rooms: 22 doubles, 8 suites
Rates: Doubles $55-60, Suites $65
Payment: AE, MC, and Visa
Children: Welcome
Dogs: Welcome with prior approval, the innkeeper prefers that guests with
  dogs stay in rooms on the ground floor
Open: All year

Historic Fredericksburg is one of the older cities in America, having been founded in 1727. Moreover, this region is rich in additional Civil War heritage with five known battlefields and numerous historic buildings and attractions situated in the nearby area. The Colonial city of Fredericksburg is literally bursting with historic landmarks, in fact there are more than 350 buildings over 125 years old that are still standing. Set just a few blocks from the heart of the downtown area, the Fredericksburg Colonial Inn also offers some of its own historic charm.

The sprawling two-story yellow clapboard inn is set just off Princess Anne Street between the Rappahannock Canal and River. Although the inn is not historic, there is a sense of history preserved within its walls. The cavernous lobby is furnished with an assortment of Colonial and American antiques that are set amidst collectibles and other memorabilia. A central staircase dominates the space, also serving to create intimate alcoves to either side. One of these contains a piano and another, a comfortable sitting area where guests can read or watch television.

Bowser is welcome in any of the guest rooms on the first floor. One chamber of particular note is Room 102, which has a pair of queen-size, wood-framed beds and a marble-topped dressing table. All of the furnishings are set on an Oriental carpet that covers the hardwood floor. As is the case with all the bedrooms, modern conveniences include a television, clock radio, and refrigerator. Additionally, there are a handful of first floor guest rooms located down a hallway off the main lobby. These are more contemporary in appearance than their upstairs counterparts, although they do maintain a similar historic tone through the use of four-poster beds and Queen-Anne style furnishings. Those traveling without a dog might opt for the chambers found at the top of the wide central staircase, which splits at a landing into two hallways that lead guests to their respective rooms. As guests ascend the stairs, they should note the two antique tall clocks which grace this landing. The second floor chambers are decorated and furnished in much the same manner as the first floor, with floral curtains at the windows and Bates spreads covering antique and canopy beds. The bathrooms offer additional character, with marble bathroom sinks retrofitted onto the top of the wooden cabinets. Families will appreciate those chambers that are either spacious enough to hold a queen-size sofabed or that connect through a central bathroom.

While there is a Continental breakfast served at the inn, there is not a full-service restaurant on the premises. Guests need only travel a short distance to find a variety of fine dining establishments or casual eateries. When it comes time to take Bowser for a walk, the Rappahannock Canal and Old Mill Park can be found within steps of the inn. A short drive will also bring visitors to the historic battlefields that have been preserved as open spaces. Fishing and boating are also options in the Fredericksburg area. Whatever reason visitors have for coming to Fredericksburg, they are sure to discover that while the Fredericksburg Colonial Inn is not a frilly or quaint country inn, it is clean, centrally located, and offers a very homey atmosphere that guests are certain to find appealing.

SLEEPY HOLLOW FARM

16280 Blue Ridge Turnpike
Gordonsville, Virginia 22942
(703) 832-5555, Fax: (703) 832-2515
Host: Beverley Allison
Rooms: 6 doubles, 1 cottage
Rates: Doubles $60-125, Cottage $75-225
Payment: MC and Visa
Children: Welcome
Dogs: Welcome only with prior approval
Open: All year

The Sleepy Hollow Farm is, true to its name, nestled into a small hollow of land off a winding back country road lined with rock walls and split-rail fences. Rolling pastures and fields surround the hollow containing this charming 18th-century, two-story clapboard and brick house. As guests approach the homestead, and one of its many terraces, a large black lab and a half-blind albino sheepherding dog will undoubtedly act as the welcoming committee. They may even show Bowser where the sheltered kennel is situated (located a few steps from the house), where Bowser may wish to sleep at night.

While the house and its adjacent slave quarters date back to the 1700s, each has been expanded over the years to meet different owners' needs. The main house is almost a puzzle of rooms, some being added as late as the 1940s to what is otherwise an antique structure. The heart of the home is the kitchen and sitting room whose wall of windows, coupled with the warmth of the woodstove, can make even the coldest day seem quite bearable. This spacious common area leads to the intimate, beamed ceiling dining room with its blue manteled fireplace and Oriental rug covering the hardwood floor. The house offers many nooks and crannies, two of our favorites are the lovely coral pink garden room and the den with its television.

One of the first floor bedrooms is good sized, offering a four-poster bed, sitting room, and a private bath. A second guest room, perfect for couples, offers an antique mahogany bed, a fireplace, and a Jacuzzi. The upstairs suite has two connecting bedrooms with a private bathroom, which is ideal for a family or two couples. The other chamber is located across the hall from the suite and has terrific views of the pond. A country decor predominates in each space, enhanced through the use of pine antique side tables, cedar sweater chests, and assorted country collectibles. Braided area rugs covering the hardwood floors complete the effect. The bathrooms vary in size and their appointments, although several have old-fashioned claw-footed tubs.

The adjacent Chestnut Cottage is just a few steps from the kitchen door. This converted slave-quarters' shed is yellow clapboard and has been beautifully refurbished using the original chestnut boards to recreate the beamed ceilings, walls, and stairs. The cottage can be rented in its entirety or as two suites. The Kitchen Suite offers a large sitting room with a sofabed and woodstove, along with a full-kitchen. A deck allows guests to enjoy the warmth of the outdoors. The Slave Quarters also provides a sitting room with a fireplace, but does not have kitchen facilities. When guests are ready to retire at night, they ascend a steep central staircase, holding on to the brass banister for support, to the two bedrooms. One of these has an iron bedstead, accented with pink trim, set amidst other comfortable furnishings. The other chamber is more spacious and airy due, in part, to the two skylights set in the eaves. This room is also charmingly decorated and has a wooden bed with a navy blue handmade quilt.

Each morning guests are invited to partake in a hearty country breakfast. While we could go on and on about the wide variety of delicacies that could be served, we won't because it is better left as a surprise. We will just say that Beverley's recipes are so innovative and delicious that they are included in a B&B cookbook. During breakfast, or at some other point during the stay, Beverley is certain to hint at the existence of the house's friendly ghost, which guests may, or may not, want her to elaborate upon.

The property is a little jewel, beautified with herb and flower gardens and a small spring-fed pond. A dock leads out beyond the water's edge to a charming gazebo. Children will delight in the small play area with swings and a sandbox, or they may choose to visit the Black Angus cows grazing in the pastures. We recommend visitors jump in the car and drive along the back country roads that meander past beautiful homesteads, which are all part of Virginia's National Historic District.

There are many reasons for visiting scenic and rural Orange County, and we feel that a stay at the Sleepy Hollow Farm is certain to be a memorable part of this vacation in the country.

THE TIDES INN

P.O. Box 339
King Carter Drive
Irvington, Virginia 22480
(800) TIDES-INN, (804) 438-5000
Innkeepers: R.L. Stephens and Family
Rates: $191-630 (MAP)
Payment: AE, DSC, MC, and Visa
Children: Welcome—those under 4 years of age are free of charge (cribs,
            babysitting, cots, and children's programs are available)
Dogs: Dogs are welcome with advance notice in specific units for an $8 per day
      fee
Open: Mid-March to January

The Tides Inn is the formal counterpart to The Tides Lodge, and together they share a portion of the scenic Rappahannock River in Irvington. The Inn's entrance is flanked by two white pillars, which guests must drive through to enter the resort's private 25-acre compound. The small road leading to the Inn wends through the nine-hole par 3 golf course and tennis facilities, eventually leading to the water. Here, the sprawling main inn and outbuildings are nestled next to the river, which eventually feeds into the Chesapeake Bay. Those arriving by yacht will need to follow the river for eight miles from the Bay before coming upon the Inn.

The actual accommodations and dining rooms are located in three-story clapboard and white-washed brick buildings which are reflective of the classic and quiet way of life at The Tides Inn. Its roots date back to the mid-1940s when the Stephens bought an overgrown peninsula jutting into the Rappahannock River. Over the next few years they cleared away trees and vines, uncovering and recovering a little piece of paradise. As the beauty of the peninsula began to unfold, the Stephens started to contemplate ways of sharing it with others. They talked about opening an inn, although Mr. Stephens claims that he and his wife were "amateurs" who knew nothing about the hotel business. Perhaps what they lacked in experience, they made up for in vision, eventually creating a resort that generations of return guests enjoy year after year. Originally, the Stephens went to Europe to acquire the Brussels carpets, fine silver, and oil paintings that were to grace the inn for so long. Today, that same old world charm and sophistication predominates, although some of the original furnishings have, by necessity, been replaced. Another subtle change took place when subsequent generations of Stephens took over the management of the Inn, but fortunately they have taken care to preserve the gentle hospitality and graciousness The Tides Inn is renowned for.

The intimate sitting areas are furnished with formal camelback sofas and chintz covered wing chairs set on Oriental rugs. A traditional Pembroke table is topped with a brass lamp, while Chippendale chairs are set around a pedestaled dining room table. Rattan couches and chairs are well-placed in various sitting areas to take advantage of either the water views through the picture windows or of the fireplace which is often crackling on cool evenings. Meals are served in the two lovely dining rooms, which also offer magnificent water views. The garden room is cheerful, with its white latticework across the ceiling and green accents. The second chamber is more English in feeling with wallpaper murals and Breton red chairs surrounding the white clothed tables. Dinner guests are assigned a table for the duration of their stay, which is a wonderful old-world tradition. The dress is informal, except during the dinner hour when patrons are asked to wear appropriate evening attire. After dinner, there are many inviting and private patios that offer a bit of solitude and quiet along with peaceful water views.

Most of the guests at The Tides Inn don't sit around for too long, opting instead for some activity. Many look forward to the cocktail or sunset cruise on the 127-foot yacht, Miss Ann, named after Mr. Stephen's wife. Tennis can be enjoyed on the clay and all-weather courts, and afterwards swimming in the Olympic-size saltwater and freshwater pools or from the inn's sandy beach is another favorite pastime. There are also sailboats, paddleboats, and canoes that guests are encouraged to borrow for exploring all of the inlets and eddies along the river. Bicycles are terrific for land-based excursions. More passive pursuits include shuffleboard and croquet. The children's playground offers recreational choices for the younger set, along with the Summer House Play Room, where children can enjoy Ping-Pong, pool, shuffleboard, and video games. Finally, there is the nationally ranked Golden Eagle Golf Course, that is as enjoyable as it is challenging.

When guests finally retire at the end of the day, they find attractive rooms awaiting them. Those traveling with a dog are asked to stay in the three-story white brick and clapboarded Garden House, which is a separate but integral part of the main complex. Each of the chambers, here, is traditionally decorated and appointed, with coordinated fabrics on the beds and at the windows. English hunt, botanical, and waterfowl prints cover the walls of these chambers. While the decor and furnishings of the rooms are decidedly inviting, the wonderful views of the pond, lush gardens, and cove are what make this a truly special spot. Shutters between each patio provide some additional privacy. Guests are made even more comfortable by the always attentive and accommodating staff at the Inn. Those who inadvertently forget a toiletry, can ask one of the housekeepers for a replacement. Box lunches can be arranged as easily as dry cleaning and laundry. Check-in is as simple and painless as check-out with bags quickly disappearing and reappearing at their ultimate destination. This leaves guests free to thoroughly enjoy the peaceful surroundings, delightful accommodations and amenities, and the warm hospitality which the Stephens so graciously offer year after year at The Tides Inn.

THE TIDES LODGE

P.O. Box 309
1 St. Andrews Lane
Irvington, Virginia 22480
(800) 24-TIDES, (804) 438-6000
Innkeeper: E. A. Stephens, Jr.
Rates: $79-364 (MAP)
Payment: AE, DSC, MC and Visa
Children: Welcome—those under 4 years of age are free of charge (cribs, cots,
    babysitting, and children's programs are available)
Dogs: Small dogs are welcome with advance notice in specific units for an $8
    per day fee
Open: Mid-March to January

The Tides Lodge is the sister resort to the more formal Tides Inn, both
offering a bit of Southern hospitality in the rural coastal town of Irvington.
Those arriving by water will discover the Lodge has a 41-slip marina, while
those traveling by car will wend through the 175-acre complex until they reach
the Lodge and its handful of outbuildings. The rather contemporary, weathered
shingle main building rests at the end of the peninsula on the water's edge,
protected on three other sides by dense stands of trees and lovely flowering
gardens.

Guests are immediately struck by the strong Scottish theme and decor that
is evident from the moment they enter the reception area. The darkly stained
vertical board walls are offset by the colorful tartan-patterned carpeting, a
profusion of potted plants, and walls of windows looking out to the surrounding
grounds and waterways. A hallway, found just off this area, is festooned with
an assortment of golf memorabilia and leads to the Royal Stewart Dining
Room. This is the most formal restaurant at the Lodge, particularly in the
evening when coats are required for the men and dresses for the women. The
menu is enticing, beginning with an appetizer selection which could include
miniature crab cakes, Chesapeake crab puffs, or oysters on the half shell with
a lobster/mushroom topping. Innovative soup selections are plentiful and
include apple with nutmeg croutons, cream of oyster and spinach, cream of
Virginia peanut and artichoke soups. The wide assortment of entrees capitalize
on local seafood and shellfish. The native crabmeat Remick, broiled flounder
with a caviar sauce, and the coquille of Atlantic scallops are supplemented by
heartier fare consisting of prime rib, roasted duckling, and rack of lamb. Most
guests have difficulty passing up the desserts, which include Lodge chocolate
chess pie, homemade apple pie, or the lemon ice box pie. While the food is
always excellent, guests are also certain to fondly remember the views of the
grounds and the marina through the greenhouse windows that front the dining
room. The more informal Binnacles is ideal for a casual lunch, offering items

like a native lump crab sandwich or a thick hamburger with all the toppings. Breakfast is not to be missed either, if only for the hot coffee, the rum buns, and the old-fashioned spoon bread.

The 60 accommodations at the Lodge are not as varied or as elegant as those found at The Tides Inn, but they are equally as attractive. Some of these rooms are set in a wing of the main building, while others are located in another two-story building on the property. The good-sized bedrooms are nicely appointed with Chippendale wing chairs covered in leather and good quality reproduction Queen Anne chairs set around a small, glass breakfast table. The artwork usually reflects a golfing theme, again with a touch of Scotland thrown in for good measure. Hunter green carpeting and coordinated bedspreads and draperies tie the entire room's decor together. The small, private patios and decks are favorite gathering spots as they offer scenic views of the grounds or waterway. Some of our favorite rooms are 410 and 411, not only for their size but also because they have an abundance of natural light. Any of the chambers situated at the end of the building provide a great deal of privacy as well.

Although the guest rooms and food are exceptional, people (and Bowser) are often drawn to The Tides Lodge for recreation — most importantly, golf. While Bowser cannot romp along the golf course, golfers can enjoy a very challenging 18 holes on the Tartan Course. Afterwards, it is easy to pick up Bowser and take him/her for a walk along the water's edge or through the expansive property. There are three lighted tennis courts, salt and fresh water swimming pools, and putting greens and practice ranges. Children will delight in the swing sets, slides, volleyball, and numerous lawn games available to them. The Children's Playhouse offers Ping-Pong and video games, as well as an ice cream parlor, for indoor amusements. The Tides Lodge has become a family favorite over the years because they offer extensive children's programs during the summer months for those between the ages of 5 - 12. Adult guests can also choose from an assortment of recreational options, ranging from sailing, canoeing, or cruising on the yacht to bicycling, dancing, or just taking in the nightly entertainment or movie. When it comes time to rejuvenate tired muscles, the full service sauna is awaiting.

Much of the success of the Lodge would not be possible without its exemplary staff — who are without pretense and make every effort to meet the needs of the guests. The fact that there is a 1:1 staff-to-guest ratio, ensure that guests needs are quickly and quietly attended to at the Lodge. The attentive staff, the low-key atmosphere, the abundance of recreational diversions, and the picturesque coastal setting all combine to make The Tides Lodge a natural vacation destination for guests and their canine cohorts.

WELBOURNE

Middleburg,Virginia 22117
(703) 687-3201
Hostess: Sherry Morison
Rooms: 4 doubles, 2 cottages
Rates: $85-105
Payment: Personal checks
Children: Older children are welcome
Dogs: Well-behaved dogs are welcome provided they stay off the furniture
Open: All year

One need only travel along the winding back roads that lead to the charming hamlet of Middleburg to gain an appreciation for the beautiful and rural countryside which characterizes this part of the United States. Lined with sprawling gentlemen's farms, vineyards, and miles of white rail fences, Virginia's renowned hunt country has an atmosphere unto itself. While B&B guests could stay in any one of many accommodations, it seems only appropriate that when visiting the hunt country, one should stay in one of the original manor houses.

A back road just outside of town leads visitors to one gravel road after another until arriving at the entrance to Welbourne. The 550-acre estate lies beyond the stone pillars complete with bronze statues of attacking geese, which flank the entrance to the winding driveway. As guests proceed, the park-like setting is enhanced by ancient shade trees which conceal much of what lies ahead. The yellow manor house with windows framed by green shutters and a veranda fronted by six huge columns soon appears in a clearing. As guests park their car along the circular drive, and walk to the front door, they will pass by old stone hitching posts lining the edge of the lawn. Upon entering the house, new arrivals will be greeted by Sherry or one of her staff.

This beautiful home, a Virginia Historic Landmark dating back to 1775, has been in the Morison's family for seven generations. The building, which Sherry describes as "an old English country house with a faded elegance," is not in disrepair, it is just in need of a little paint and some touching up around the edges. When Sherry speaks with prospective guests on the telephone, she is very clear about what people can expect and is quick to "deflect those who are in search of perfection." This is not a contrived inn or charming B&B filled with reproduction furnishings and coordinated decorator fabrics. This is a real house, filled with touchable antiques in an environment steeped in family history. Those with an interest in the multi-generational South, and who have a true love of antiques, will fall in love with this grand old house.

The three enormous sitting rooms are filled with classic English antique tables and chairs resting on Oriental carpets. A Steinway piano occupies one part of a room, while another features an antique game table. Fine French china and crystal are displayed next to original works of art, exquisite collectibles, and assorted family portraits and heirlooms. The first floor living and sitting rooms give guests some indication of what they will find throughout the house. Here, there is little pretense. Most of the collection has been bequeathed to the family over the years. It has been used and appreciated over time, therefore, if an antique bed is a little too short because of an oversized footboard, or if the claw-footed bathtub is a little worn, then hopefully guests will find a way to adapt. The Morison's are quite attached to their home and its sense of history and they enjoy sharing it with their guests. In many ways the estate and its grounds are like a fine painting — one needs to understand its background and appreciate its detail to fully savor the experience.

The F. Scott Fitzgerald Room or the Thomas Wolf Room (both have been visitors to the house and guests can call it either name, depending upon their literary preferences) lies on the first floor. The large chamber is furnished with antiques and dominated by a four poster bed. Up the stairs, lined with Oriental carpets, there are several other lovely twin and queen bedded rooms, each with a working fireplace. While the bedrooms in the main house might be somewhat worn around the edges, they are filled with antique treasures. Partner's desks, highboys, dressing tables fitted with mirrors, and canopied beds, are just some of the many highlights. The bathrooms are also spacious and offer antique claw footed bathtubs, more contemporary showers, and thick cotton towels.

Those in search of a little more privacy might want to stay in one of the two cottages. These are accessed by way of overgrown walkways that lead through colorful gardens. One is a rather rustic, diminutive yellow cottage, which actually dates back further than the main house. Coziness is found in the extreme here; we couldn't decide whether it was the green floral wallpaper or the six and a half foot ceilings that made this chamber appear so intimate. The double brass bed is adorned with a simple Bates spread, while an Oriental rug covers the hardwood floor. A small sitting area is dotted with tables and chairs. A ladder formed from rough hewn logs leads to a loft which curious guests may need to investigate. A small kitchen is available for storing food and beverages. The other cottage is substantially larger and has a more refined ambiance about it, with 14-foot ceilings and two bedrooms furnished with a pair of twin beds and a double bed, respectively. The good-sized kitchen is a nice addition. However, the fireplaced living room with its built-in bookshelves, sofa, and side chairs is really what makes this cottage something special.

Each day begins with an irresistible, hearty Southern breakfast. This lovely affair is set on a pedestaled dining room table complete with all the fine china, silver, and crystal one might expect in a house of this stature. Afterwards, many choose to explore the grounds and gardens surrounding the manor, as well as take Bowser for a romp through the fields. The Morisons have six coon hounds who might be interested in meeting Bowser, as well. Whether planning to spend either just a night or several days, we highly recommend Welbourne to anyone who is interested in capturing a glimpse into the traditions of the Virginia hunt country and its residents.

INN AT MONTROSS

Courthouse Square
Montross, Virginia 22520
(800) 321-0979, (804) 493-9097
Innkeepers: Eileen and Michael Longman
Rooms: 6 doubles
Rates: $75-125
Payment: AE, DSC, MC, and Visa
Children: Not suitable for small children
Dogs: Welcome with prior approval and a $5 fee
Open: All year

For travelers who are investigating the eastern shore of Virginia, or who are trying to see all the historic sights between Mount Vernon and Williamsburg, The Montross Inn and Restaurant is a great overnight destination. Originally built in 1683, the building was owned by John Minor and utilized as an Ordinary (tavern) for many years. The original handwritten grant, which gave Mr. Minor permission to operate such a facility, is still displayed in the inn. Over the decades, the building has exchanged hands several times and has been used as everything from a hotel to a home for the elderly. Unfortunately, in 1790, the building burned to the ground, but was rebuilt shortly thereafter.

The Longmans discovered the inn quite by accident. They were formerly corporate types, he a bank vice-president and she, a nursing consultant. They both shared a passion for sailing, as well as a dream of opening an inn along the inland waterway that boaters could use as a way station. After searching for years, they stumbled upon a real estate advertisement for an inn that was for sale. Without much further ado, they bought what is now known as the Inn at Montross. Their backgrounds are quite diverse, Michael is British and Eileen an American from Baltimore, but they shared a common goal. Both wanted to create an inn that was reminiscent of the ones they had visited in Europe. In Europe, a inn or hostelry was truly a reflection of the hosts, who not only lived on the premises but also furnished the accommodations in the same manner they would their own home. Theirs would not be a place decorated by a designer and filled with period reproductions. It would be a comfortable, homey spot, where guests felt completely at ease in the unpretentious surroundings. They have succeeded with the Inn at Montross.

Set a block off the main street of Montross, this three-story, white clapboarded building is accented with black shuttered windows set into the walls and eaves of the building. Guests make their way up a path, lined with small perennial gardens, to the front porch. Once inside the inn, new arrivals will undoubtedly be greeted by the innkeepers' two golden retrievers. The small office, where guests register, is set off to the right, with the main dining room found at the rear of the inn behind the central staircase. Look carefully for the 1886 Sohmer Grand Piano, which Michael has restored. Wood paneled walls in the common areas serve as the backdrop for the eclectic array of collectibles and furnishings. There are antiques and reproductions intermixed, along with African sculptures, primitive and modern art, and porcelains. It is well worth spending the extra time to examine some of the treasures the Longmans have acquired during their travels.

The upstairs guest chambers are all good-sized and furnished with four poster beds. Floral curtains frame the windows and comfortable reproductions combine with a few antiques to comprise the majority of the furnishings. A color television, individual climate controls, and a private bathroom are standards in each of the chambers. A guest room on the third floor is not only the largest in the house, but also has a deck with a private entrance to the yard below. The Longmans have remained true to their original premise, creating guest chambers that are not only comfortable but are also unpretentious and inviting.

The Inn at Montross and Restaurant has also developed quite a fine reputation for its excellent food, and guests will undoubtedly want to sample the delicious cuisine served here. The entrees range from Chesapeake crab meat saute and scallops of veal to noisetes of beef tenderloin and English shepherds' pie. Afterwards, many patrons meander downstairs into the original cellar of the house, where they will find John Minor's Ordinary. This is an extension of the upstairs pub, but is set in an even more relaxed environment. Two of the highlights for some are the competitive dart playing and a large screen television.

During the day, many choose to explore the picturesque coastline, take ferry rides out to Smith and Tangier islands, or visit Westmoreland State Park. The nearby wineries are always popular, as are the many other historic sites that dot the region. The Inn at Montross might not live up to the Longmans' original dream of provisioning sailors, but they do a fine job keeping landlubbers quite satisfied.

WIDOW KIP'S SHENANDOAH INN

Box 117, Route 1
Mount Jackson, Virginia 22842
(703) 477-2400
Hosts: Betty and Bob Luse
Rooms: 5 doubles, 2 cottages
Rates: Doubles $65-70, Cottages $75-85
Payment: MC and Visa
Children: Welcome
Dogs: Welcome in the two cottages
Open: All year

The Widow Kip's Shenandoah Inn is a charming 1830s Colonial home set in the rural community of Mount Jackson. A country road leads guests to the blue grey clapboard house and two cottages situated on a small knoll. Views from this vantage point are of the seven acres of land that look out onto a fork of the Shenandoah River and beyond to the distant Shenandoah Valley Massanutten Mountains. A front walk, lined by mature plantings and shaded by enormous trees, leads new arrivals to the front door.

The Widow Kips was once owned by THE Widow Kip, who was renowned as much for her B&B as she was for selling some of its antique furnishings and collectibles to her overnight guests. In 1991 Bob and Betty bought it, changed the name slightly, and moved their own Victorian pieces into the house (these are not for sale). The living room is one of the most comfortable common rooms in the B&B and is well equipped with modern conveniences that include a television, VCR, and game table. The fireplace is often well stoked in the winter months creating an even more welcoming atmosphere. The Luses' have collected an array of antiques over the years, including a noteworthy partner's desk, all of which they prominently display throughout the house. The dozens of family photographs and framed needlepoint samplers complement this traditional decor.

The central staircase leads guests to the four upstairs bed chambers in the main house, which are decorated with period and antique furnishings set on Oriental rugs. One room has an eight-foot Lincoln bed, while two others are furnished with a sleigh bed and canopy bed, respectively. A wide array of colorful antique quilts nicely complement the blue and yellow, peach and green, and mauve color schemes. The original fireplaces in all but one bedroom create additional interest, particularly when soft armchairs are pulled up in front of them. What most people remember though are the lovely views of the surrounding valley and the refreshing summer breezes which flow through the windows. The bedrooms are also individually air conditioned should the weather become too hot. Much to one person's amazement, and the innkeepers as well, when the guest decided to open a window for some fresh air, the air conditioner fell from the second to the first floor. It landed on another air conditioner, smashing both in the process. Guests needn't think about "flying" air conditioners because these units have been anchored down to prevent any further incident.

Those traveling with their canine cohorts will not be staying in the main house, but instead in the charming cottages. Betty usually escorts her guests through the rear of the kitchen and along a short walkway leading to these accommodations. The Silk Purse, a refurbished wash house, and Sow's Ear, a converted hen house, are set around a pretty Williamsburg-style courtyard. A quaint porch is one of the many memorable aspects of the Silk Purse, along with a sitting room filled with white wicker and even a trundle bed for those who want to also use it as a bedroom. The main bed chamber has been decorated in rich mauves and navy blues along with floral wallpapers. The full kitchenette is an added convenience along with the color cable television. The Sow's Ear offers a subtle sense of the English countryside, although the traditional furniture is distinctly from the 1930s. Comparatively, the bathroom seems almost contemporary. However, the double bed and lovely decor will surely make guests feel right at home in this truly private setting. Anyone staying at the Widow Kip's is invited to use the outdoor gas grill for preparing their own barbecue dinner or they may dine in one of the four restaurants situated in the nearby area.

In the morning, a delicious country breakfast is offered in the main house's dining room. The two pedestal dining room table is adorned with a white lace tablecloth, which provides an elegant setting for the meal to follow. Freshly crushed apple juice, scones or pastries (complete with homemade apple butter), and coffee or tea are an appealing way to start the repast. This is followed by the main course, which ranges from French toast stuffed with seasonal fruit to waffles and homemade sausage or bacon. It is here, that guests have the opportunity to get acquainted in an informal yet lovely family-style setting. Afterwards, some retire to the living room to read the morning newspaper, while others establish themselves on the rocking chairs found on the side porch. Of course, there is always a chaise lounge or two available next to the 32-foot swimming pool.

Bowser will probably be anxious for some exercise and will certainly enjoy a walk through the grounds or down one of the nearby country roads. The inn has bicycles available for those who want to further explore the area. Other favorite summertime activities among the locals are canoeing, hiking, and golfing. Visitors to Mt. Jackson may be interested in investigating some of the historic battlefields or spelunking through one of the many caverns. At the end of the day, guests will be comforted with the knowledge that they are staying with two gracious B&B hosts, who seem to know just what appeals to people who are on vacation.

WILLOW GROVE INN

14079 Plantation Way
Route 15 North
Orange, Virginia 22960
(800) 949-1778, (703) 672-5982
Innkeeper: Angela Mulloy
Rooms: 3 doubles, 2 suites
Rates: Doubles $95-155, Suites $125-165, MAP $195-255
Payment: Personal checks
Children: Welcome (cribs and babysitters are available)
Dogs: Small well-behaved dogs are welcome with prior approval
Open: All year

The Willow Grove Inn is a lovely old Southern manor house, and as is the case with many historic buildings, there is the original home and one that was added many years later. Joseph Clark built the Federal portion of the house in 1778, hiring the same people who were responsible for building Montpelier. Some forty years later, his son added the impressive brick wing to the original home. This classic Jeffersonian-style edifice is rather imposing, with its four large columns rising three stories to support a fourth floor eave, which is fitted with a semi-circular window. Little has changed about the antebellum home over the years. It survived both the Revolutionary and Civil Wars relatively unscathed, with the exception of a cannon ball that was recently extricated from one of the eaves. Today, Willow Grove is listed on the National Register of Historic Places and is designated a Virginia Historic Landmark.

The setting is idyllic, with 37-acres of sprawling fields and grounds replete with formal gardens and large willow and magnolia trees shading the sloping lawns. The expansive pale yellow house with black shutters is set at the end of a winding drive. As people make their way through the plantation, they will see the old war trenches that are still in evidence, along with several historic outbuildings. Upon entering the restored home, guests will begin to gain a sense of the many treasures it contains. Whether it be a common room, tavern, or bedroom, each has been decorated with impressive English and American antiques. Aside from the exquisite architectural details and the impressive furnishings, this is not a formal "museum-style" inn. This is, instead, a comfortable old Southern plantation where guests are not so much pampered as they are made to feel completely at home.

Each of the bedrooms is named after one of the Virginian-born Presidents. Delicate handmade antique quilts decorate the many four poster and brass and iron bedsteads. These beds are not only attractive, but are also exceptionally comfortable having been triple sheeted and adorned with down comforters and a handful of fluffy pillows. The subtle color scheme nicely complements the decorative prints on the walls and many of the home's original features which include hand-carved fireplace mantles, wide-pine floors, and elaborate moldings. The paned windows are framed by swags, which draw one's eye out to the formal gardens. A pair of wine glasses are thoughtfully placed on a tray alongside a bottle of spring water. The private bathrooms are outfitted with large cotton towels and an assortment of imported toiletries and bath gels. This inn is a place where many guests feel inclined to sleep in. This is one of the primary reasons why Angela often arranges for a tray of hot coffee and the morning paper to be brought to the room, rather than making guests get up any earlier than they are prepared to, to enjoy the full breakfast. This hearty repast can be accompanied by homemade muffins and breads, fresh fruit, granola, and yogurt.

No one, but no one, misses the Sunday brunch, which is a multi-course affair featuring true, Southern-style delicacies. There are no grits on the menu, just plenty of local meats, fish, seasonal fruits, and vegetables all of which are presented in a light and healthy manner. Guests will also thoroughly enjoy the inn's dinners (a $100 credit toward this meal is included in the room price). Many have been known to sip a mint julep on the veranda or enjoy the peaceful setting from the hammock before finally deciding to come in for this delicious evening meal. This repast can be enjoyed in the casual Clark's Tavern (formerly an old root cellar) with its full bar and pub setting, or in the Dolly Madison dining room. The latter is a formal chamber, where tables are covered with linen tablecloths and set with fine china, crystal, and silver. If weather permits, some may choose to keep their place on the veranda and enjoy their dinner outside. On the weekends, soft piano music is played for guests and many find it is a delightful way to end a most enjoyable evening. During the week, the restaurant is closed, but as the weekend approaches things begin to pick up considerably and the entire inn once again shifts into high gear.

During the day, guests and their canine cohorts will stay very busy exploring the grounds, visiting the old stone barns, and walking through the lovely gardens. In addition to playing badminton, bocci, and croquet, many people also enjoy visiting the beautiful lakes, picturesque Blue Ridge Mountains, and interesting vineyards this region is known for.

CHESTER

Box 57
Route 4
Scottsville, Virginia 24590
(804) 286-3960
Hosts: Dick Shaffer and Gordon Anderson
Rooms: 5 doubles
Rates: $65-100
Payment: AE
Children: Children over the age of eight are welcome
Dogs: Welcome provided they get along with other dogs, and if they prove to be a bit too rambunctious they may stay in the kennel facilities on the premises
Open: All year

For travelers looking for a weekend getaway in the country, or a central location for trips to such historic sites as Monticello and Ash Lawn, Chester is an ideal destination. This wonderful Greek Revival home, complete with a grand portico and tall formal columns, was constructed in 1847 by Joseph C. Wright. He was a retired landscape architect from Chester, England, and was responsible for amassing the exquisite collection of plantings that can be found on the property today. The 9-acres of land is home to 50 different varieties of trees and shrubs planted in and around century old boxwood hedges. Two of the most noteworthy specimens are the enormous holly and white pine trees — both of which are thought to be the largest of their kind in the region.

The house itself also has some interesting history attached to it, one story in particular should be appealing to Civil War buffs. In 1865, it was occupied by the seriously wounded Major James Hill, a Confederate Army Commander. General Sheridan and his aide General George Custer (best known for his last stand at Little Big Horn) visited Chester to arrest the Commander, but because he was so gravely ill they opted to let him die in peace. Surprisingly, Major Hill survived his wounds and after the war he subsequently became the editor of the local paper. The house remained in the same family for 100 years, before being sold to yet another family who resided there for 35 years, and then in 1987 Dick and Gordon bought it.

History aside, today's guests will be delighted with the current estate. A mailbox, highlighted with a dog motif, marks the entrance to the circular drive that leads to the house, which is set back from the road behind a white fence and immense shade trees. Bowser will undoubtedly be anxious to explore the expansive property; however, he should be prepared for a meeting with the eight resident Borzois (Russian Wolfhounds). Three of them consider themselves "lap" dogs and live at the house, and the others are housed in a large kennel on the property. The house is truly a treasure trove of antiques and works of art the two men have collected over the years. Oriental and Persian rugs cover the hardwood floors and Chinese vase lamps adorn the antique tables. The living room and dining room are the most formal and impressive chambers in the house. The dining room is one of the first spaces guests pass through. A mahogany sideboard contains decanters of sherry and candles. The room is often illuminated at night by the light of the fireplace and the crystal chandelier hanging from the high ceiling. The multi-pedestal table is covered with linen, and set with fine china, silver, and crystal for the opulent dinners and full English breakfasts that are presented each day. Just around the corner, is the equally notable living room. Here, designer fabrics of silk and cotton cover the couches and armchairs, and various collectibles are artfully displayed on both the mantel and on the round, tiered table.

From these dramatic entry rooms, guests will then come to Chester's most popular bedroom. This first floor chamber is furnished with a pencil-post bedstead situated at just the right angle to take advantage of the warmth and comfort emanating from the fireplace. Best of all, this is the only room that has a private bathroom. The decor in all of the bedrooms is fairly reflective of the common areas. These are not cluttered spaces, quite the reverse, they are thoughtfully appointed with important pieces that fill a need. This includes a finial four poster bed in one room and a Queen Anne armchair in another. With one exception, each of the upstairs bedrooms has a fireplace, and they all share bathrooms. Some have marble pedestal sinks in the bedroom for added convenience. The fir floors are covered with area rugs and the fireplace mantels are adorned with candle sticks and some collectibles. The very subtle color schemes complement the lovely furnishings, and the overall ambiance is further enhanced with the lovely views of the grounds, which can be had from just about every window.

Chester is often a rather social B&B, where guests can spend much of their time visiting with other guests and the hosts. The second floor library is one favorite place, where an abundance of books can be borrowed. A stereo provides soft background music, while a large screen television is also available for those who want to catch a favorite show. Others might prefer to relax on one of the rocking chairs that can be found on any of the four porches. The sprawling lawn, set with white iron furniture, can be equally as inviting.

Each morning guests are invited to partake in a full English breakfast. The menu often includes Swedish popover pancakes served with seasonal fruits and freshly ground coffee or English teas. Zucchini breads and an assortment of homemade muffins usually accompany this repast. The menu changes daily, with offerings of egg dishes, pancakes, and waffles. Those who do not have plans for dinner, and enjoy a family-style affair, should consider sampling an exquisite meal at Chester. Dick and Gordon not only do the cooking, but also dine with their guests. This makes everyone feel as though they are attending an intimate dinner party, as the four-course meal often stretches long into the evening, driven by great conversation and full wine glasses. A sampling of the menu for the night might include a poached chicken breast coupled with fresh vegetables and an endive salad, a charcoal-grilled roast beef with all the fixings, or a grilled loin of pork stuffed with prunes, apricots, and apples.

Chester is a terrific destination, particularly for those who want to enjoy a wonderful weekend in a beautifully refurbished home, that is as lovely as it is warm and inviting. The combination of interesting people, tranquil surroundings, and elegant accommodations is certain to be a hit with all who stop here.

HIGH MEADOWS VINEYARD AND MOUNTAIN SUNSET INN

High Meadows Lane
Route 4, Box 6
Scottsville, Virginia, 24590-9706
(800) 232-1832, (804) 286-2218
Innkeepers: Mary Reilly and Roddy Hiduskey
Rooms: 7 doubles, 5 suites
Rates: Doubles $85-145, Suites $110-145
Payment: MC and Visa
Children: Welcome
Dogs: Welcome in the ground floor rooms with prior approval
Open: All year

Scottsville is situated at the base of the Blue Ridge Mountains on a bend of the James River. Once the county seat for this region, this town has nicely mellowed with age, providing a special spot for a romantic retreat. One of the most inviting country inns in the area is High Meadows, which has seen many changes during its 170 years. Peter White, a local surveyor, built the Federalist portion of this expansive inn in 1832. Fifty years later, Charles Harris added the Victorian section to the homestead. Then in 1905, a lumberman named W.F. Paulette constructed the Queen Anne Mountain Sunset Manor. It was not until 1985, that Peter and Jae connected the homes through a very careful and extensive restoration process — including the addition of electricity and plumbing! The turned newel post and balustrade staircase, mahogany burl graining on much of the moldings and doors, and original ornamental plaster medallions which join much of the woodwork, are just a few of the details that have been preserved. Today, the inn is a showplace that is listed on the National Register of Historic Homes.

Peter, retired from the Royal Navy, and Jae, a financial analyst, have maintained the integrity of each section by decorating and furnishing the rooms in keeping with their intrinsic details. One chamber offers a windowed alcove and a fireplace, providing the perfect setting for the high four-poster bed draped with a sheer fabric and the many period pieces. Another bedroom has beamed ceilings overhead and hardwood floors covered with woven rugs, creating the right environment for the stenciled walls and a massive four-poster bed covered by a fringed bedspread. Guests are also certain to find many individually selected, period antiques throughout the inn, which include writing desks, end tables, and carved sitting chairs. While each bedroom may be different, there are certain constants. A small decanter of port is set out with two wine glasses, which guests can enjoy while they peruse the leather-bound book filled with pre- and post-restoration photographs. In their reading, they will also come across a history of the inn, and information on important pieces of furniture found throughout the buildings. Peter and Jae have not overlooked a few of the modern comforts, incorporating whirlpool bathtubs, air-conditioning, and televisions with VCRs into some of the chambers. The Cedar Carriage House, another accommodation option, is modern in feeling but very private and has some of the most impressive views of the property.

After a good night's sleep, guests are treated to a sumptuous English breakfast. This is as creative as it is filling, with an ever-changing gourmet egg dish complemented by homemade muffins, breads, and scones. Fresh fruit and an assortment of juices, teas, and coffees round out the offerings. In the afternoon, guests are invited to partake in tea, while others might want to save their appetites for the early evening Virginia wine tasting accompanied by a selection of hors d'oeuvres. Weekend guests can take part in an extravagant dining experience at the inn, a delicious six-course meal prepared by Peter and enjoyed by all. The fare during the week is simpler, but in some ways much more intriguing because it arrives in a European supper basket. Guests might dine on lasagna, quiche, or crepes. Or, perhaps, Cornish game hens, a salad, and a torte or chocolate mousse might be on the menu for that night. Fresh flowers and even a book of poetry have also been known to make their way into the dinner basket.

As unique as the inn is, what surrounds it will undoubtedly be of more interest to Bowser. Although 50 acres of Pinot Noir-producing vineyards are part of the property, the grounds adjacent to the inn are filled with large trees shading the sprawling lawns and lining the paths that lead to rose gardens and two spring-fed ponds. While there are plenty of lovely areas to enjoy on the premises, there are also seasonal wine festivals, county fairs, and the Montpelier or Foxfield races to investigate, as well. In the Fall, many guests like to canoe along the James River and enjoy some of the foliage colors. But, by far, the most popular time to visit is in August, when the grapes are harvested and placed into vats. These ultimately are made into the wine that is bottled under the High Meadows Vineyard's private label.

It is not often that travelers get to experience such richness of texture in a country inn. The combination of historical authenticity, fine foods and wines, and lovely grounds truly require a visit, a visit that may well become an annual tradition.

THE CONYERS HOUSE

Slate Mills Road
Sperryville, Virginia 22740
(703) 987-8025
Hosts: Sandra and Norman Cartwright-Brown
Rooms: 6 doubles, 1 suite, 2 cottages
Rates: Doubles $100-150, Suite $195, Cottages $160-170
Payment: Personal checks
Children: Not appropriate for young children
Dogs: "Civilized, non-shedding dogs" are welcome with advance notice in
     both of the cottages and The Cellar Kitchen for a fee of $30 per night.
Open: All year

Tucked away on a hillside in the Blue Ridge Mountains, the charming Conyers House is situated in the heart of Virginia's hunt country. This is an unpretentious place, loaded with the Cartwright-Brown's collection of country antiques and lots of character. It is thought that a part of this antique house was built in 1776 by Hessian prisoners of war. In 1815 it was moved to its current location and attached to a house which Samuel Conyers built in 1810. The combined homesteads served for many years as a succession of general stores and, in the 1970s, were transformed into a hippie commune. It wasn't until a few years later that the current owners bought this rundown house and property and began to restore it. After two years of painstaking work on what was originally going to be their weekend retreat, the Cartwright-Browns decided to open their home to B&B guests.

Today, visitors will enjoy traveling along the winding, back country roads that meander by rolling hills and sprawling farms on the way to The Conyers House. As guests head up the gravel drive, they will first come to the charming two-story, coffee colored clapboard main house. Up the rather steep hillside to the left, lie the two smaller cottages. New arrivals usually ascend the stairs to the small wraparound porch, where saddles hang from their pegs, and then pass through the front door. The hallway provides a glimpse of what guests will soon discover is a treasure trove of fine antiques, lovely furniture, and interesting collectibles. Antique clocks rest on mahogany tables, needlepoint pillows are placed upon wing chairs, and vases of fresh and dried flower arrangements provide colorful accents. The formal yet comfortable dining room, with its Chippendale pedestaled table and sideboard set with a silver tea service, is the first chamber guests will pass by. Three mounted pheasants adorn the mantel of the oversized fireplace. Walk further into the house and discover the living room, complete with walls of books, overstuffed couches for enjoying them, and Oriental rugs covering the hardwood floor. In addition to the abundance of well worn antiques and family heirlooms, the common areas are also filled with hunt prints and a variety of memorabilia centering upon horseback riding. Guests won't be surprised to learn that Sandra is an accomplished rider and enjoys the seasonal "hunts" that lure many equestrians to the area.

Upon further inspection, it is evident that the comfortable formal feeling of the common rooms is also reflected in the guest chambers. Canopy and four-poster beds rest upon Oriental rugs, antique clocks are set on fireplace mantels, and small writing desks are placed next to windows framed with balloon shades. Each of these chambers have private bathrooms of varying size. For those traveling with their canine companions, there are three room configurations from which to choose. The first and possibly the most unique is the subterranean chamber known as the Cellar Kitchen. Although the centerpiece for this spacious room is a huge cooking fireplace, guests are equally intrigued with the high-beamed ceilings and thick stone walls. A waist-high bedstead is complemented by other comfortable furnishings. It is easy for guests and their canine cohorts to come and go through the separate entrance. While some might find this chamber a little dark at times, others are so charmed by the antique surroundings they hardly even notice.

A second option is The Hill House, situated just "30-paces" up the hillside from the main house. This offers a secluded and romantic setting, along with a host of modern amenities. The suite is not huge, but the low ceilings and abundance of windows do give it a good deal of charm. There is more than enough room to comfortably hold the four-poster bed and a small sitting area, while the side porch provides a little extra elbow room and wonderful views. The Franklin fireplace is usually stoked on cool nights, giving guests the chance to choose a snack from the small refrigerator and perhaps watch one of the videos from Sandra's "eclectic" collection. One of our favorite features of The Hill House is the double Jacuzzi bathtub, where many a guest has soothed his/her aching muscles at the end of a long day horseback riding or just exploring this picturesque region.

Further up the hill, there is The Old Spring House, which was moved to its current location in 1990. This chamber has the nicest views of the valley, and the melodic sound of rain falling upon the tin roof often lulls guests to sleep at night. What this cottage may lack in antiques and exquisite decor, it more than makes up for in ambiance. The beamed-ceilinged sitting area is furnished with a wood framed sofa set next to a whimsical Basset Hound table, and is warmed by the charming pot belly stove. A cassette player can provide the musical backdrop and a television and a VCR are available for visual diversions. There is a refrigerator which can store drinks and snacks to accompany the entertainment. Overhead, there is the cozy loft (set under the eaves) which contains a bed covered with a hunter green comforter. The good-size bright green bathroom is a most festive chamber, nicely appointed with a claw-footed bathtub, antique wash basin, and floral curtains. Keep in mind, this is horse country and do not be too surprised if, while enjoying the view from your porch, a horse or two comes sauntering up to pay you a visit.

Guests of the The Conyers House will discover there are almost always things laid out for them to munch on. In the afternoon, tea and baked goodies (along with sherry) are set out for those returning at the end of the day. While dinner is not a part of the B&B price, Sandra does create exquisite seven-course meals that she serves in the intimate dining room on fine china amid soft candlelight. Dinner guests choose their entrees ahead of time, and Sandra then decides which appetizers and secondary dishes will best complement the main course. This gourmet feast could include local rainbow trout in a dill and lemon sauce, pork tenderloin braised in cider with sauerkraut and apples, or venison with a rich wine cream sauce. Other entree choices include Cornish game hen with an herbal bread dressing and chutney, breast of duck in an orange sauce, and brace of quail with wild and brown rice dressing and chutney. These dishes are interspersed with soup, salad, pasta, sorbet, dessert, and coffee. Four different wines are also offered over the course of the evening, along with after-dinner drinks. Each morning, an equally impressive and most filling breakfast is offered. This repast may include buckwheat pancakes with maple syrup accompanied by an apple and sausage stuffing, or a lighter egg dish.

While guests will undoubtedly savor the delicious meals presented at The Conyers House, most are thoroughly taken in with the picturesque rural setting, the low-key atmosphere, the impressive antiques, and the overall sense of privacy they feel while staying here.

ASHTON COUNTRY HOUSE

1205 Middlebrook Avenue
Staunton, Virginia 24401
(800) 296-7819, (703) 885-7819
Hosts: Shelia Kennedy and Stanley Polanski
Rooms: 4 doubles
Rates: $75-90
Payment: Personal checks
Children: Not appropriate for children under 16 years of age
Dogs: Certain, well-behaved-dogs are welcome with prior approval provided there are not any guests staying at the B&B who are allergic to dogs.
Open: Weekends and holidays—September through May, seven-days-a-week through the summer

The Ashton Country House not only is surrounded by 20-acres of pastures dotted with stands of ancient shade trees, but also offers lovely views of the Allegheny and Blue Ridge Mountains. After many years of imagining what a country Bed and Breakfast should be like and how guests should be treated, Sheila and Stan found the perfect house for their venture in 1987. By 1990, they had opened the 1860 Greek-Revival Ashton Country House to guests, who were as impressed with the personalized attention they received as they were with the gracious surroundings.

A new arrival's first impressions are usually of the columned veranda and the 40-foot center hall and staircase. Empire furnishings dot the hall, while antique maps line the walls. Although the house is quite old, it is clear that it was built to last as all of the walls, interior and exterior, are constructed of brick. Whether sitting in the living room listening to Stan play the piano, dining in front of the fireplace, or wandering about the house in search of a peaceful alcove or an inviting chair on the porch, guests will find a comfortable mix of antiques, reproductions, and family heirlooms. The house is also rich in color, with roses and greens accenting some of the common areas and pastel yellow and blue hues brightening others.

Each of the upstairs bedrooms is equally appealing, although they differ markedly in character. The Master Suite is the largest and most formal chamber, and is dominated by the four poster bed. This bedroom connects with another room that features a distinctive Empire sleigh bed, complete with "bed stairs." The flavor of the Garden Room is quite different, with its brass and iron bedstead and mirrored oak armoire. The soft colors in the floral wallpaper and mauve accents gives this space a distinctly Victorian feel. The Audubon Room, named for the bird motifs on the wallpaper, lamps, and assorted collectibles in the chamber, is furnished with a pencil post bed and an English armoire. Those who are traveling with their canine cohort will undoubtedly be most comfortable in the Cottage Room, which is situated just above the kitchen off a second story porch. This chamber is reminiscent of a Maine cottage, although there is a Victorian twist. The rather simple Faux woodgrain-finished furnishings include a double bedstead, a dresser, and a comfortable wing chair. This bedroom is not only a terrific spot from which to take in the rich aroma of the freshly brewed morning coffee, but it also gives Bowser an easy way to get outside quickly without disturbing the other guests at the B&B.

It is the special touches that guests often remember fondly, long after their stay at the Ashton Country House. What most people certainly appreciate, in addition to the private oversized modern bathrooms with showers, is that beds are outfitted with flannel sheets and thick quilts in the winter and chambray cotton sheets in the summer. Ceiling fans keep the air circulating on warm summer nights, or more often, the cooling breeze and the sounds of the creek are just what guests need to lull them to sleep.

While some come to the Ashton Country House to relax and unwind, others choose to spend their time actively. A few of the popular recreational options include bicycling along country roads, or playing tennis or golf. Many also like to investigate the many natural wonders nearby such as the natural chimneys and caverns, the hot springs, or the harvest of fruits and maple sap which goes into making many wonderful apple and maple products found at the various festivals in Monterey. Some settle in for the duration of the stay, content to explore the grounds and visit with the animal menagerie, which consists of almost a dozen cats, two dogs, and a goat. Whether you are out and about or relaxing at the inn, afternoon tea and lemonade are set out for guests' enjoyment, along with an abundance of baked goodies.

The afternoon tea is just a sampling of what guests may expect for the following morning's meal. Most breakfast goers are usually very impressed with Sheila's culinary skills. In addition to being a grade school teacher, she has also trained at the New York Restaurant School. The ever changing morning repast includes a daily egg specialty coupled with bacon and/or sausage, fried potatoes, and homemade muffins and breads. The fresh fruit varies seasonally as do the juices. Stan and Sheila are well versed in a variety of subjects, bringing as much great conversation to the breakfast table as they do delicious food.

Finally, we realize there are a number of criteria to meet in order for travelers to bring their dog. However, we thought the Ashton Country House to be a terrific choice for a vacation destination with a very well-behaved Bowser and a rejuvenating one for the rest of his/her family, as well.

HOTEL STRASBURG

201 Holiday Street
Strasburg, Virginia 22657
(800) 348-8327, (703) 465-9191
Manager: Garry Rutherford
Rooms: 17 doubles, 10 suites
Rates: Doubles $69, Suites $72-149
Payment: AE, DC, MC, and Visa
Children: Welcome
Dogs: Well-behaved dogs are welcome with prior approval
Open: All year

Strasburg is only an hour's drive west of Washington, D.C., but it feels as though it is hundreds of miles away from the city. Located near the base of Massanutten Mountain and the entrance to the picturesque Skyline Drive, this sleepy town is home to the Hotel Strasburg. Built in the 1890s as a private hospital, its use changed dramatically in the 1900s when it was converted into an inn. Since then, the inn has offered a constant stream of travelers charming Victorian accommodations and good food. Today, the Hotel Strasburg stands intact as a delightful four story, white clapboard building with a wraparound porch. Once inside the hunter green foyer, guests can begin to peruse the public areas. Here, the Victorian era, with all of its heavy and elaborately carved furnishings and dark fabrics, is proudly displayed. The same feeling is extended to the upstairs bedrooms.

These chambers range from intimate doubles to rather spacious suites that offer the modern comforts of king-size beds and Jacuzzi bathtubs. Situated off a long hallway, each of these bedrooms, in contrast to the downstairs area, is quite bright. The natural board ceilings have been painted white, with the walls papered in charming floral prints and windows framed by delicate lace curtains. The antique Victorian furnishings are standouts, whether they be simple marble-topped tables, elaborately carved headboards, or immense oak armoires. Some of the pieces are even available to purchase, having been supplied by the Strasburg Antiques Emporium. Bates bedspreads top the brass, white iron, or canopy bedsteads. Sitting areas have comfortable armchairs, barrel tables, and standing lamps. Antique wash basins and other collectibles also dot the bedrooms. One of our favorite chambers is 210, with its burgundy floral wallpaper setting the decorative tone for the king-size bed that is surrounded by some of the hotel's Victorian antiques. Guests who want the most in privacy and modern comfort, should look into one of the four newly renovated suites in the adjacent Taylor House, which feature private bathrooms with Jacuzzi bathtubs.

Guests who choose to dine at the inn have a choice of three, interconnected dining rooms on the first floor of the main building. Dark green accent colors provide the perfect visual backdrop to the large, carved sideboards which rest on Oriental rugs. Windsor chairs surround the small tables clad with white linens. Entree selections range from the more traditional offerings such as filet mignon, tournedos Zinfandel, and veal Marsala to some local and nouvelle specialities including North Valley pork chops, chicken Shenandoah, and chicken and shrimp pesto. Afterwards, some people choose to retire to the pub for an evening libation. Those who want to bypass dinner at the inn, in favor of another restaurant, can just enjoy the Continental breakfast that is served here each morning.

Bowser will undoubtedly enjoy being so close to the mountains. While some visitors opt to explore the many natural caverns in the area (some are very commercial), others prefer to get out and hike or fish in the Shenandoah National Forest. There are also many areas off the Blue Ridge Parkway, where visitors can pull off and explore the many, less commercial, natural wonders. The Strasburg Emporium (reputed to hold the state's largest antique collection) is also an interesting place to look for a treasure or two. Whatever attracts guests to this region, they are certain to enjoy the warm hospitality, authentic accommodations, and reasonable prices at the Hotel Strasburg.

GRAVES MOUNTAIN LODGE

General Delivery
Route 670
Syria, Virginia 22743-4231
(703) 923-4231, Fax: (703) 923-4312
Innkeepers: Rachael and Jim Graves
Rooms: 53
Rates: $50-100 per person (AP)
Payment: MC and Visa
Children: Welcome
Dogs: Welcome in all accommodations except the motel units and 3 cottages
Open: All year

The Blue Ridge Mountains have long been popular with sightseers and naturalists eager to take in their pristine beauty. Situated to the east of the scenic Skyline Drive, lies a small rural town called Syria. After meandering along the country road that leads through town, visitors will come upon the Graves Mountain Lodge nestled up on a hillside. The lodge and its many outbuildings are set on expansive grounds that are enclosed by very old-fashioned post-less fencing, where each section is placed at a converse angle to the next enabling the rails to rest upon themselves. As new arrivals drive up to the main buildings for check-in, they will pass by a tennis court, children's playground, snack bar, and a pair of swimming pools.

The grey stained, vertical-board lodge is a sprawling two-story building that houses a dining room, recreational lounges, and a gift shop. Because it is centrally located to the rest of the complex, many guests find it is a natural place to congregate, whether in front of the large stone fireplaces, on the first floor covered patio set with rockers and comfortable chairs, or out on the second floor deck with its panoramic valley views. The front desk is the heartbeat for the lodge, outfitted with trophies, placards of the family crest, and other memorabilia. The adjacent gift shop offers a variety of collectibles, ranging from crafts and Indian carvings to jewelry, gift baskets, and assorted preserves made right on the premises. A helpful staff member is always on hand to direct people to one of the two game rooms situated at either end of the lodge. Here, Ping-Pong and pool tables are two of the more popular indoor diversions. A piano, television, board games, and an abundance of books and magazines complete the options.

The dining room is comprised of a handful of long tables which set the scene for the hearty "all you can eat" family-style meal. The attached side porch has additional tables and some of the most panoramic views of the valley. This is good old-fashioned home cooking and entrees range from fried chicken, roast beef, and country ham to rainbow trout, rib eye steak, and, the ever popular, pot luck selection. These are hearty meals that the kids will like too.

Most people come to the Graves Mountain Lodge for the outdoors and the relaxed atmosphere; the simple and rather rustic accommodations are almost secondary. The unpretentious, family-oriented ambiance is enhanced by an abundance of diversions and activities along with a good selection of comfortable accommodations. Some guests like the idea of staying in a cottage, where they can either supply their own linens or make use of the lodge's for an extra fee. The white clapboard Peon Palace farmhouse offers three bedrooms furnished with both double and bunk beds. There is also a kitchen, a pair of bathrooms, and a living room complete with a wood stove. Guests, who intend on staying for a week or more, may be interested in the Lower Cabin, which is probably one of the most rustic of the accommodations offered. The stone foundation, timber walls, and covered front porch set the tone for this intimate abode situated next to the Rose River. There is a common room with a fireplace, three upstairs bedrooms, a kitchen, and one bathroom. Of all the accommodations available at the lodge, the eight cottages appear to be the overall favorites among returning guests. Not only do they provide the most privacy, but they also give guests a little more living space by offering such options as porches, living rooms, and kitchens.

In addition to both the junior Olympic swimming pool and toddler's pool, there is a tennis court, an extensive choice of lawn games, and access to golf. Some guests may also be interested in hiking, hunting, and fishing. A guide is available for these activities if one wishes. One of the many great things about the lodge is that it serves as an ideal base for visiting the Lurray Caverns, Monticello, and the Wilderness Battlefield. Skyline Drive's scenic beauty is also easily accessible. The lodge has a working farm on the premises with cows, pigs, horses, a variety of fowl, and over 300 acres of orchards. The harvested fruits are turned into desserts, mixes, preserves, and jellies that are canned at the lodge's cannery.

Those looking for a completely relaxed vacation destination, where having a good time seems to be the primary thought on people's minds, will certainly want to look into a stay at the Graves Mountain Lodge.

BLUE BIRD HAVEN BED AND BREAKFAST

8691 Barhamsville Road (Highway 30 South)
Williamsburg-Toano, Virginia 23168
(804) 566-0177
Host: June Cottle
Rooms: 3 doubles
Rates: $50-65
Payment: Personal checks
Children: Welcome
Dogs: Welcome with prior approval
Open: All year

The Blue Bird Haven is an unpretentious B&B, one where guests will enjoy true Southern hospitality for a reasonable price. Set just nine miles from the center of Historic Williamsburg, this intimate white clapboard, ranch-style home, is well located for day trips throughout the area. Guests will know they have arrived in the right spot when they see the colorful pineapple flag hanging next to the back stoop. New arrivals follow the path to the front door, where they will be greeted by the affable June, and instantly made to feel at ease in her home.

Guests are encouraged to make use of the cozy wood-paneled den, complete with a television and woodstove, which is set just off the entry way. A breakfast room and separate kitchen can be found in the rear of the house. June spends much of her time over at The College of William and Mary working in the catering department. While this has proved to be a full-time job, she still enjoys taking care of her guests, particularly at mealtimes. Each morning, a full Southern-style breakfast is served and often features such dishes as cheese grits, Virginia ham, blueberry pancakes, eggs strata, and granola accompanied by an assortment of fresh fruits, muffins, pastries, and breads.

The bedrooms are located down a side hallway, with two chambers sharing a bathroom that has a shower/tub combination. The camel colored York Room offers a pair of wicker bedsteads covered with simple Bates spreads. The James Room, just down the hall, is decorated with a double four poster bed set against a blue backdrop. Shutters and draperies frame the windows, offering a great deal of privacy for this first floor room. The most spacious chamber is the Tidewater Room, which is found in the newer addition overlooking the backyard. This guest room has a queen-size four poster bed, a sitting area, and a private bathroom. There is even enough extra space for a roll away bed, should it be necessary. If the weather is particularly hot and humid, the air conditioning certainly will be appreciated; however, more often than not, guests are content to let the ceiling fans cool the rooms. June has added several personal touches to each of the chambers, ranging from placing handmade quilts on the beds to vases of fresh flowers on the dressers. In the evening, there is even a bed-time dessert tray set out for guests to enjoy.

Bowser won't find acres of land to romp on here, but might enjoy sitting on the screened-in porch and inspecting the variety of birds fluttering back and forth between the bird bath and the numerous bird feeders. The Blue Bird Haven B&B offers simple and intimate accommodations, friendly hospitality, and a terrific value in addition to providing easy access to Williamsburg, Busch Gardens, Jamestown, Virginia Beach, and a variety of other historic attractions.

As a final note, because June is now running the B&B on her own, she has had to cut back on the amount of last minute B&B business she can accept; however, she still loves to entertain her guests and looks forward to doing so with advance notice.

ANDERSON COTTAGE

Old Germantown Road
Warm Springs, Virginia 24484
(703) 839-2975, Fax: (703) 839-3058
Host: Jean Randolph Bruns
Rooms: 2 suites, 1 cottage
Rates: Suites $55-75, Cottage $110
Payment: Personal checks
Children: Older children are welcome in main house and younger children
        are more comfortable in the cottage
Dogs: Small, well-behaved dogs are welcome with advance notice and prior
        approval
Open: The Main House is closed from December until early March, the
        Cottage is open all year

Warm Springs is famous for its therapeutic hot springs and picturesque rural setting. Almost a half-century after the "medicinal" qualities of the warm springs were discovered, portions of the Anderson Cottage were constructed. The first structure to be built on the property was the brick kitchen in the 1820s. It was recently renovated and is now being utilized as a guest cottage. The rambling main house came next, but this is actually an 18th-century log tavern combined with an 1870s clapboard addition. The original historic character has been preserved, mostly due to the diligence of Jean's family who have owned the property for the last 100 years. Interestingly enough, for 80 of those years, the buildings have functioned as an inn.

The gardens surrounding the B&B are almost as interesting as the history behind the Anderson Cottage. Set just five miles from the renowned Hot Springs and Homestead Hotel, the two acres of lawn and gardens has its own warm springs running through it — 95 degrees to be exact. Guests have been known to spend hours sitting by the stream and either reading or just taking a little nap under one of the shade trees. Once inside the home, it is clear that this is a well loved place. The walls are a little out of plumb, hardwood floors are canted, and narrow hallways are charming. Filled with many of the family's original furnishings and other collectibles, this abode is very endearing. This house is in no way overdecorated with designer fabrics and untouchable antiques, it is instead a truly personal collection that Jean and her family have acquired over the years.

One of the guest chambers, situated on the first floor, is particularly appropriate for Bowser because it has a private entrance. The ample suite, aside from offering a queen-size bedroom and private bath, has an intimate living room with a fireplace. The suite on the second floor has a queen-size bedroom that is joined to a parlor containing a twin-size bed. The private bathroom even contains a wonderful antique tub. Of the remaining two upstairs guest chambers, one offers a double bed and the charm of a fireplace, along with the convenience of an extra twin bed. The other provides queen-bedded accommodations and a private bathroom. Each have their own unique views of the lovely grounds.

For those who prefer a little more privacy, we recommend the Kitchen Cottage. These intimate quarters do not have all of the same antique features as found in the rooms at the main house, but the Cottage does provide guests with a pair of bedrooms, a combination sitting room/kitchen, and a living room. The queen-size bed in one chamber, and the twin beds in another, make this an ideal configuration for families or couples traveling together. The living room is quite inviting and open, with garden views visible through the three walls of windows. Bowser will certainly like the idea of curling up in front of the fireplace at the end of the day, as well as the ease of access to the outdoors.

Those looking for some additional diversions will want to wander over to the main house where they will find thousands of books to choose from in the library. There are also parlors where some enjoy a game of backgammon, card games, or the chance to put together a jigsaw puzzle. The piano is also an attraction for some guests. During the warm weather, many gravitate to the intimate porches where they can read a favorite book or watch some of the other guests play a game of badminton or croquet. Those who want to travel further afield, might try the golfing at one of The Homestead's courses, fishing in the local streams and rivers, and trail riding at River Ridge. There are also wonderful lakes for swimming and good trails for hiking. Of course, there are also many cultural attractions, along with craft and specialty shops in the area.

We have found that most people fall into the quiet routine of the household, rising late and enjoying one of Jean's English breakfasts. Some mornings, guests are treated to pancakes covered with real maple syrup and accompanied by sausage. Other days, it is the more traditional eggs, herbed tomatoes, and bacon along with homemade preserves for topping the fresh breads and rolls.

THE PINK HOUSE BED AND BREAKFAST

Waterford, Virginia 22190
(703) 882-3453
Hosts: Charles and Marie Anderson
Rooms: 1 suite
Rates: $95-100
Payment: Personal checks
Children: Those over twelve years of age are welcome
Dogs: "Well-restrained dogs that are housebroken" welcome with prior approval
Open: All year

Those who are searching for an historic village, uncluttered with boutiques or an overabundance of tourists, will find Waterford, Virginia to be ideal. Waterford, which is listed as a National Historic Landmark, was founded in 1733 by Quakers who emigrated from Bucks County, Pennsylvania. Most of the buildings and homes were built by the Quakers in the early 1800s and provide the historic framework, charm, and feeling of simplicity which is integral to this area. It is surprising to discover that the town has somehow resisted modernization and development, remaining much the way it did a century ago. The Pink House Bed and Breakfast lies in the heart of this historic village. The three-story brick abode is painted a faded Bermudian pink and accented with black shutters and an expansive wraparound deck that overlooks the street and the gardens.

Although The Pink House formerly offered two suites, it now has just one since Marie transformed the other into her office. The Opera Suite is a three room chamber, furnished with classic 18th-century European antiques set amid more contemporary American pieces. A baby grand piano is the focal point for one sitting room, while another is furnished with a Chippendale sofa and matching armchairs set around the fireplace and the wall of built-in bookshelves. Hardwood floors are covered with dark red area rugs and coordinated swags are draped at a pair of side-by-side windows. In contrast, the bedroom seems rather Spartan. A few collectibles grace the white walls which are accented by calico fabrics framing the windows and a colorful handmade quilt folded over a wooden towel rack. Beyond the footboard of the double bed, is an original cooking fireplace. The large bathroom has an assortment of toiletries and, best of all, is equipped with a whirlpool tub. Those traveling with Bowser will appreciate the private entrance, which leads to the gardens and beyond to the fields around Waterford.

Hearty appetites will be happy to know that Marie likes to "start the day with a good feed." Although this was said rather tongue-in-cheek, breakfast truly is a delightful English-style repast. It begins with fresh fruit and is followed by an egg dish created from farm fresh eggs (bought from neighboring farms). The grilled tomatoes are reminiscent of an English B&B, and are complemented by Irish soda bread, scones, or biscuits complete with a variety of preserves. This meal is often served on the ivy covered terrace overlooking the gardens, which is one of the few places that Bowser might catch a glimpse of the two cats who spend most of their time outside. After breakfast, the formal gardens will tantalize even those with only a passing interest in things botanical. Or, there are many fine spots available for those just content to read the paper and relax in the warmth of the morning sun.

People do not usually come to Waterford seeking boutiques or trendy restaurants, but would rather unwind and rejuvenate in a peaceful setting for a couple of days. The quaint village is often described in such periodicals as *National Geographic*, which delve into the town's unique history, as well as explore its picturesque surroundings. Those who happen to visit in early

October, will find that most of the town turns out for the Waterford Foundation Homes Tour and Craft Exhibit. This was originally started to raise money for restoring portions of the historic village, and not only gives visitors the opportunity to see the interiors of some of these charming houses, but also gives them the chance to purchase some of the many local crafts that are on display.

WEST VIRGINIA

THE CURRENT

HC 64, Box 135
Denmar Road
Hillsboro, West Virginia 24946
(304) 653-4722
Hostess: Leslee McCarty
Rooms: 3 doubles, 1 suite
Rates: Doubles $50, Suite $75
Payment: MC and Visa
Children: Welcome (roll-away beds and babysitters are available)
Dogs: Well-behaved small dogs are welcome if the house is not too full
Open: All year

Hillsboro is a sleepy town situated off a scenic country route, about 30 miles from both Virginia's Hot Springs and West Virginia's White Sulphur Springs. While these larger towns are known for their therapeutic mineral springs, this region is equally popular with hikers and bicyclists who enjoy the picturesque countryside and the Greenbrier River Trail.

Somewhat of an activist, Leslee first came to this part of the state to work on a community development project. What was supposed to be a temporary venture, turned out to be much more of a commitment as she ended up meeting John, getting married, and settling down in this rural community. Their home, and B&B, was formerly known as the Beard farmhouse, but has now been renamed The Current. Originally built in 1905, the rambling house is located on a winding country road. Guests find it by traveling past the town center's playing fields and the Denmar State Hospital, until they arrive at a small, Presbyterian Church. Across the way is The Current. Leslee has recently purchased the church and eventually plans to refurbish it to accommodate overnight guests and small groups.

For the time being, guests all stay in the charming farmhouse, which is situated near the banks of the Greenbrier River. It is easy to understand why this place is such a favorite overnight destination for bicyclers and hikers. The pastoral setting, delightful accommodations, and affable nature of Leslee make it a natural choice for B&B enthusiasts looking for a relaxed environment. Physically, the house reflects its simple past with the oak woodworking around the doors and the oak windows framed by white lace curtains. An assortment of family heirlooms and regional crafts make for an especially warm and inviting atmosphere. There are a number of rooms to choose from, the largest being the first floor suite. When we last spoke with Leslee, her parents were in residence in this particular room, but once their house is completed (a project Leslee is helping out with) it should be available on a regular basis. For the time being, guests are welcome to stay here when her parents are traveling (which is frequently). This spacious chamber has a large room with a queen-bed, a sitting room with a television, and a private bathroom. The three spacious upstairs guest rooms vary in layout with combinations of doubles and pairs of twin beds. As with the first floor common areas, the collection of antiques and family collectibles, country quilts, handcrafts, and fresh flower arrangements provide just the right environment for a delightful B&B experience. A half-bath on the second floor, shared by these chambers, is convenient; however, most opt to use one of the two full baths situated on the first floor.

Each morning a full breakfast is offered to guests in the dining room, which is often warmed by a woodstove. This hearty meal includes such dishes as blueberry pancakes, quiche, French toast, scrambled eggs, and omelets. Fresh fruit, cereals, and homemade breads and preserves are welcome complements to this delicious meal. Leslee is also happy to adapt the menu to meet the needs of vegetarians, for a small additional fee. With a substantial meal under one's belt, guests can spend the day in as energetic or relaxed a fashion as they choose.

As we mentioned, there are terrific bicycling and hiking options right down the road, as well as canoeing, golf, and tennis facilities in the nearby area. Literary enthusiasts might be interested in investigating the birthplace of Pearl S. Buck, located nearby. At the end of the day, many return to The Current and relax on the deck, which offers some of the loveliest views of the property. The hot tub is another favorite place to sooth tired muscles, particularly after a day of hiking, bicycling, cross-country skiing, or just sightseeing.

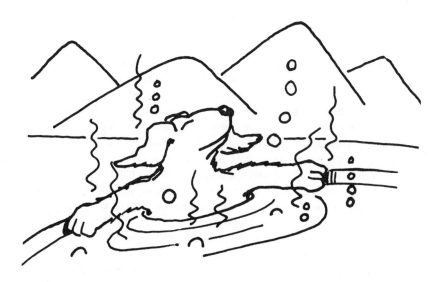

THE GENERAL LEWIS

301 East Washington Street
Lewisburg, West Virginia 24901
(800) 628-4454, (304) 645-2600
Innkeeper: Rodney Fisher
Rooms: 24 doubles, 2 suites
Rates: Doubles $55-70, Suites $80
Payment: AE, MC, and Visa
Children: Welcome, children under 10 are free of charge
Dogs: Welcome with prior approval and a $5 fee
Open: All year

Lewisburg is located along the eastern border of West Virginia, in the lush Greenbrier Valley. This historic region has long been of great interest to both Revolutionary and Civil War historians, but even non-historians will be enamored with this lovely old-fashioned town. Gracious old brick and wood frame homes, set amid historic stone churches, parks, and museums, have been so carefully preserved over the years that the entire town has been entered into the National Register of Historic Places. One of the dwellings that occupies center stage in Lewisburg is the rather extraordinary General Lewis. An antique stage coach rests to the side of the semi-circular drive, which leads to the inn. Although the coach is now considered a museum piece, its duties at one time included taking travelers to the numerous fresh water springs that lined the James River.

Today, there is still a sense of history at the inn. Guests ascend the front steps leading to the two-story veranda which spans the middle section of the inn. Supported by massive pillars, the veranda is enhanced with comfortable rocking chairs. The inn's foyer is filled with impressive antiques, lovely heirlooms, and a variety of historic treasures and memorabilia. At times, guests have the feeling they are visiting a museum rather than staying at an inn. The hand-carved walnut and pine front desk was actually moved from another historic hotel and it has been said that Patrick Henry and Thomas Jefferson once registered at this desk. Those who want to just relax for a few minutes and soak in the antiquity of the inn might choose the beamed-ceiling living room, that is also furnished with a variety of American antiques collected by the inn's founders, Randolph and Mary Hock. A pillar and scroll clock, spinning wheel, harvest table, and corner hutch are just a few of the countless pieces of interest. The hardwood floors are covered with Oriental rugs, the walls are adorned with works of art and pottery, all of which can be enjoyed from the comfortable rocking and armchairs. Anyone with an interest in history will truly enjoy Memory Hall located next to the central staircase. Here, a fascinating array of antique guns, farm tools, cooking implements, musical instruments, household utensils, and a collection of pottery and glassware line the walls.

The guest chambers are decorated in keeping with the common rooms at the inn. These are located off long hallways that are also appointed with country antiques and memorabilia. The good-sized bed chambers have hardwood floors covered with braided or Oriental rugs. Floral wallpapers, in subdued colors, enhance the walls above the wainscotings. High bedsteads are covered with Bates spreads, some of these are modified four poster and others canopied. Accents include brass sconces and standing iron lamps, along with vases of fresh flowers. The rockers and wing chairs aptly reflect the period as well. Some of the modern concessions are ceiling fans, color televisions, air conditioning, telephones, and private bathrooms. Those who are interested in one of the two-bedroom suites will find they are exceptionally spacious, located in the original 1834 home, and have nice views of the inn's garden.

The inn is actually comprised of several sections, each built during different time periods. The dining room is part of the original 1834 home, and aside from serving terrific meals, it also has many notable architectural features. The doorways leading from the lobby were once windows, the original front door now serves as the inn's main front door, and the hand-hewn beamed ceilings were formerly used in the slaves' quarters. Subdued lighting and white tablecloths provide a tranquil, yet unpretentious, setting. The entrees are not only a good value, but are also served in the hearty Southern tradition. The specialties of the house are the mountain trout and fried chicken.

Although the inn does not offer many diversions for guests and their canine cohorts, there are plenty of other things to do in the area. The Greenbrier River Hiking and Bicycling Trail, the Lost World Caverns, and white water rafting are just some of the options. Of course, visitors might be interested in paying a visit to some of the last remaining springs. A leisurely walking tour of town, with Bowser, will also reveal the Civil War cemetery, the General Andrew Lewis Park, the 1796 Old Stone Presbyterian Church, the 1820 John Wesley Methodist Church, and the oldest house in town, an authentic log cabin.

SMOKE HOLE LODGE

P.O. Box 953
Petersburg, West Virginia 26847
No telephone, but messages may be left at Alt's Grocery (304) 257-4774
Host: Edward Stifel
Rooms: 2 dorms, 5 doubles
Rates: $100 for the first person, $85 for each additional person (AP)
Payment: Personal checks
Children: Welcome (those under 4 years of age are free of charge)
Dogs: Welcome with prior approval provided they do not bother the lodge's
     animals
Open: Early May through October

Many an adventurous traveler has wondered what it would be like to leave the pressures and complications of the modern world and escape to a simpler lifestyle. Doing without the conveniences that many take for granted, such as electricity and telephones, travelers could instead focus on blending in with their natural surroundings and enjoying the intrinsic beauty of an area. Backpacking and hiking through remote regions is one way to achieve this feeling; however, for those who want a bed to sleep in and walls around them, there is a rustic retreat in the hills of West Virginia known as the Smoke Hole Lodge.

Originally built in 1981 by Edward Stifel, the lodge is set amid 1,500 acres in West Virginia's Smoke Hole gorge region. The gorge is surrounded by mountains and remains basically undisturbed by modern man. The history of this site dates back to pre-Colonial times, when the area was a popular hunting ground for the native Indians. Here, along with various other natural wonders, they discovered a remote cave that contained a natural flu which was ideal for smoking their meat.

Today, it is difficult not to be impressed by the unadulterated natural beauty of the area. However, don't try to just drop by and investigate the Smoke Hole Lodge — it's virtually impossible. Those who know how to get to Petersburg are off to a good start; however, the directions from there are almost incomprehensible. Therefore, trust Ed when he suggests using the lodge's "Super Truck" to navigate the 5-miles of very bumpy dirt back roads. These virtual "cartpaths" have led even the most experienced off-road drivers into a ditch or two. The hour and twenty minute trip from Petersburg (one hour on the dirt road) is worth every bump though, because the ultimate destination is a remarkable, unspoiled wilderness retreat.

Once at the lodge, the mountains provide the backdrop for the dense foliage and ancient forests that rise around the lodge. Regardless of the season, there are crystal clear mountain streams for fishing and uncrowded hiking trails, and there is an abundance of wildlife who clearly are the keepers of the land. Humanity is the interloper here. While there are no organized diversions like golf or tennis, there is three-mile frontage on the south branch of the Potomac River, which offers great tubing, fishing, swimming, and canoeing opportunities. During the quieter times of the day or evening, guests are likely to find foraging deer, hawks hunting for prey, and possibly even run across an occasional bear who inadvertently wanders through the property. The lodge also has a large domesticated population, including dogs, cats, geese, chickens, and cows.

The lodge itself is rather rustic, but exceptionally clean, offering a choice of five double bedrooms and two dormitories, the latter of which accommodate four to five guests each. All of the rooms have a private bathroom and come equipped with fresh linens and towels. The few modern conveniences are powered by kerosene, wood, and bottled gas. When guests aren't exploring the out of doors, they are apt to gather in the large living room and warm themselves in front of the fireplace. There are rarely more than eight guests at any one time, making for a convivial atmosphere in which everyone soon feels right at home with one another. The before-dinner social hour can be enjoyed on either of the two porches, where folks can visit, sample a few hors d'oeuvres, and watch the spectacular sunsets. All of the hearty, family-style meals are served in the dining room, where the simple atmosphere is enhanced by views of the river.

Granted, a vacation at the Smoke Hole Lodge is not for everyone. But for those who are enamored with the idea having only stars from the night sky to light their way and the sounds of the wind and the water to lull them to sleep, this will prove to be a genuine piece of paradise.

THE REST
OF THE BEST

DELAWARE

DEWEY	Atlantic Oceanside Motel	(302) 227-8811
BEACH	1700 Hwy 1	
DOVER	Dover Budget Inn	(302) 734-4433
	1426 North Dupont Hwy	
	Holiday Inn Dover	(302) 734-5701
	348 North DuPont Hwy	
	Sheraton Inn	(302) 678-8500
	1570 North DuPont Hwy	
NEWARK	Best Western	(302) 738-3400
	260 Chapman Rd	
	Howard Johnson	(302) 368-8521
	1119 South College Ave	
	Comfort Inn	(302) 368-8715
	1120 South College Ave.	
	Red Roof Inn	(302) 292-2870
	415 Stanton Christiana Rd	
	Residence Inn-Marriott	(302) 453-9200
	240 Chapman Rd	
NEW	Econo Lodge	(302) 322-4500
CASTLE	232 South Dupont Hwy	
	Econo Lodge	(302) 654-5775
	3 Memorial Dr.	
	Howard Johnson Motor Lodge	(302) 656-7771
	2162 New Castle Ave	
	New Castle Travelodge	(302) 654-5544
	1213 West Ave	
	Quality Inn	(302) 328-6666
	147 North Dupont Hwy	
	Ramada Inn	(302) 658-8511
	Rte 13	
	Rodeway Inn	(302) 328-6246
	111 South Dupont	
REHOBETH	Atlantic Budget Inn	(302) 227-9446
BEACH	154 Rehobeth Ave	
SEAFORD	Comfort Inn	(302) 629-8385
	1450 Beaver Dam Rd	
WILMINGTON	Best Western	(302) 656-9436
	1807 Concord Pike	
	Guest Quarters Suite Hotel	(302) 656-9300
	707 North King St	
	Holiday Inn	(302) 655-5488
	King & 7th streets	

Raddison Hotel	(302) 478-6000
4727 Concord Pike	
Sheraton Suites	(302) 654-8300
422 Delaware Ave	
Wilmington Hilton	(302) 792-2700
630 Naamans Rd	

WASHINGTON D.C.

Best Western (202) 457-0565
 1121 New Hampshire Ave NW
Clarion (202) 232-8000
 1315 16th St NW
Capitol Hilton (202) 393-1000
 16th and K Streets NW
The Carlton (202) 638-2626
 923 16th St at K St NW
Embassy Suites (202) 362-9300
 4300 Military Rd NW
Grand Hotel (202) 429-0100
 2350 M Street NW
Guest Quarters (202) 785-2000
 801 New Hampshire Ave NW
Guest Quarters (202) 333-8060
 2500 Pennsylvannia Ave NW
Hilton and Towers (202) 483-3000
 1919 Connecticut NW
Holiday Inn (202) 479-4000
 555 C St SW
Holiday Inn (202) 483-2000
 1501 Rhode Island Ave NW
Holiday Inn (202) 338-4600
 2101 Wisconsin Ave NW
Holiday Inn (202) 737-1200
 1155 14th St NW
Hotel Washington (202) 638-5900
 Pennsylvannia Ave at 15th Street NW
Marriott (202) 872-1500
 1221 22nd St NW
Omni Shoreham Hotel (202) 234-0700
 2500 Calvert St NW
One Washington Circle Hotel (202) 872-1680
 One Washington Circle
Park Hyatt (202) 789-1234
 1201 24th St NW
Pullman Highland Hotel (202) 797-2000
 1914 Connecticut Ave NW
Quality Hotel (202) 638-1616
 415 New Jersey Ave NW
Quality Hotel (202) 332-9300
 1900 Connecticut Ave NW

Radisson Park Terrace Hotel	(202) 232-7000
1515 Rhode Island Ave NW	
Savoy Suites	(202) 337-9700
2505 Wisconsin Ave NW	
Sheraton	(202) 328-2000
2660 Woodley Rd NW	
Washington	(202) 638-5900
515 15th St	
Washington Court on Capitol Hill	(202) 628-2100
525 New Jersey Ave NW	
Washington Rennaissance	(202) 898-9000
999 Knight St NW	
Washington Vista	(202) 429-1700
1400 M Street NW	
Willard Intercontinental	(202) 628-9100
1401 Pennsylvania Ave NW	
Wyndham Bristol Hotel	(202) 955-6400
2430 Pennsylvania Ave NW	

MARYLAND

ABERDEEN	Days Inn	(410) 272-8500
	783 West Bel Air Ave	
	Holiday Inn	(410) 272-8100
	1007 Beards Hill Rd	
	Howard Johnson's Lodge	(410) 272-6000
	793 West Bel Air Ave	
	Sheraton Inn	(410) 273-6300
	Rte 22	
ANNAPOLIS	Holiday Inn	(410) 224-3150
	210 Holiday Court	
	Loews Annapolis	(410) 263-7777
	126 West St	
	Residence Inn	(410) 573-0300
	170 Admiral Cochrane Dr	
BALTIMORE	Admiral Fell Inn	(410) 522-7377
	888 South Broadway	
	Marriott Inner Harbor Hotel	(410) 962-0202
	110 South Eutah St	
	Best Western	(410) 633-9500
	5625 O'Donnell St	
	Doubletree Inn	(410) 235-5400
	4 West University Pkwy	
	Holiday Inn	(410) 265-1400
	1800 Belmont Ave	
	Holiday Inn	(410) 485-7900
	6510 Frankfort Ave	
	Ramada Hotel	(410) 265-1100
	1701 Belmont Ave	
	Ramada Inn Inner Harbor	(410) 539-1188
	8 North Howard St	
	Sheraton Inner Harbor Hotel	(410) 962-8300
	300 South Charles St	
	Sheraton International Hotel (BWI)	(410) 859-3300
	7032 Elm Rd	
	Tremont Hotel	(410) 576-1200
	8 East Pleasant St	
	Tremont Plaza	(410) 727-2222
	222 St. Paul	
BELTSVILLE	Holiday Inn	(301) 937-4455
	4095 Powder Mill Rd	

BETHESDA	Marriott	(301) 897-9400
	5151 Pooks Hill Rd	
	Marriott Suites	(301) 897-5600
	6711 Democracy Blvd	
	Ramada Hotel	(301) 654-1000
	8400 Wisconsin Ave	
	Residence Inn by Marriott	(301) 718-0200
	7335 Wisconsin Ave	
BOWIE	Econo Lodge	(301) 464-2200
	4502 Crain Highway	
CAMP	Days Inn	(301) 423-2323
SPRINGS	5001 Mercedes Blvd	
CATONSVILLE	Econo Lodge West	(410) 744-5000
	5801 Baltimore Nat. Pike	
CHEVERLY	Howard Johnsons Lodge	(301) 779-7700
	5811 Annapolis Rd	
COLUMBIA	Columbia Inn	(410) 730-3900
	10207 Wincopin Circle	
CUMBERLAND	Holiday Inn	(301) 724-8800
	100 South George St	
DELMAR	Atlantic Budget Inn	(410) 896-3434
	Route 13	
EASTON	Atlantic Budget Inn	(410) 822-2200
	8058 Ocean Gateway	
	Comfort Inn	(410) 820-8333
	8523 Ocean Gateway	
	The Tidewater Inn	(410) 822-1300
	101 East Denver St	
EDGEWOOD	Best Western	(410) 679-9700
	1709 Edgewood Rd	
	Days Inn	(410) 671-9990
	2116 Emmorton Park Rd	
ELKTON	Knights Inn	(410) 392-6680
	262 Belle Hill Rd	
FREDERICK	Comfort Inn	(301) 695-6200
	420 Prospect Blvd	
	Days Inn	(301) 694-6600
	5646 Buckeyestown Pike	
	Frederick Super 8	(301) 695-2881
	5579 Spectrum Drive	
	Holiday Inn	(301) 694-7500
	5400 Holiday Drive	
	Holiday Inn	(301) 662-5141
	999 West Patrick St	

	Knights Inn	(301) 698-0555
	6005 Urbana Pike	
	Red Horse Motor Inn	(301) 662-0281
	998 West Patrick St	
FROSTBURG	Comfort Inn	(301) 689-2050
	Route 36	
GAITHERSBURG	Hilton	(301) 977-8900
	620 Perry Pkway	
	Holiday Inn	(301) 948-8900
	2 Montgomery Village Ave	
GLEN BURNIE	Hampton Inn	(410) 761-7666
	6617 Ritchie Hwy	
	Holiday Inn	(410) 761-8300
	6600 Ritchie Hwy	
	Holiday Inn	(410) 636-4300
	6323 Ritchie Hwy	
GRANTSVILLE	Holiday Inn	(301) 895-5993
	Highway 68	
GREENBELT	Marriott	(301) 441-3700
	6400 Ivy Lane	
	Holiday Inn	(301) 982-7000
	7200 Hanover Drive	
HAGERSTOWN	Best Western	(301) 791-3560
	18221 Mason Dixon Rd	
	Best Western	(301) 733-0830
	431 Dual Highway	
	Holiday Inn	(301) 739-9050
	900 Dual Highway	
	Motel 6	(301) 582-4445
	11321 Massey Blvd	
	Ramada Inn	(301) 733-5100
	901 Dual Highway	
HANOVER	Red Roof Inn	(410) 712-4070
	7306 Parkway Dr	
HUNT VALLEY	Embassy Suites Hotel	(410) 584-1400
	213 International Circle	
	Hampton Inn	(410) 527-1500
	11200 York Rd	
	Marriott	(410) 785-7000
	245 Shawan	
	Residence Inn	(410) 584-7370
	10710 Beaver Dam Rd	
JESSUP	Red Roof Inn	(410) 796-0380
	8000 Washington Blvd	

LANDOVER HILLS	Comfort Inn 6205 Annapolis Rd	(301) 322-6000
LANHAM	Holiday Inn 5910 Princess Garden Pkwy	(301) 459-1000
	Red Roof Inn 9050 Lanham Severn Rd	(301) 731-8830
LA PLATA	Best Western 6900 Crain Highway	(301) 934-4900
LAUREL	Comfort Suites Hotel 14402 Laurel Place	(301) 206-2600
	Holiday Inn 3400 Fort Meade Rd	(301) 498-0900
LINTHICUM	Comfort Inn 6921 Baltimore Annapolis Blvd	(410) 789-9100
	Holiday Inn 890 Elkridge Landing Rd	(410) 859-8400
	Marriott (Airport) 1743 West Nursery Rd	(410) 859-8300
	Red Roof Inn 827 Elkridge Landing Rd	(410) 850-7600
NEW CARROLLTON	Sheraton Hotel 8500 Annapolis Rd	(301) 459-6700
OCEAN CITY	Days Inn 4201 Coastal Highway	(410) 289-6488
	Fenwick Inn 13801 Coastal Highway	(410) 250-1100
	Sheraton Fontainebleau 10100 Ocean Highway	(410) 524-3535
OXON HILL	Red Roof Inn 6170 Oxen Hill Rd	(301) 567-8030
PIKESVILLE	Holiday Inn 1721 Reisterstown Rd	(410) 486-5600
POCOMOKE CITY	Days Inn 1540 Ocean Highway	(410) 957-3000
	Quality Inn 825 Ocean Highway	(410) 957-1300
PRINCESS ANNE	Econo Lodge 10936 Market Lane	(410) 651-9400
ROCKVILLE	Potomac Inn 3 Research Court	(301) 840-0200
	Ramada Inn 1775 Rockville Pike	(301) 881-2300
	Woodfin Suites Hotel 1380 Piccard Dr	(301) 590-9880

ST. MICHAELS	Best Western	(410) 745-3333
	1228 South Talbot	
SALISBURY	Comfort Inn	(410) 543-4666
	Route 11	
	Days Inn	(410) 749-6200
	Route 13N	
	Hampton Inn	(410) 546-1300
	1735 N. Salisbury Blvd	
	Holiday Inn	(410) 742-7194
	Route 11	
	Sheraton Inn	(410) 546-4400
	300 S. Salisbury Blvd	
SILVER	Holiday Inn	(301) 589-0800
SPRING	8777 Georgia Ave	
SNOW HILL	River House Inn	(410) 632-2722
	201 East Market St	
SOLOMONS	Holiday Inn Hotel	(410) 326-6311
	1555 Holiday Ave	
THURMONT	Rambler Motel	(301) 271-2424
	Route 15	
TIMONIUM	Red Roof Inn	(410) 666-0380
	111 West Tomonium Rd	
TOWSON	Days Inn	(410) 882-0900
	8801 Walkraven Blvd	
	Holiday Inn	(410) 823-4410
	1100 Cromwell Bridge Rd	
WALDORF	HoJo Inn	(301) 932-5090
	3125 Crain Highway	
	Holiday Inn	(301) 645-8200
	1 St. Patricks Dr	
WESTMINSTER	Comfort Inn	(410) 857-1900
	451 Western Maryland College Dr.	
	Days Inn	(410) 857-0500
	2500 S. Cranberry Rd	
WILLIAMSPORT	Days Inn	(310) 582-3500
	310 E. Potomac St	

VIRGINIA

ALEXANDRIA	Best Western 625 First St	(703) 548-6300
	Comfort Inn US 1	(703) 765-2325
	Comfort Inn I-95	(703) 922-0132
	Quest Quarters Suites 1900 Diagonal Rd	(703) 684-5900
	Holiday Inn 2460 Eisenhower Ave	(703) 960-3400
	Holiday Inn 480 King St	(703) 549-6080
	Howard Johnsons 5821 Richmond Hwy	(703) 329-1400
	Ramada Hotel 901 N. Fairfax St	(703) 683-6000
	Ramada Inn 4641 Kenmore Ave	(703) 751-4510
	Red Roof Inn 5975 Richmond Hwy	(703) 960-5200
ALTAVISTA	Comfort Suites 1558 Main St	(804) 369-4000
ARLINGTON	Renaissance Hotel 950 N. Stafford St	(703) 528-6000
	Doubletree Hotel 300 Army Navy Dr	(703) 416-4400
	Holiday Inn 4610 N. Fairfax Dr	(703) 243-9800
	Howard Johnsons 2650 Jefferson Davis Hwy	(703) 684-7200
	Hyatt Hotel 1325 Wilson Blvd	(703) 525-1234
	Marriott Hotel 1700 Jefferson Davis Hwy	(703) 920-3230
ASHLAND	Comfort Inn 101 Cottage Greene Dr	(804) 752-7777
BEDFORD	Best Western Hotel 921 Blue Ridge Ave	(703) 586-8266
BLACKSBURG	Best Western 900 Plantation Ave	(703) 552-7770

	Marriott Hotel	(703) 552-7001
	900 Prices Fork Rd	
	Comfort Inn	(703) 951-1500
	3705 S. Main St	
	Holiday Inn	(703) 951-1330
	3503 Holiday La.	
BLAND	Big Walker Hotel	(703) 688-3331
	I-77	
BRISTOL	Days Inn	(703) 669-6974
	1014 Old Airport Rd	
	Econo Lodge	(703) 466-2112
	912 Commonwealth Ave	
	Holiday Inn	(703) 669-7171
	Euclid St	
BUCHANAN	Wattstull Inn	(703) 254-1551
	Rte 1	
CARMEL CHURCH	Comfort Inn	(804) 448-2828
	Rte 207	
	Days Inn	(804) 448-2011
	Carmel Church Rd	
CARROLLTON	Econo Lodge	(804) 357-9057
	20080 Brewers Neck Blvd	
CHANTILLY	Comfort Inn	(703) 818-8200
	4050 Westfax Dr	
	Marriott (Airport) Hotel	(703) 471-9500
	333 W. Service Rd	
CHARLOTTSVILLE	Best Western	(804) 296-8111
	105 Emmett St	
	Best Western	(804) 296-5501
	1613 Emmett St	
	Comfort Inn	(804) 293-6188
	1807 Emmett St	
	Holiday Inn	(804) 293-9111
	1600 Emmett St	
	Holiday Inn	(804) 977-5100
	1200 5th St SW	
	Knight's Inn	(804) 973-8133
	1300 Seminole Tr	
CHESAPEAKE	Days Inn	(804) 487-8861
	1439 George Washington	
	Wellesley Inn	(804) 366-0100
	Greenbrier Pkwy	
CHESTER	Days Inn	(804) 748-5871
	Rte 10	

CHRISTIANSBURG	Days Inn	(703) 382-0261
	Hwy 460	
	Econo Lodge	(703) 382-6161
	2430 Roanoke St	
COLLINSVILLE	Dutch Inn	(703) 647-3721
	633 Virginia Ave	
	Econo Lodge	(703) 647-3941
	800 S. Virginia Ave	
COVINGTON	Comfort Inn	(703) 962-2141
	Mallow Rd	
	Holiday Inn	(703) 962-4951
	I-64	
	Knight's Court	(703) 962-7600
	Valley Ridge Rd	
CULPEPPER	Comfort Inn	(703) 825-4900
	890 Willis Ln	
	Holiday Inn	(703) 825-1253
	Rte 29 (Bus)	
DALEVILLE	Best Western	(703) 992-1234
	235 Roanoke Rd	
DANVILLE	Strattford Inn	(804) 793-2500
	2500 Riverside	
DUBLIN	Bell's B&B	(703) 674-6331
	13 Giles Ave	
DUMFRIES	Holiday Inn	(703) 221-1141
	Rte 234	
EMPORIA	Best Western	(804) 634-3200
	1100 W. Atlantic Ave	
	Comfort Inn	(804) 348-3282
	1411 Skippers Rd	
	Days Inn	(804) 634-9481
	921 W. Atlantic Ave	
	Hampton Inn	(804) 634-9200
	1207 W. Atlantic Ave	
	Holiday Inn	(804) 634-4191
	I-95	
FAIRFAX	Comfort Inn	(703) 591-5900
	11180 Main St	
	Holiday Inn	(703) 591-5500
	3535 Chain Bridge Rd	
	Holiday Inn	(703) 352-2525
	11787 Lee Jackson Hwy	
	Hyatt	(703) 818-1234
	12777 Fair Lakes Cr.	

	Wellesley Inn	(703) 359-2888
	10327 Lee Hwy	
FALLS CHURCH	Marriott Hotel	(703) 849-9400
	3111 Fairview Dr	
	Ramada Hotel	(703) 893-1340
	7801 Leesburg Pike	
FANCY GAP	Doe Run Lodge	(703) 398-2212
	Rt 2	
FREDERICKSBURG	Best Western	(703) 371-5050
	2205 William St	
	Best Western	(703) 373-0000
	543 Warrenton Rd	
	Best Western	(703) 786-7404
	Rte 3	
	Days Inn	(703) 898-6800
	5316 Jefferson Davis Hwy	
	Dunning Mills Inn	(703) 373-1256
	2305 C Jefferson Davis Hwy	
	Hampton Inn	(703) 371-0330
	2310 William St	
	Holiday Inn	(703) 898-1102
	5324 Jefferson Davis Hwy	
	Holiday Inn	(703) 371-5550
	564 Warrenton Rd	
	Ramada Inn	(703) 786-8361
	Rte 3	
	Sheraton Inn	(703) 786-8321
	Rte 3	
FRONT ROYAL	Scottish Inn	(703) 636-6168
	533 S. Royal	
	Super 8	(703) 636-4888
	111 South St	
HAMPTON	Arrow Inn	(804) 865-0300
	7 Semple Farm Rd	
	Days Inn	(804) 826-4810
	1918 Colliseum Dr	
	Econo Lodge	(804) 723-0741
	1781 N. King St	
	Hampton Inn	(804) 838-8484
	1813 W. Mercury	
	La Quinta	(804) 827-8680
	2138 W. Mercury	
	Red Roof	(804) 838-1870
	1925 Colliseum Dr	

	Sheraton Inn	(804) 838-5011
	1215 W. Mercury	
HARRISONBURG	Comfort Inn	(703) 433-6066
	1440 E. Market	
	Days Inn	(703) 433-9353
	1131 Ferrett Hill Rd	
	Econo Lodge	(703) 433-2576
	1703 E. Market	
	Hojos	(703) 434-6771
	Port Republic Rd	
	Ramada Inn	(703) 434-9981
	1 Pleasant Valley Rd	
	Sheraton Hotel	(703) 433-2521
	1400 E. Market	
	Village Inn	(703) 434-7355
	Rte 1	
HERNDON	Holiday Inn	(703) 478-9777
	485 Elden	
	Renaissance Hotel (airport)	(703) 478-2900
	Rte 28	
	Marriott	(703) 435-0044
	315 Elden	
HILLSVILLE	Econo Lodge	(703) 728-9118
	I-77	
HOPEWELL	Comfort Inn	(804) 452-0022
	5380 Oaklawn Blvd	
KEYSVILLE	Sheldon's Motel	(804)736-8434
	Rte 2	
LEESBURG	Best Western	(703) 777-9400
	726 E. Market	
LEXINGTON	Comfort Inn	(703) 463-7311
	Rte 11 N.	
	Days Inn	(703) 463-2143
	Rte 60	
	Econo Lodge	(703) 463-7371
	Rte 11	
	Holdiay Inn	(703) 463-7351
	Rte 11	
	Howard Johnson Hotel	(703) 463-9181
	Rte 11	
	Ramada Inn	(703) 463-6666
	Rte 11	
LURAY	In-Town Motel	(703) 743-6511
	410 W. Main	

	Ramada Inn	(703) 743-4521
	Rte 211	
LYNCHBURG	Best Western	(804) 237-2986
	2815 Candlers Mtn Rd	
	Comfort Inn	(804) 847-9041
	Odd fellows Rd	
	Raddisson Hotel	(804) 528-2500
	601 Main St	
MANASSAS	Best Western	(703) 368-7070
	8640 Mathis Ave	
	Holiday Inn	(703) 335-0000
	10800 Van Dor Lane	
	Ramada Inn	(703) 361-0221
	10820 Balls Ford Rd	
	Red Roof Inn	(703) 335-9333
	10610 Automotive Dr	
MARION	Holiday Inn	(703) 783-3193
	1424 N. Main St.	
MARTINSVILLE	Best Western	(703) 632-5611
	Rte 220 N.	
MCCLEAN	Best Western	(703) 734-2800
	8401 Westpark Dr.	
	Ritz Carlton	(703) 506-4300
	1700 Tysons Blvd	
MIDDLEBURG	Red Fox Inn	(703) 687-6301
	2 E. Washington St	
MIDLOTHIAN	Brandermill Inn	(804) 739-8871
	13550 Harbour Point Pkwy	
MT. JACKSON	Best Western	(703) 477-2911
	I-81	
NATURAL BRIDGE	Natural Bridge Resort	(703) 291-2121
	I-81	
NELLYS FORD	Meander Inn at Penny Lane Farm	(804) 361-1121
	Rte 151	
NEWMARKET	Days Inn	(703) 740-4100
	9360 George C. Cullins Pkwy	
NEWPORT NEWS	Comfort Inn	(804) 249-0200
	12330 Jefferson Ave	
	Days Inn	(804) 874-0201
	14747 Warwick Blvd	
	Days Inn	(804) 873-6700
	11829 Fishing Point Dr	
	Host Inn	(804) 599-3303
	985 Jay Clyde Morris Blvd	

	Newport News Inn	(804) 826-4500
	6128 Jefferson Ave	
NORFOLK	Comfort Inn	(804) 623-5700
	930 Virginia Beach Blvd	
	Days Inn	(804) 583-4521
	1631 Bayville St.	
	Econo Lodge	(804) 480-9611
	9601 Fourth View St	
	Quality Inn	(804) 461-6251
	6280 Northampton Blvd	
PETERSBURG	Best Western	(804) 733-1776
	405 E. Washington St.	
	Comfort Inn	(804) 732-2900
	11974 S. Crater Rd	
	Days Inn	(804) 733-4400
	12208 S. Crater Rd	
	Econo Lodge	(804) 862-2717
	16905 Parkdale Rd.	
	Flagship Inn	(804) 861-3470
	815 S. Crater Rd.	
	Holiday Inn	(804) 733-0730
	Washington St.	
	Travelodge	(804) 526-4611
	2201 Ruffin Mill Rd.	
	Quality Inn	(804) 733-1152
	16600 Sunnybrook Rd.	
	Quality Inn	(804) 733-0600
	I-95	
PORTSMOUTH	Holiday Inn	(804) 393-2573
	8 Crawford Pkwy	
RADFORD	Best Western	(703) 639-3000
	1501 Tyler Ave	
	Comfort Inn	(703) 639-4800
	1501 Tyler Ave	
	Dogwood Lodge	(703) 639-9338
	Rte 11	
RAPHINE	Quality Inn	(703) 377-2604
	I-81	
RICHMOND	Best Western	(804) 346-4000
	8008 West Broad St	
	Best Western	(804) 222-2780
	5700 Williamsburg Rd	
	Comfort Inn	(804) 751-0000
	2100 W. Hundred Rd	

	Comfort Inn	(804) 359-4061
	3200 West Broad St	
	Days Inn	(804) 353-1287
	I-95	
	Days Inn (Airport)	(804) 222-2041
	5500 Williamsburg Rd	
	Days Inn	(804) 276-6450
	6346 Midlothian Tnpk	
	HoJo Inn	(804) 266-8753
	E. Parham Rd	
	Holiday Inn (Airport)	(804) 222-6450
	5203 Williamsburg Rd	
	Holiday Inn	(804) 275-7891
	4303 Commerce Rd	
	Holiday Inn	(804) 359-9441
	3207 N. Blvd	
	Holiday Inn	(804) 359-6061
	2000 Staples Mill Rd	
	Holiday Inn	(804) 285-9951
	6531 W. Broad St.	
	Holiday Inn	(804) 644-9871
	301 West Franklin	
	Howard Johnson Lodge	(804) 353-0116
	1501 Robinhood Rd	
	La Quinta Inn	(804) 745-7100
	6910 Midlothian Turnpike	
	Marriott	(804) 643-3400
	Fifth and E. Broad Streets	
	Ramada Inn	(804) 285-9061
	Parham Rd	
	Red Roof Inn	(804) 745-0600
	100 Gresham Wood Pl	
	Red Roof Inn	(804) 271-7240
	4350 Commerce Rd	
	Residence Inn	(804) 285-8200
	2121 Dickens Rd	
	Sheraton Inn	(804) 226-4300
	4700 S. Laburnum Ave	
	Sheraton Hotel	(804) 323-1144
	9901 Midlothian Turnpike	
ROANOKE	Colony House Motor Lodge	(703) 345-0411
	3560 Franklin Rd. SW	
	Comfort Inn	(703) 563-0229
	3695 Thirlane Rd NW	

	Days Inn	(703) 342-4551
	535 Orange Ave	
	Holiday Inn (Airport)	(703) 366-8861
	6626 Thirlane Rd	
	Holdiay Inn	(703) 343-0121
	1927 Franklin Rd. SW	
	Holiday Inn	(703) 342-8961
	Orange Ave NE	
	Holiday Inn	(703) 774-4400
	4468 Starkey Rd	
	Marriott	(703) 563-9300
	2801 Hershberger Rd NW	
	Sheraton Inn (Airport)	(703) 362-4500
	2727 Ferndale Dr NW	
	Sleep Inn	(703) 772-1500
	4045 Electric Rd	
	Travelodge	(703) 992-6700
	2444 Lee Highway S	
ROCKY MNT	Franklin Motel	(703) 483-9962
	Rte 220	
SALEM	Arborgate Inn	(703) 389-0280
	301 Wildwood Rd	
	Blue Jay Budget Host Inn	(703) 380-2080
	5399 W. Main St	
	Comfort Inn	(703) 387-1600
	151 Wildwood Rd	
	Holiday Inn	(703) 389-7061
	1671 Skyview Rd	
	Quality Inn	(703) 562-1912
	179 Sheraton Dr	
SANDSTON	Hampton Inn	(804) 222-8200
	5300 Airport Square Lane	
S. BOSTON	Best Western	(804) 572-4311
	2001 Seymour	
S. HILL	Econo Lodge	(804) 447-7116
	623 Atlantic St	
	Holiday Inn	(804) 447-3123
	Rte 58	
SPRINGFIELD	Best Western	(703) 922-9000
	6550 Loisdale Ct	
	Hilton	(703) 971-8900
	Rte 644 E.	
STAFFORD	Days Inn	(703) 659-0022
	2868 Jefferson Davis Hwy	

STAUNTON	Comfort Inn	(703) 886-5000
	1302 Richmond Ave	
	Days Inn	(703) 337-3031
	I-81	
	Econo Lodge	(703) 885-5158
	1031 Richmond Rd	
	Hessian Econo Lodge	(703) 337-1231
	Rte 11	
	Holiday Inn	(703) 248-5111
	Rte 275	
	Super 8	(703) 886-2888
	1015 Richmond Rd	
STEELS	The Osceola Mill Country Inn	(703) 377-6455
TAVERN	Rte 56	
STEPHENS	Comfort Inn	(703) 869-6500
CITY	167 Town Run Lane	
STERLING	Hampton Inn	(703) 471-8300
	45440 Holiday Dr	
	Holiday Inn	(703) 471-7411
	1000 Sully Rd.	
STUART	Virginian Motel	(703) 694-4244
	Blue Ridge St	
SUFFOLK	Holiday Inn	(804) 934-2311
	2864 Pruden Blvd	
TROUTVILLE	Comfort Inn	(703) 992-5600
	2654 Lee Highway	
	Howard Johnsons	(703) 992-3000
	Rte 220 N	
VIENNA	Residence Inn	(703) 893-0120
	8616 Westwood Center Dr.	
VIRGINIA	Executive Inn	(804) 420-2120
BEACH	717 S. Military Hwy	
	Holiday Inn	(804) 464-9351
	5725 Northampton Blvd	
	La Quinta Inn	(804) 497-6620
	192 Newtown Rd	
	Ocean Holiday Motel	(804) 425-6920
	2417 Atlantic Ave	
	Princess Anne Inn	(804) 428-5611
	2501 Atlantic Ave	
	Red Roof Inn	(804) 490-0225
	196 Ballard Court	
	Thunderbird Motor Lodge	(804) 428-3024
	Atlantic Ave	

	Travelodge	(804) 473-9745
	4600 Bonney Rd	
WARRENTON	Comfort Inn	(703) 349-8900
	6633 Lee Highway	
	Hampton Inn	(703) 349-4200
	501 Blackwell Rd	
	HoJo Inn	(703) 347-4141
	6 Broadview Ave	
WAYNESBORO	Comfort Inn	(703) 942-1171
	640 W. Broad St	
	Days Inn	(703) 943-1101
	2060 Rosser Ave	
	Deluxe Budget Motel	(703) 949-8253
	2112 West Main St	
	Holiday Inn	(703) 942-5201
	I-64	
WILLIAMSBURG	Best Western	(804) 253-1222
	111 Penniman Rd	
	Best Western	(804) 229-9540
	York St	
	Best Western	(804) 229-1655
	900 Capitol Landing Rd	
	Best Western	(804) 229-3003
	Rte 60	
	Comfort Inn	(804) 229-2000
	120 Bypass Rd	
	The Commonwealth Inn	(804) 253-1087
	1233 Richmond Rd	
	Days Inn	(804) 565-0090
	6488 Richmond Rd	
	Embassy Suites	(804) 229-6800
	152 Kingsgate Pkwy	
	George Washington Inn	(804) 220-1410
	500 Merrimac Tr.	
	Governor's Inn	(804) 229-1000
	506 N. Henry St	
	Heritage Inn	(804) 229-6220
	1324 Richmond Rd	
	Holiday Inn	(804) 229-0200
	814 Capitol Landing Rd	
	Holiday Inn	(804) 565-2600
	3032 Richmond Rd	
	Quality Inn	(804) 565-1000
	6483 Richmond Rd	

	Quarterpath Inn	(804) 220-0960
	620 York St	
	Ramada Inn	(804) 229-4100
	351 York St	
	Ramada Inn	(804) 565-2000
	5351 Richmond Rd	
	Rodeway Inn	(804) 229-2981
	1420 Richmond Rd	
	Williamsburg Center	(804) 220-2800
	600 Bypass Rd	
	York Street Hotel	(804) 229-4100
	351 York St	
WINCHESTER	Best Western	(703) 662-4154
	711 Millwood Ave	
	Budgetel Inn	(703) 678-0800
	800 Millwood Ave	
	Holiday Inn	(703) 667-3300
	1050 Millwood Pike	
	Mohawk Motel	(703) 667-1410
	2754 Northwestern Pike	
	Quality Inn	(703) 667-2250
	603 Millwood Ave	
	Super 8 Motel	(703) 665-4450
	1077 Millwood Pike	
WOODBRIDGE	Days Inn	(703) 494-4433
	14619 Potomac Mills Rd	
WOODSTOCK	Budget Host Inn	(703) 459-4086
	Rte 2	
WYTHEVILLE	Days Inn	(703) 228-5500
	150 Malin Dr	
	Econo Lodge	(703) 228-5517
	1190 E. Main St	
	Holiday Inn	(703) 228-5483
	Rte 11	
	Ramada Inn	(703) 228-6000
	955 Peppers Ferry Rd	
	Red Carpet Inn	(703) 228-5525
	280 Lithia Rd	
YORKTOWN	York Town Motor Lodge	(804) 898-5451
	8829 George Washington Hwy	

WEST VIRGINIA

BECKLEY	Comfort Inn	(403) 255-2161
	1909 Harper Rd	
BLUEFIELD	Holiday Inn	(304) 325-6170
	Rte 460	
BRIDGEPORT	Holiday Inn	(304) 842-5411
	100 Lodgeville Rd	
	Knight's Inn	(304) 842-7115
	1235 W. Main St	
CHARLESTON	Holiday Inn	(304) 344-4092
	600 Kanawha	
	Holiday Inn	(304) 343-4661
	1000 Washington St	
	Knight's Inn	(304) 925-0451
	6401 MacCorkle Ave SE	
	Ramada Inn	(304) 744-4641
	Montross Dr	
	Red Roof Inn	(304) 925-6953
	6305 MacCorkle Ave SE	
DAVIS	Deerfield Village Resort	(304) 866-4698
	Courtland Rd	
ELKINS	Econo Lodge	(304) 636-5311
	Rte 33 E	
FAIRMONT	Holiday Inn	(304) 366-5500
	East Grafton Rd	
	Red Roof Inn	(304) 366-8600
	Rte 250	
FAYETTEVILLE	Comfort Inn	(304) 574-3443
	Laurel Creek Rd	
HUNTINGTON	Econo Lodge	(304) 529-1331
	3325 Rte 60	
	Radisson Hotel	(304) 525-1001
	1001 3rd Ave	
	Red Roof Inn	(304) 733-3737
	5190 Rte 60 E	
HURRICANE	Red Roof Inn	(304) 757-6392
	Putnam Dr	
	Smiley's Motel	(304) 562-3346
	419 Hurricane Creek Rd	
JANE LEW	Wilderness Plantation Inn	(304) 884-7806
	Box 96	
LEWISBURG	Brier Inn	(304) 645-7722
	540 N. Jefferson St	

	Super 8 Motel	(304) 647-3188
	550 N. Jefferson St	
MARTINSBURG	Arborgate Inn	(304) 267-2211
	1599 Edwin Miller Blvd	
	Econo Lodge	(304) 274-2181
	Rte 2	
MORGANTOWN	Econo Lodge	(304) 599-8181
	3506 Monongahela Blvd.	
	Holiday Inn	(304) 599-1680
	1400 Saratoga Blvd	
	Ramada Inn	(304) 296-3431
	Rte 119	
NITRO	Best Western	(304) 755-8341
	4115 1st Ave	
PARKERSBURG	Red Roof Inn	(304) 485-1741
	3714 7th St	
PRINCETON	Days Inn	(304) 425-8100
	Rte 460	
RIPLEY	Econo Lodge	(304) 372-5000
	1 Hospitality Dr	
S. CHARLESTON	Red Roof Inn	(304) 744-1500
	4006 MacCorkle AvE SW	
ST. ALBANS	Days Inn	(304) 766-6231
	6210 MacCorkle Ave SW	
SUMMERSVILLE	Best Western	(304) 872-6900
	1203 Broad St	
	Comfort Inn	(304) 872-6500
	903 Industrial Dr North	
WEIRTON	Best Western	(304) 723-5522
	350 Three Springs Dr	
WESTON	Comfort Inn	(304) 269-7000
	Rte 33	
WHEELING	Comfort Inn	(304) 547-1380
	I-70	
	Days Inn	(304) 547-0610
	I-70	
WHITE SULPHER	Old White Motel	(304) 536-2441
SPRINGS	865 E. Main St	

NEW JERSEY

BEACH HAVEN	Engleside Inn	(609) 492-1251
	30 Engleside Ave	
BLACKWOOD	HoJo Inn	(609) 228-4040
	832 N. Black Horse Pike	
BORDENTOWN	Best Western	(609) 298-8000
	Rte 206	
	Days Inn	(609) 298-6100
	Rte 206	
BRIDGEPORT	Holiday Inn	(609) 467-3322
	Center Square Rd	
CARTERET	Holiday Inn	(908) 541-9500
	1000 Roosevelt Ave	
CHERRY HILL	Hampton Inn	(609) 346-4500
	121 Laurel Oak Rd	
	Holiday Inn	(609) 663-5300
	Sayer Ave	
	Residence Inn	(609) 429-6111
	1821 Old Cuthburt Rd	
CLIFTON	Howard Johnson	(201) 471-3800
	680 Rte 3	
DAYTON	Days Inn	(908) 329-3000
	2316 Rte 130	
E. HANOVER	Ramada Hotel	(201) 386-5622
	130 Rte 10	
E. ORANGE	Royal Inn	(201) 677-3100
	120 Evergreen Place	
E. RUTHERFORD	Days Inn	(201) 507-5222
	850 Rte 120	
	Sheraton	(201) 896-0500
	2 Meadowlands Plaza	
E. WINDSOR	Ramada Inn	(609) 448-7000
	399 Monmouth St	
EATONTOWN	Crystal Motor Lodge	(908) 542-4900
	170 Rte 35	
EDISON	Red Roof Inn	(908) 248-9300
	860 New Durham Rd	
	Wellesley Inn	(908) 287-0171
	831 Rte 1	
ELIZABETH	Holiday Inn	(908) 355-1700
	1000 Spring St	
	Sheraton Inn	(908) 527-1600
	901 Spring St	

ENGLEWOOD	Radisson Hotel	(201) 871-2020
	401 S. VanBrunt St	
FAIRFIELD	Best Western	(201) 575-7700
	216 Rte 46	
	Ramada Inn	(201) 575-1742
	38 Two Bridges Rd	
FT. LEE	Holiday Inn	(201) 461-3100
	2117 Rte 4	
HASBROUCK	Sheraton Hotel	(201) 288-6100
HEIGHTS	650 Terrace Ave	
HAZLET	Wellesley Inn	(908) 888-2800
	3215 Rte 35	
HIGHTSTOWN	Town House Motel	(609) 448-2400
	Rte 33	
KENILWORTH	Holiday Inn	(908) 241-4100
	S. 31st St	
LAKEWOOD	Best Western	(908) 367-0900
	1600 Rte 70	
LAWRENCEVILLE	Howard Johnson	(609) 896-1100
	2995 Brunswick Pike	
	Red Roof Inn	(609) 896-3388
	2303 Brunswick Pike	
LYNDHURST	Novotel	(201) 896-6666
	1 Polito Ave	
MAHWAH	Comfort Inn	(201) 512-0800
	160 Rte 17 S	
	Sheraton Hotel	(201) 529-1660
	1 International Blvd	
MIDDLETOWN	Howard Johnson	(908) 671-3400
	750 Rte 35	
MONMOUTH	Red Roof Inn	(908) 821-8800
JCT.	208 New Road	
	Residence Inn	(908) 329-9600
	4225 Rte 1	
MORRISTOWN	Madison Hotel	(201) 285-1800
	1 Convent Rd	
MT. HOLLY	Best Western	(609) 261-3800
	Rte 541	
	Howard Johnsons	(609) 267-6550
	Rte 541	
MT. LAUREL	Red Roof Inn	(609) 234-5589
	603 Fellowship Rd	
	Travelodge	(609) 234-7000
	Rte 73	

NEWARK	Holiday Inn	(201) 589-1000
	160 Holiday Plaza	
	Ramada Hotel	(201) 824-4000
	Rte 1	
N. BERGEN	Executive Days Inn	(201) 348-3600
	2750 Tonnelle Ave	
PARAMUS	Howard Johnson Lodge	(201) 265-4200
	393 Rte 17	
	Radisson Inn	(201) 262-6900
	601 From Rd	
PARK RIDGE	Marriott	(201) 307-0800
	300 Brae Blvd	
PARSIPPANY	Days Inn	(201) 335-0200
	3159 Rte 46	
	Hampton Inn	(201) 263-0095
	3535 Rte 46	
	Parsippany Hilton	(201) 267-7373
	One Hilton Ct	
	Red Roof Inn	(201) 334-3737
	855 Rte 46	
PENNS GROVE	Howard Johnson	(609) 299-3800
	10 Howard Johnson Ln	
PHILLIPSBURG	Howard Johnson	(908) 454-6461
	1315 Rte 22	
PISCATAWAY	Embassy Suites Hotel	(908) 980-0500
	121 Centennial Ave	
PRINCETON	Novotel	(609) 520-1200
	100 Independence Way	
	Ramada Hotel	(609) 452-2400
	4355 Rte 1	
	Summerfield Suites Hotel	(609) 951-0009
	4375 Rte 1	
RAMSEY	Howard Johnsons Motor Lodge	(201) 327-4500
	1255 Rte 17	
	Wellesley Inn	(201) 934-9250
	946 Rte 17	
REDBANK	Oyster Point Hotel	(908) 530-8200
	146 Bodman Place	
ROCHELLE PARK	Ramada Hotel	(201) 845-3400
	375 W. Pasaic	
RUNNEMEDE	Comfort Inn	(609) 939-6700
	101 Ninth Ave	
	Holiday Inn	(609) 939-4200
	109 Ninth Ave	

SADDLEBROOK	Holiday Inn	(201) 843-0600
	50 Kenney Pl	
	Marriott Hotel	(201) 843-9500
	Rte 80	
SECAUCUS	Meadowlands Hilton	(201) 348-6900
	2 Harmon Plaza	
	Red Roof Inn	(201) 319-1000
	15 Meadowlands Pkwy	
SOMERSET	Holiday Inn	(908) 356-1700
	195 Davidson Ave	
	Radisson Hotel	(908) 469-2600
	200 Atrium Dr	
	Ramada Inn	(908) 560-9880
	Weston Canal Rd	
	Summerfield Suites Hotel	(908) 356-8000
	260 Davidson Ave	
SOMERS POINT	Residence Inn	(609) 927-6400
	Mays Landing Rd	
S. PLAINFIELD	Comfort Inn	(908) 561-4488
	Stelton Rd	
	Holiday Inn	(908) 753-5500
	4701 Stelton Rd	
SPRINGFIELD	Holiday Inn	(201) 376-9400
	304 Rte 22	
TINTON FALLS	Days Inn	(908) 389-4646
	11 Center Plaza	
	Residence Inn	(908) 389-8100
	90 Park Rd	
TOMS RIVER	Holiday Inn	(908) 244-4000
	290 Hwy 37	
	Howard Johnsons	(908) 244-1000
	955 Hooper Ave	
	Ramada Hotel	(908) 905-2626
	2373 Rte 9	
WARREN	Sommerset Hills Hotel	(908) 647-6700
	200 Liberty Corner	
WAYNE	Holiday Inn	(201) 256-7000
	334 Rte 46	
	Howard Johnson	(201) 696-8050
	1850 Rte 23	
WEEHAWKEN	Ramada Suite Hotel	(201) 617-5600
	500 Harbor Blvd	
W. ATLANTIC CITY	Travelodge	(609) 641-3131
	1760 Tilton Rd.	

WHIPPANY	Marriott 1401 Rte 10	(201) 538-8811
WOODCLIFF **LAKE**	Hilton 210 Tilton	(201) 391-3600

PENNSYLVANIA

ALLENTOWN	Days Inn 1151 Bulldog Dr	(215) 395-3731
	Microtel 1880 Steelstone Rd	(215) 266-9070
	Motel Allenwood 1058 Houseman Rd	(610) 395-3707
	Red Roof Inn 1846 Catasauqua Rd	(215) 264-5404
ALTOONA	Econo Lodge 2906 Pleasant Valley Rd	(814) 944-3555
	HoJo Inn 1500 Sterling St	(814) 946-7601
BARKEYVILLE	Days Inn I-80	(814) 786-7901
BARTONSVILLE	Holiday Inn Rte 611	(717) 424-6100
BEAVER FALLS	Holiday Inn Rte 18	(412) 846-3700
BEDFORD	Best Western Rte 220	(814) 623-9006
	Motel Townhouse 200 South Richard St	(814) 623-5138
	Quality Inn Rte 220	(814) 623-5188
	Super 8 Motel Rte 220	(814) 623-5880
BENSALEM	Comfort Inn 3660 Street Rd	(215) 245-0100
BETHLEHEM	Comfort Inn 3191 Highfield Dr	(215) 865-6300
	Comfort Suites 120 W. Third St	(215) 882-9700
BLOOMSBURG	Econo Lodge 189 Columbia Mall Dr.	(717) 387-0490
	Quality Inn 1 Buckhorn Rd	(717) 784-5300
BLUE MTN	Kenmar Motel 17788 Cumberland Hwy	(717) 423-5195
BREEZEWOOD	Comfort Inn Rte 30	(814) 735-2200

	Ramada Inn	(814) 735-4005
	Rte 30	
BROOKVILLE	Econo Lodge	(814) 849-8381
	235 Allegheny Blvd	
	Super 8 Motel	(814) 849-8840
	251 Allegheny Blvd	
BUTLER	Super 8 Motel	(412) 287-8888
	128 Pittsburgh Rd	
CARLISLE	Best Western	(717) 243-5411
	1245 Harrisburg Pike	
	Days Inn	(717) 258-4147
	101 Alexander Spring Rd	
	Econo Lodge	(717) 249-7775
	1460 Harrisburg Pike	
	Holiday Inn	(717) 245-2400
	1450 Harrisburg Pike	
	Howard Johnsons	(717) 243-6000
	1255 Harrisburg Pike	
	Knights Inn	(717) 249-7622
	1153 Harrisburg Pike	
	Rodeway Inn	(717) 249-2800
	1239 Harrisburg Pike	
CHADDS FORD	Brandywine River Hotel	(215) 388-1200
	Rte 1	
CHAMBERSBURG	Travelodge	(717) 264-4187
	565 Lincoln Way East	
	Holiday Inn	(717) 263-3400
	1095 Wayne Ave	
CLARION	Holiday Inn	(814) 226-8850
	Rte 68	
	Knights Inn	(814) 226-4550
	Rte 3	
CLEARFIELD	Best Western	(814) 765-2441
	I-80	
	Days Inn	(814) 765-5381
	Rte 879	
CORAOPOLIS	Best Western	(412) 262-3800
	1 Airport Rd	
	Days Inn	(412) 269-0990
	1170 Thornrun Rd	
	Embassy Suites	(412) 269-9070
	550 Cherrington Pkwy	
	La Quinta	(412) 269-0400
	1433 Beers School Rd	

	Marriott	(412) 788-8800
	100 Aten Rd	
	Red Roof Inn	(412) 264-5678
	1454 Beers School Rd	
	Royce Hotel	(412) 262-2400
	1160 Thornrun Rd	
DANVILLE	Red Roof Inn	(717) 275-7600
	Rte 54	
DENVER	Black Horse Lodge	(717) 336-7563
	2180 North Reading Rd	
	Econo Lodge	(717) 363-4649
	2015 North Reading Rd	
	Holiday Inn	(717) 336-7541
	Rte 272	
	Pennsylvania Dutch Motel	(717) 336-5559
	2275 North Reading Rd	
DUBOIS	Holiday Inn	(814) 371-5100
	Rte 219	
	Ramada Inn	(814) 371-7070
	Rte 255	
EASTON	Days Inn	(215) 253-0546
	Rte 22	
E. STROUDSBURG	Budget Motel	(717) 424-5451
	Rte 80	
ERIE	Days Inn	(814) 868-8521
	Rte 97	
	Holiday Inn	(814) 456-2961
	18 W. 18th St	
	Holiday Inn	(814) 864-4911
	8040 Perry Hwy	
	Howard Johnsons	(814) 864-4811
	7575 Peach St	
	Microtel	(814) 864-1010
	8100 Peach St	
	Ramada Inn	(814) 825-3100
	6101 Wattsburg Rd	
	Red Roof Inn	(814) 868-5246
	7865 Perry Hwy	
ESSINGTON	Comfort Inn	(215) 521-9800
	53 Industrial Hwy	
	Holiday Inn	(215) 521-2400
	45 Industrial Hwy	
EXTON	Holiday Inn	(215) 524-9000
	120 N. Pottstown	

FRACKVILLE	Econo Lodge	(717) 874-3838
	501 S. Middle St	
GETTYSBURG	Comfort Inn	(717) 337-2400
	871 York Rd	
	Heritage Motor Lodge	(717) 334-9281
	64 Steinwehr Ave	
	Holiday Inn	(717) 334-6211
	516 Baltimore St	
	Howard Johnsons	(717) 334-1188
	301 Steinwehr Ave	
	Quality Inn	(717) 334-1103
	380 Steinwehr Ave	
GRANTVILLE	Holiday Inn	(717) 469-0661
	I-81	
GREENTREE	Best Western	(412) 922-7070
	875 Greentree Rd	
	Hampton Inn	(412) 922-0100
	555 Trumbull Dr	
	Hawthorn Suites	(412) 279-6300
	700 Mansfield Ave	
HAMLIN	Comfort Inn	(717) 689-4148
	I-84	
HARRISBURG	Best Western	(717) 652-7180
	300 N. Mountain Rd	
	Best Western	(717) 558-9500
	765 Eisenhower Blvd	
	Budgetel Inn	(717) 540-9339
	200 N. Mountain Rd	
	Budgetel Inn	(717) 989-8000
	990 Eisenhower Blvd	
	Comfort Inn	(717) 561-8100
	4021 Union Deposit Rd	
	Econo Lodge	(717) 545-9089
	150 Nationwide Dr	
	Holiday Inn	(717) 939-7841
	4751 Lindle Rd	
	Holiday Inn	(717) 697-0321
	5401 Carlisle Pike	
	Knights Inn	(717) 774-5990
	300 Commerce Dr	
	Quality Inn	(717) 233-1611
	525 S. Front St	
	Quality Inn	(717) 732-0785
	501 N. Enola Rd	

	Radisson Hotel	(717) 763-7117
	1150 Camp Hill Bypass	
	Ramada Hotel	(717) 774-2721
	Pennsylvania Trnpke	
	Red Roof Inn	(717) 657-1445
	400 Corp. Circle	
	Red Roof Inn	(717) 939-1331
	950 Eisenhower Blvd	
	Residence Inn	(717) 561-1900
	4480 Lewis Rd	
	Sheraton Inn	(717) 561-2800
	800 E. Park Dr	
	Super 8 Motel	(717) 233-5891
	4125 N. Front St	
HAZLETON	Comfort Inn	(717) 455-9300
	Rte 93	
	Econo Lodge	(717) 788-5887
	Rte 93	
	Forest Hill Inn	(717) 459-2730
	Rte 93	
	Hampton Inn	(717) 454-3449
	Rte 93	
	Holiday Inn	(717) 455-2061
	Rte 309	
HERMITAGE	Holiday Inn	(412) 981-1530
	3200 S. Hermitage	
HUNTINGDON	Days Inn	(814) 643-3934
	Rte 22	
	Huntingdon Motor Inn	(814) 643-1133
	Rte 22	
INDIANA	Best Western	(412) 349-9620
	1545 Wayne Ave	
	Holiday Inn	(412) 463-3561
	1395 Wayne Ave	
JOHNSTOWN	Comfort Inn	(814) 266-3678
	455 Theatre Dr	
	Holiday Inn	(814) 535-7777
	250 Market St	
	Super 8 Motel	(814) 266-8789
	1440 Scalp Ave	
KING OF PRUSSIA	Comfort Inn	(215) 962-0700
	550 W Dekalb Pike	
	Hampton Inn	(215) 962-8111
	530 Dekalb Pike	

	Holiday Inn	(215) 265-7500
	260 Goddard Blvd	
	Residence Inn	(215) 640-9494
	600 W Swedesford Rd	
	Sheraton Plaza Hotel	(215) 265-1500
	1150 First Ave	
KINTNERSVILLE	Light Farm	(215) 847-3276
	2042 Berger Rd	
KUTZTOWN	Campus Inn	(610) 683-8721
	15080 Cutztown Rd	
	Lincoln Motel	(610) 683-3456
	Main St	
LAMAR	Comfort Inn	(717) 726-4901
	Rte 64	
LANCASTER	Best Western	(717) 569-6444
	222 Eden Rd	
	Days Inn	(717) 299-5700
	30 Keller Ave	
	Hotel Brunswick	(717) 397-4801
	Chestnut St	
	Ramada Inn	(717) 393-5499
	2250 E Lincoln Hwy	
	Super 8 Motel	(717) 393-8888
	2129 E Lincoln Hwy	
	Travelodge	(717) 397-4201
	2101 Columbia Ave	
LEWISBURG	Days Inn	(717) 523-1171
	Rte 15	
LEWISTOWN	Holiday Inn	(717) 248-4961
	Rte 322	
LIONVILLE	Comfort Inn	(215) 524-8811
	5 N. Pottstown Pike	
	Hampton Inn	(215) 363-5555
	4 N. Pottstown Pike	
	Holiday Inn	(215) 363-1100
	815 N. Pottstown Pike	
LOCKE HAVEN	Days Inn	(717) 748-3297
	Rte 220	
MANSFIELD	Comfort Inn	(717) 662-3000
	300 Gateway Dr	
	Mansfield Inn	(717) 662-2136
	Rte 15	
	Oasis Motel	(717) 659-5576
	Rte 15	

MARS	Days Inn	(412) 772-2700
	909 Sheraton Dr	
	Hampton Inn	(412) 776-1000
	210 Executive Dr	
	Red Roof Inn	(412) 776-5670
	Rte 19	
MATAMORAS	Best Western	(717) 491-2400
	900 Rte 6	
MEADVILLE	Days Inn	(814) 337-4264
	240 Conneaut Lake Rd	
	Super 8 Motel	(814) 333-8883
	845 Conneaut Lake Rd	
MERCER	Howard Johnsons	(412) 748-3030
	835 Perry Hwy	
MIDDLETOWN	Rodeway Inn	(717) 939-4147
	800 Eisenhower Blvd	
MIFFLINVILLE	Super 8	(717) 759-6778
	I-80	
MILFORD	Myer Motel	(717) 296-7223
	Rte 6	
MONROEVILLE	Days Inn	(412) 856-1610
	2727 Mosside Blvd	
	Radisson Hotel	(412) 373-7300
	101 Mall Blvd	
	Red Roof Inn	(412) 856-4738
	2729 Mosside Blvd	
MONTGOMERYVILLE	Comfort Inn	(215) 361-3600
	678 Bethlehem Pike	
MOOSIC	Days Inn	(717) 457-6713
	I-81	
MORGANTOWN	Holiday Inn	(215) 286-3000
	Pennsylvania Turnpike	
NEW CASTLE	Comfort Inn	(412) 658-7700
	1740 New Butler Rd	
NEW COLUMBIA	Comfort Inn	(717) 568-8000
	Rte 15	
NEW HOPE	Holiday Inn	(215) 862-5221
	Rte 202	
NEW STANTON	Howard Johnson Lodge	(412) 925-3511
	I-76	
OAKDALE	Comfort Inn	(412) 787-2600
	7011 Old Steubenville Park Rd	
OAKLAND	Hampton Inn	(412) 681-1000
	Forbes Ave	

	Howard Johnsons	(412) 683-6100
	3401 Blvd of the Allies	
OIL CITY	Holiday Inn	(814) 677-1221
	1 Seneca St	
PHILADELPHIA	Holiday Inn	(215) 561-7500
	18th St	
	Ramada Suites	(215) 922-1730
	1010 Race St	
	Chestnut Hill Hotel	(215) 242-5905
	8229 Germantown Ave	
	Marriott (Airport)	(215) 365-4150
	I-95	
PINE GROVE	Econo Lodge	(717) 345-4099
	Rte 443	
PITTSBURGH	Holiday Inn	(412) 247-2700
	915 Brinton Rd	
	Holiday Inn	(412) 682-6200
	100 Lytton Ave	
	Holiday Inn	(412) 922-8100
	401 Holiday Dr	
	Holiday Inn	(412) 366-5200
	4859 McKnight Rd	
	Hilton Hotel	(412) 391-4600
	Commonwealth Place	
	Marriott	(412) 922-8400
	101 Marriott Dr	
	Red Roof Inn	(412) 787-7870
	Rte 60	
	Sheraton Inn	(412) 343-4600
	164 Ft. Couch Rd	
	Vista International Hotel	(412) 281-3700
	1000 Penn Ave	
POTTSTOWN	Comfort Inn	(215) 326-5000
	Rte 100	
	Days Inn	(215) 970-1101
	29 High St	
	Holiday Inn	(215) 327-3300
	1600 Industrial Hwy	
POTTSVILLE	Quality Hotel	(717) 622-4600
	100 S. Center St	
PUNXSUTAWNEY	Pantall Hotel	(814) 938-6600
	135 E. Mahoning St	
READING	Dutch Colony Inn	(610) 779-2345
	4635 Perkiomen Ave	

	Holiday Inn 2545 Fifth St	(215) 929-4741
SCRANTON	Best Western Rte 11	(717) 346-7061
	Days Inn Rte 347	(717) 348-6101
	Econo Lodge 1175 Kane St	(717) 348-1000
	Econo Lodge 1027 O'Neil Hwy	(717) 346-8782
SELINSGROVE	Comfort Inn Rte 11	(717) 374-8880
	Days Inn Rte 11	(717) 743-1111
SEWICKLEY	Swickley Country Inn 801 Ohio River Blvd	(412) 741-4300
SOMERSET	Days Inn 220 Waterworks Rd	(814) 445-9200
	Holiday Inn I-76	(814) 445-9611
	Ramada Inn I-76	(814) 443-4646
STATE COLLEGE	Autoport Motel 1405 S. Atherton St	(814) 237-7666
	Days Inn 240 S Pugh St	(814) 238-8454
	Hampton Inn 1101 E. College Ave	(814) 231-1590
	Holiday Inn 1450 S. Atherton St	(814) 238-3001
STROUDSBURG	Sheraton Inn 1220 W. Main	(717) 424-1930
TREVOSE	Ramada Hotel 2400 Old Lincoln Hwy	(215) 638-8300
	Red Roof Inn 3100 Lincoln Hwy	(215) 244-9422
TURTLE CREEK	James Street Guest House Rte 22	(412) 372-8060
UNIONTOWN	Holiday Inn 700 W. Main St	(412) 437-2816
	Lodge at Chalk Hill Rte 40	(412) 438-8880
WARREN	Holiday Inn 210 Ludlow St	(814) 726-3000

WASHINGTON	Holiday Inn	(412) 222-6200
	340 Racetrack Rd	
	Red Roof Inn	(412) 228-5750
	1399 West Chestnut St	
WAYNESBORO	Best Western	(717) 762-9113
	239 W. Main St	
WAYNESBURG	Econo Lodge	(412) 627-5544
	350 Miller Lane	
	Super 8 Motel	(412) 627-8880
	80 Miller Lane	
WELLSBORO	Canyon Motel	(717) 724-1681
	18 E. Ave	
	Foxfire B&B	(717) 724-5175
	Hills Creek St	
	Sherwood Motel	(717) 724-3424
	2 Main St	
WESTCHESTER	Westchester Inn	(215) 692-1900
	943 S. High St	
WEST MIDDLESEX	Comfort Inn	(412) 342-7200
	Rte 18	
WEXFORD	Econo Lodge	(412) 935-1000
	109 VIP Drive	
WHITE HAVEN	Days Inn	(717) 443-0391
	Rte 940	
WILKES-BARRE	Best Western	(717) 823-6152
	77 E. Market	
	Hampton Inn	(717) 825-3838
	1063 Hwy 315	
	Howard Johnson Motel	(717) 824-2411
	500 Kidder St	
	Howard Johnson Motor Lodge	(717) 654-3301
	307 Rte 315	
	Knights Inn	(717) 654-6020
	310 Rte 315	
WILLIAMSPORT	City View Inn	(717) 326-2601
	Rte 15	
	Econo Lodge	(717) 326-1501
	2401 E. Third St	
	Genetti Hotel	(717) 326-6600
	200 W Fourth St	
	Sheraton Hotel	(717) 327-8231
	100 Pine St	
WINDGAP	Travel Inn	(215) 863-4146
	Rte 512	

WYOMISSING	Econo Lodge	(215) 378-5101
	635 Spring St	
	Inn at Reading	(215) 372-7811
	1040 Park Rd	
	Sheraton Hotel	(215) 376-3811
	422 W. Papermill Rd	
	Wellesley Inn	(215) 374-1500
	910 Woodland Ave	
YORK	Best Western	(717) 767-6931
	1415 Kenneth Rd	
	Econo Lodge	(717) 846-6260
	125 Arsenal Rd	
	Hampton Inn	(717) 840-1500
	1550 Mt Zion Rd	
	Holiday Inn	(717) 755-1966
	2600 E Market St	
	Howard Johnsons	(717) 843-9971
	Rte 30	
	Ramada Inn	(717) 846-4940
	1650 Toronita St	
	Red Roof Inn	(717) 843-8181
	323 Arsenal Rd	
	Super 8 Motel	(717) 852-8686
	40 Arsenal Rd	

NEW YORK

ALBANY	Econo Lodge	(518) 456-8811
	1632 Central Ave	
	Howard Johnson Lodge	(518) 462-6555
	Rte 9 W	
	Red Roof Inn	(518) 459-1971
	188 Wolf Rd	
AMHERST	Red Roof Inn	(716) 689-7474
	42 Flint Rd	
	Residence Inn	(716) 632-6622
	100 Maple Rd	
AMSTERDAM	Holiday Inn	(518) 843-5760
	10 Market St	
	Valley View Motor Inn	(518) 842-5637
	Rte 5S	
ARMONK	Ramada Inn	(914) 273-9090
	Westchester Bus. Park	
AUBURN	Days Inn	(315) 252-7567
	37 William St	
	Holiday Inn	(315) 253-4531
	75 North St	
	Irish Rose B&B	(315) 255-0196
	102 S. St	
AVOCA	Goodrich Center Motel	(607) 566-2216
	Rte 415	
BATAVIA	Crown Inn	(716) 343-2311
	8212 Park Rd	
	Treadway Inn	(716) 343-1000
	8204 Park Rd	
BATH	Old National Hotel	(607) 776-4104
	13 E Steuben St	
BINGHAMTON	Comfort Inn	(607) 722-5353
	1156 Front St	
	HoJo Inn	(607) 724-1341
	690 Old Front St	
	Holiday Inn	(607) 722-1212
	2 Holly St	
	Holiday Inn	(607) 729-6371
	4105 Vestal Pkwy	
	Hotel deVille	(607) 722-0000
	80 State St	
	Motel 6	(607) 771-0400
	1012 Front St	

BRIGHTON	Wellesley Inn	(716) 427-0130
	797 E. Henrietta	
BROCKPORT	Econo Lodge	(716) 637-3157
	6575 Fourth Section Rd	
BUFFALO	Buffalo Exit 53 Motor Lodge	(716) 896-2800
	475 Dingens St	
	Hilton	(716) 845-5100
	120 Church St	
	Holiday Inn	(716) 896-2900
	601 Dingens St	
	Holiday Inn	(716) 886-2121
	620 Delaware Ave	
	Hyatt Regency	(716) 856-1234
	2 Fountain Plaza	
	Journeys End Suites	(716) 854-5500
	601 Main St	
	Lord Amherst Motor Hotel	(716) 839-2200
	5000 Main St	
	Marriott	(716) 689-6900
	1340 Millersport Hwy	
CALCIUM	Microtel	(315) 629-5000
	8000 Virginia Smith Dr	
CAMBRIDGE	Townhouse Motor Inn	(518) 677-5524
	Rte 22	
CANANDAIGUA	Econo Lodge	(716) 394-9000
	170 Eastern Blvd	
	Inn on the Lake	(716) 394-7800
	770 S. Main St	
CHEEKTOWAGA	Wellesley Inn	(716) 631-8966
	4630 Genesee St	
CLAYTON	Westwinds Motel	(315) 686-3352
	Rte 2	
CLIFTON PARK	Comfort Inn	(518) 373-0222
	Rte 146	
COBBLESKILL	Best Western	(518) 234-4321
	12 Campus Dr	
COLONIE	Comfort Inn	(518) 783-1216
	866 Albany Shaker Rd	
	Hampton Inn	(518) 438-2822
	10 Ulenski Dr	
	Marriott	(518) 458-8444
	189 Wolf Rd	
CORNING	Best Western	(607) 692-2456
	Rte 15	

	Hilton	(607) 962-5000
	125 Dennison Pkwy E.	
CORTLAND	Econo Lodge	(607) 753-7594
	3775 Rte 11	
DELHI	Buena Vista Motel	(607) 746-2135
	Andes Rd	
DUNKIRK	Days Inn	(716) 673-1351
	10455 Bennett Rd	
	Econo Lodge	(716) 366-2200
	310 Lakeshore Dr	
EAST HAMPTON	Dutch Motel	(516) 324-4550
	488 Montauk Hwy	
EAST NORWICH	East Norwich Inn	(516) 922-1500
	Rte 25A	
EAST SYRACUSE	Embassy Suites	(315) 446-3200
	6646 Old Collamar Rd	
	Hampton Inn	(315) 463-6443
	6605 Old Collamar Rd	
	Holiday Inn	(315) 437-2761
	6501 College Place	
	Motel 6	(315) 433-1300
	6577 Court St Rd	
	Residence Inn	(315) 432-4488
	6420 Yorktown Circle	
	Marriott Hotel	(315) 432-0200
	6302 Carrier Pkwy	
ELMIRA	Holiday Inn	(607) 739-3681
	602 Corning Rd	
	Holiday Inn	(607) 734-4211
	1 Holiday Plaza	
	Motel 6	(607) 739-2525
	151 Rte 17	
	Red Jacket Motor Inn	(607) 734-1616
	Rte 17	
ELMSFORD	Days Inn	(914) 592-5680
	200 Tarrytown Rd	
	Ramada Inn	(914) 592-3300
	540 Sawmill River Rd	
ENDICOTT	Best Western	(607) 754-1533
	749 W. Main St	
FAIRPORT	Trail Break Motor Inn	(716) 223-1710
	7340 Pittsburgh-Palmyra Rd	
FARMINGTON	Best Western	(716) 924-2131
	6108 Loomis Rd	

	Budget Inn	(716) 924-5020
	6001 Rte 96	
FISHKILL	Residence Inn	(914) 896-5210
	2481 Rte 9	
	Wellesley Inn	(914) 896-4995
	2477 Rte 9	
FULTON	Fulton Motor Lodge	(315) 598-6100
	163 S. First St	
	Quality Inn	(315) 593-2444
	930 S. First St	
GENEVA	Motel 6	(315) 789-4050
	485 Hamilton St	
GLENS FALLS	Queensbury Hotel	(518) 792-1121
	88 Ridge St	
GRAND ISLAND	Cinderella Motel	(716) 773-2872
	2797 Grand Island Blvd	
GREECE	Marriott (Airport)	(716) 225-6880
	1890 West Ridge Road	
	Wellesley Inn	(716) 621-2060
	1635 West Ridge Road	
GREENPORT	Silver Sands Resort	(516) 477-0011
	Silver Mirror Rd	
HAMBURG	HoJo Inn	(716) 648-2000
	6245 Camp Rd	
	Red Roof Inn	(716) 648-7222
	5370 Camp Rd	
HAUPPAUGE	Radisson Hotel	(516) 232-3000
	3635 Express Dr. N	
HEMPSTEAD	Best Western	(516) 486-4100
	80 Clinton St	
HENRIETTA	Econo Lodge	(716) 427-2700
	940 Jefferson Rd	
	Marketplace Inn	(716) 475-9190
	800 Jefferson Rd	
	Microtel	(716) 334-3400
	905 Lehigh Station Rd	
	Red Roof Inn	(716) 359-1100
	4820 W. Henrietta Rd	
	Residence Inn	(716) 272-8850
	1300 Jefferson Rd	
HERKIMER	Herkimer Motel	(315) 866-0490
	100 Marginal Rd	
HIGHLAND FALLS	Best Western	(914) 446-9400
	Rte 218	

HOLTSVILLE	Best Western	(516) 758-2900
	1730 N. Ocean Ave	
HORSEHEADS	Best Western	(607) 739-3891
	Rte 14	
	Howard Johnsons	(607) 739-5636
	Rte 17	
	Huck Finn Motel	(607) 739-3807
	101 Westinghouse Rd	
ITHACA	Best Western	(607) 272-6100
	1020 Ellis Hollow Rd	
	College Town Motor Lodge	(607) 273-3542
	312 College Ave	
	Comfort Inn	(607) 272-0100
	356 Elmira Rd	
	Econo Lodge	(607) 257-1400
	2303 N. Triphammer Rd	
	Holiday Inn	(607) 272-1000
	222 S. Cayuga St	
	Howard Johnsons	(607) 257-1212
	2300 N. Triphammer Rd	
	Meadow Court Inn	(607) 273-3885
	529 S. Meadow St	
JAMESTOWN	Comfort Inn	(716) 664-5920
	2800 N. Main St	
	Holiday Inn	(716) 664-3400
	150 W. Fourth St	
	Motel 6	(716) 665-3670
	1980 E. Main St	
JOHNSON CITY	Best Western	(607) 729-9194
	569 Harry L Drive	
	Red Roof Inn	(607) 729-8940
	590 Fairview St	
JOHNSTOWN	Holiday Inn	(518) 762-4686
	308 N. Comrie Ave	
KINGSTON	Holiday Inn	(914) 338-0400
	503 Washington St	
	Ramada Inn	(914) 339-3900
	Rte 28	
LAKE GEORGE	Balmoral Motel	(518) 668-2673
	444 Canada St	
	Best Western	(518) 668-5701
	Luzerne Rd	
	Diamond Cove Cottages	(518) 668-5787
	Lake Shore Dr	

	Econo Lodge 431 Canada St	(518) 668-2689
	Ft. William Henry Motor Inn Canada St	(518) 668-3081
	Travelodge Rte 9	(518) 668-5421
LAKE PLACID	Art Devlin's Olympic Inn 350 Main St	(518) 523-3700
	Best Western 150 Main St	(518) 253-3353
	Edge of the Lake Motel 56 Saranac Ave	(518) 523-9430
	Holiday Inn 1 Olympic Dr	(518) 523-2556
	Howard Johnsons 90 Saranac Ave	(518) 523-9555
	Northway Motel 5 Wilmington Rd	(518) 523-3500
	Ramada Inn 8 Saranac Ave	(518) 523-2587
LANCASTER	Red Roof Inn 146 Maple Dr	(716) 633-1100
LATHAM	Century House Inn 997 New Loudon Rd	(518) 785-0931
	Hampton Inn 981 New Loudon Rd	(518) 785-0000
	Holiday Inn 946 New Loudon Rd	(518) 783-6161
	Howard Johnsons 611 Troy-Schenectady Rd	(518) 785-5891
	Residence Inn 1 Residence Inn Dr	(518) 783-0600
LIBERTY	Holiday Inn Rte 17	(914) 292-7171
LITTLE FALLS	Best Western 20 Albany St	(315) 823-4954
LIVERPOOL	Days Inn 400 N. Seventh St	(315) 451-1511
	Sheraton Inn 441 Electronics Pkwy	(315) 457-1122
MALONE	Econo Lodge 227 W. Main St	(518) 483-0500
	Four Seasons Motel 236 W. Main St	(518) 483-3490

MANHASSET	Royal Inn Motor Lodge	(516) 627-5300
	1177 Northern Blvd	
MELVILLE	Hilton	(516) 845-1000
	598 Broad Hollow Rd	
	Radisson Plaza	(516) 423-1600
	1350 Old Walt Whitman Rd	
MIDDLETOWN	Middletown Motel	(914) 342-2535
	501 Rte 211 E	
	Super 8 Lodge	(914) 692-5828
	563 Rte 211 E	
MT. KISCO	Holiday Inn	(914) 241-2600
	1 Holiday Dr	
NEWBURGH	Comfort Inn	(914) 567-0567
	5 Lakeside Rd	
	Holiday Inn	(914) 564-9020
	90 Rte 17	
	Howard Johnson	(914) 564-4000
	95 Rte 17	
	Ramada Inn	(914) 564-4500
	1055 Union Ave	
NEW HAMPTON	Days Inn	(914) 374-2411
	Rte 17	
NEW HARTFORD	Holiday Inn	(315) 797-2131
	1777 Burrstone Rd	
NEW YORK CITY	Drake Swissotel	(212) 421-0900
	440 Park Ave	
	Essex House	(212) 247-0300
	160 Central Park S.	
	Fort Travelodge (Airport)	(718) 995-9000
	Belt Pkwy	
	Hilton (Airport)	(718) 322-8700
	138-10 135th Ave	
	Hilton	(212) 586-7000
	1335 Ave. of the Americas	
	Holiday Inn	(212) 966-8898
	138 Lafayette	
	Holiday Inn	(212) 977-4000
	1605 Broadway	
	Hotel Millenium	(212) 693-2001
	53 Church St	
	Loews New York Hotel	(212) 752-7000
	569 Lexington Ave	
	The Mark	(212) 744-4300
	25 E. 77th St	

	Marriott (Airport)	(718) 565-8900
	102-05 Ditmars Blvd	
	Marriott	(212) 398-1900
	1535 Broadway	
	Mayflower Hotel	(212) 265-0060
	15 Central Park W	
	New York Renaissance Hotel	(212) 765-7676
	714 7th Ave	
	Novotel	(212) 315-0100
	226 W. 52nd	
	Penninsula	(212) 247-2200
	700 Fifth Ave	
	Royalton	(212) 869-4400
	44 W. 44th	
	St. Regis Hotel	(212) 753-4500
	2 E. 55th St	
	Sheraton Park Ave	(212) 685-7676
	45 Park Ave	
	The Stanhope	(212) 288-5800
	995 Fifth Ave	
NIAGRA FALLS	Best Western	(905) 356-0551
ONTARIO	5551 Murray St	
	Comfort Inn on the River	(905) 356-0131
	4009 River Rd	
	Flamingo Motor Inn	(905) 356-4646
	7701 Lundys Lane	
	Glengate Motel	(905) 357-1333
	5534 Stanley Ave	
	Holiday Inn	(905) 356-1333
	5339 Murray Hill	
	Liberty Inns	(905) 356-9452
	6408 Stanley Ave	
	Marco Polo Inn	(905) 356-6959
	5553 Ferry St	
	Niagra Family Inn	(905) 354-9844
	5612 Ellen Ave	
	Ramada Inn	(905) 356-6116
	7429 Lundys Lane	
	Sheraton Hotel	(905) 374-1077
	6755 Oaks Dr	
	Sheraton Inn	(905) 374-4142
	6045 Stanley Ave	
	Surfside Inn	(905) 295-4354
	3665 Macklem St	

	University Motor Lodge	(905) 358-6243
	6000 Stanley Ave	
	Venture Inn	(905) 358-3293
	4960 Clifton Hill	
NIAGRA FALLS	Best Western	(716) 283-7612
NEW YORK	7001 Buffalo Ave	
	Days Inn	(716) 285-9321
	201 Rainbow Blvd	
	Radisson Hotel	(716) 285-3361
	Third St	
	Travelers Budget Inn	(716) 297-3228
	9001 Niagra Falls Blvd	
N. SYRACUSE	Holiday Inn	(315) 457-4000
	6701 Buckley Rd	
NORWICK	Howard Johnsons	(607) 334-2200
	75 N. Broad St	
OGDENSBURG	Alta Courts Motel	(315) 393-6860
	Riverside Dr	
	Quality Inn	(315) 393-4550
	Riverside Dr	
	Stonefence Hotel	(315) 393-1545
	Riverside Dr	
ONEONTA	Holiday Inn	(607) 433-2250
	Rte 23	
	Super 8 Motel	(607) 432-9505
	Rte 23	
ORANGEBURG	Holiday Inn	(914) 359-7000
	329 Rte 303	
PAINTED POST	Econo Lodge	(607) 962-4444
	200 Rober Damm Dr	
	Lamplighter Motel	(607) 962-1184
	9316 Victory Hwy	
	Stiles Motel	(607) 962-5221
	9239 Victory Hwy	
PEEKSKILL	Peekskill Inn	(914) 739-1500
	634 Main St	
PEMBROKE	Econo Lodge	(716) 599-4681
	8493 Rte 77	
PLAINVIEW	Howard Johnson	(516) 349-9100
	150 Sunnyside Blvd	
	Residence Inn	(516) 433-6200
	9 Gerhard Rd	
PLATTSBURGH	Econo Lodge	(518) 561-1500
	610 Upper Cornelia St	

	Howard Johnsons	(518) 561-7750
	Rte 3	
	Super 8 Motel	(518) 562-8888
	7129 Rte 9	
QUEENSBURY	Ramada Inn	(518) 793-7701
	Aviation Rd	
	Susse Chalet	(518) 793-8891
	Big Boom Rd	
	Wakita Court Motel	(518) 792-0326
	Rte 9	
RIPLEY	Budget Host Colonial Squire	(716) 736-8000
	Shortman Rd	
ROCHESTER	Comfort Inn	(716) 436-4400
	395 Buell Rd	
	Days Inn	(716) 325-5010
	384 E. Ave	
	Hampton Inn	(716) 272-7800
	717 E. Henrietta Rd	
	Holiday Inn	(716) 328-6000
	911 Brooks Ave	
	Holiday Inn	(716) 546-6400
	120 E. Main St	
	Howard Johnson (Airport)	(716) 235-6030
	1100 Brooks Ave	
ROME	Paul Revere Motor Inn Lodge	(315) 336-1776
	7900 Turin Rd	
RONKONKOMA	Econo Lodge	(516) 588-6800
	3055 Veterans Memorian Hwy	
ROTTERDAM	Best Western	(518) 355-1111
	2788 Hamburg St	
SACKETS HARBOR	Ontario Palace Hotel	(315) 646-8000
	103 General Smith Dr	
SARANAC LAKE	Comfort Inn	(518) 891-1970
	148 Lake Flower Ave	
	Hotel Saranac	(518) 891-2200
	101 Main St	
	Lakeside Motel	(518) 891-4333
	27 Lake Flower Ave	
	Sara-Placid Motor Inn	(518) 891-2729
	120 Lake Flower Ave	
SARATOGA SPRINGS	Adelphi Hotel	(518) 587-4688
	365 Broadway	
	Holiday Inn	(518) 584-4550
	Broadway	

SAUGERTIES	HoJo Inn Rte 32	(914) 246-9511
SCHENECTADY	Holiday Inn 100 Nott Terrace	(518) 393-4141
SKANEATELES	Birds Nest Motel 1601 E. Genesee	(315) 685-5641
SPRING VALLEY	Econo Lodge Rte 59	(914) 623-3838
STAMFORD	Red Carpet Motor Inn 7 Lake St	(607) 652-7394
SUFFERN	Wellesley Inn 17 N. Airmont Rd	(914) 368-1900
SYRACUSE	Days Inn 1100 James St	(315) 472-6961
	Genessee Inn 1060 E. Genessee St	(315) 476-4212
	Holiday Inn State Fair Blvd	(315) 457-8700
	Howard Johnsons Thompson Rd	(315) 437-2711
	Red Roof Inn 6614 N. Thompson Rd	(315) 437-3309
TARRYTOWN	Hilton Inn 455 S. Broadway	(914) 631-5700
TONAWANDA	Microtel 1 Hospitality Center Way	(716) 693-8100
UNIONDALE	Marriott 101 James Doolittle Blvd	(516) 794-3800
UTICA	Best Western 175 N. Genessee St	(315) 732-4121
	Howard Johnsons 302 N. Genessee St	(315) 724-4141
	Motel 6 150 N. Genessee St	(315) 797-8743
	Radisson Hotel 200 Genessee St	(315) 797-8010
	Red Roof Inn 20 Weaver St	(315) 724-7128
	Travelodge 1700 Genessee	(315) 724-2101
VALATIE	Blue Spruce Motel Rte 9	(518) 758-9711
WATERLOO	Holiday Inn Rte 414	(315) 539-5011

WATERTOWN	Econo Lodge	(315) 782-5500
	1030 Arsenal St	
	Quality Inn	(315) 788-6800
	1190 Arsenal St	
WATKINS GLEN	Falls Motel	(607) 535-7262
	239 N. Genessee St	
WAVERLY	O'Brien's Inn	(607) 565-2817
	Rte 17	
WEEDSPORT	Best Western	(315) 834-6623
	2709 Eerie Dr	
	Port 40 Motel	(315) 834-6198
	9050 Rte 34	
WESTBURY	Holiday Inn	(516) 997-5000
	369 Old Country Rd	
WHITE PLAINS	White Plains Hotel	(914) 761-8100
	South Broadway	
WILMINGTON	High Valley Motel	(518) 946-2355
	Rte 86	
	Holiday Lodge	(518) 946-2251
	Rte 86	
	Hungry Trout Motor Inn	(518) 946-2217
	Rte 86	
	Ledgerock Motel	(518) 946-2302
	Placid Rd	
WOODBURY	Quality Inn	(516) 921-6900
	7758 Jericho Trnpke	
	Ramada Inn	(516) 921-8500
	8030 Jericho Trnpke	

MAPS

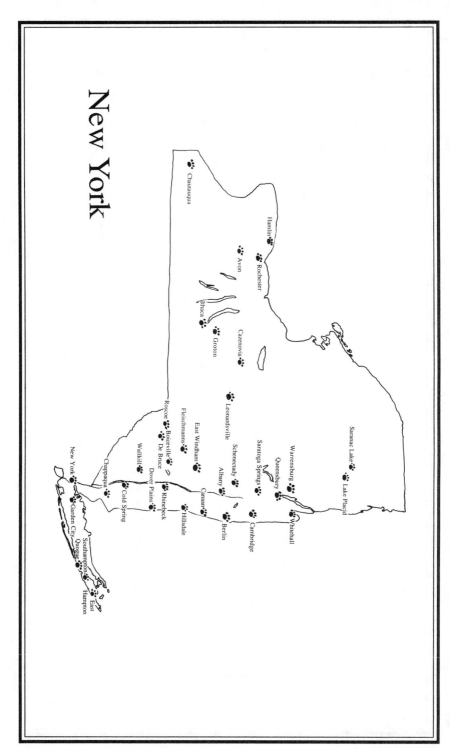

New York

Chautauqua

Hamlin

Avon
Rochester

Ithaca

Groton
Caznovia

Saranac Lake

Roscoe
Fleischmanns
Leonardsville
East Windham
Boiceville
De Bruce
Schenectady
Saratoga Springs
Warrensburg
Queensbury
Lake Placid

Wallkill
Albany
Dover Plains
Canaan
New York
Chappaqua
Rhinebeck
Cambridge
Whitehall
Cold Spring
Hillsdale
Berlin
Garden City
Quogue
Southampton
East Hampton

265

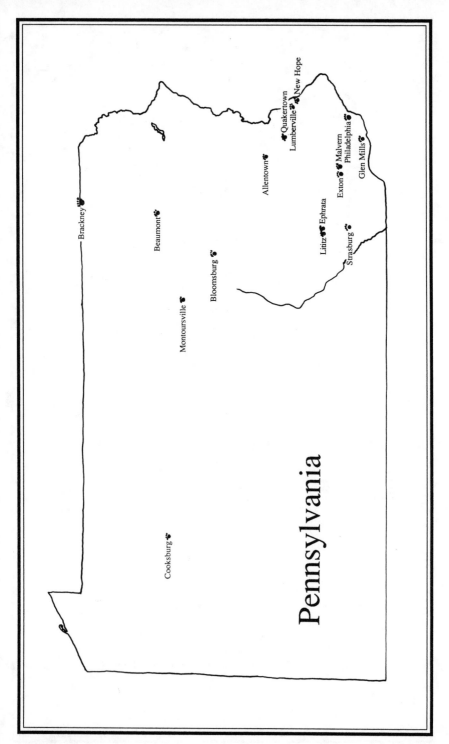

Pennsylvania

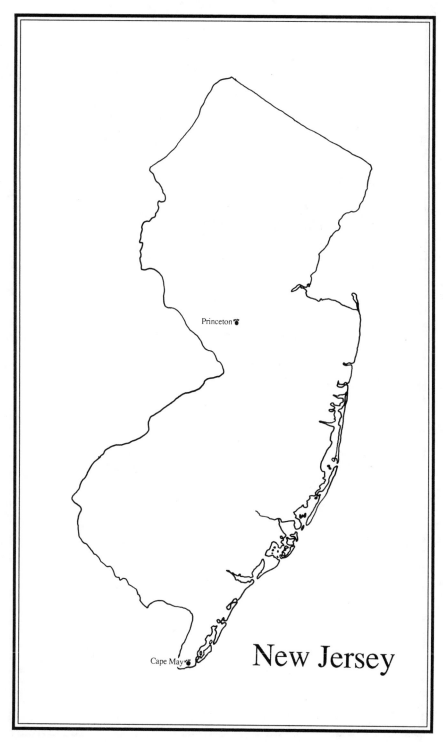

Princeton

Cape May

New Jersey

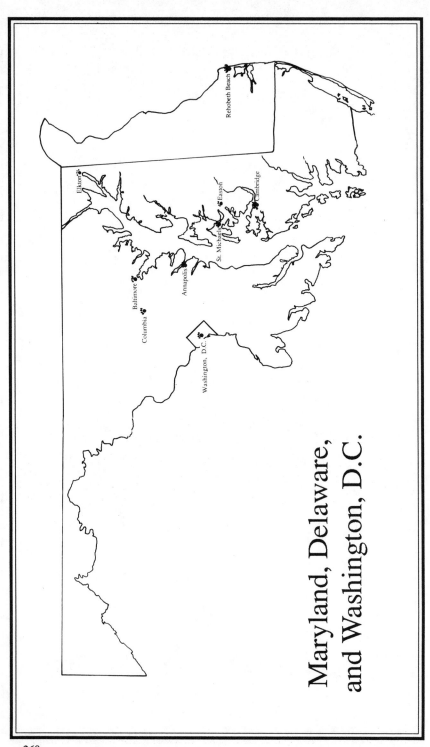

Maryland, Delaware, and Washington, D.C.

Rehoboth Beach

Elkton

Easton
Cambridge

St. Michaels

Baltimore
Annapolis

Columbia

Washington, D.C.

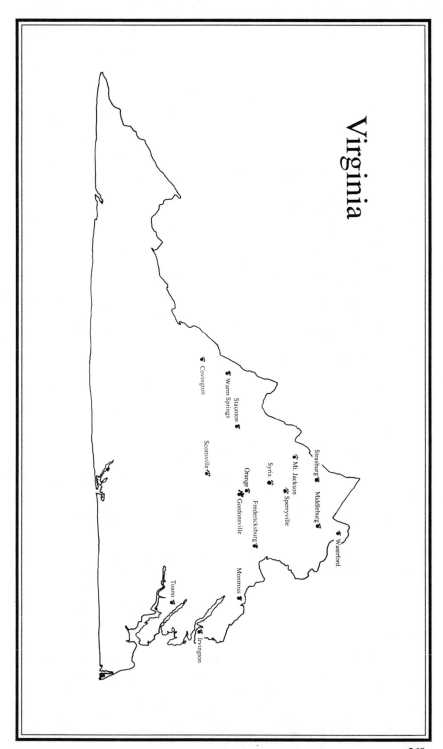

Virginia

Covington

Warm Springs

Staunton

Scottsville

Strasburg
Mt. Jackson
Middleburg
Sperryville
Syria
Orange
Fredericksburg
Gordonsville
Waterford

Toano

Montross

Irvington

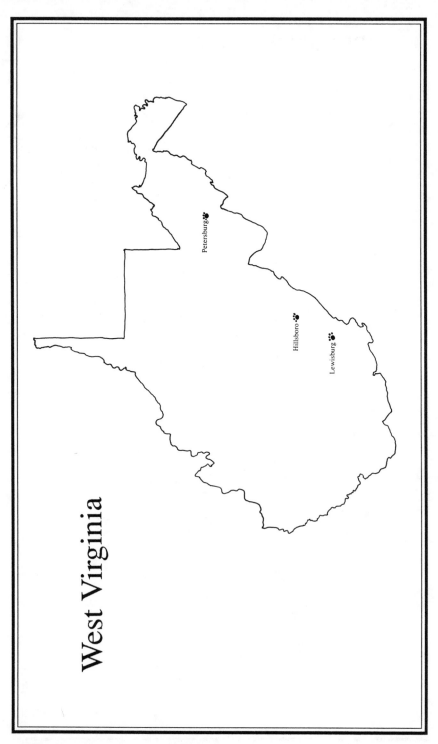

West Virginia

Petersburg

Hillsboro

Lewisburg

THE CHAINS—TOLL FREE NUMBERS

Best Western: (800) 528-1234

Budgetel Inns: (800) 4-BUDGET

Clarion Hotels: (800) CLARION

Comfort Inns: (800) 228-5150

Days Inn: (800) 325-2525

Econo Lodge: (800) 446-6900

Embassy Suites: (800) 362-2779

Four Seasons: (800) 332-3442

Guest Quarters: (800) 424-2900

Hampton: (800) HAMPTON

Hilton Hotels: (800) HILTONS

Holiday Inn: (800) HOLIDAY

Howard Johnson: (800) 654-2000

Hyatt Corp: (800) 228-9000

La Quinta: (800) 531-5900

Loews Hotels: (800) 223-0888

Marriott Hotels: (800) 228-9290

Meridien: (800) 543-4300

Omni Hotels: (800) 843-6664

Quality Inns: (800) 228-5151

Radisson Hotels: (800) 333-3333

Ramada Inns (800) 2-RAMADA

Red Carpet/Scttsh: (800) 251-1962

Red Roof Inns: (800) 843-7663

Residence Inns: (800) 331-3131

Ritz-Carlton: (800) 241-3333

Sheraton Hotels: (800) 325-3535

Stouffer Hotels: (800) HOTELS-1

Super 8: (800) 843-1991

Susse Chalet: (800) 258-1980

Travelodge: (800) 255-3050

INDEX